TELEVISION WRITING

From Concept to Contract

Revised Edition

Richard A. Blum

FOCAL PRESS
Boston • London

For Jason and Jennifer

Focal Press is an imprint of Butterworth Publishers.

Library of Congress Cataloging in Publication Data

Blum, Richard A.
  Television writing.

  Bibliography: p.
  Includes index.
  1. Television authorship. I. Title.
PN1992.7.B58 1984   808'.066791   84–4136
ISBN 0–240–51737–7

Butterworth Publishers
80 Montvale Avenue
Stoneham, MA 02180

10 9 8 7 6 5 4 3 2 1

Printed in the United States of America

Contents

Acknowledgments   v

1   Introduction   1

Part One: Program Proposals and Series Presentations   5

2   Commercial TV Presentations: Drama and Comedy   7
The Networks and Program Development • TV Series
Formats • How to Write a Series Presentation

3   The Variety Special and Quiz Show   37
The Variety Special • The Quiz Program Proposal

4   Public TV Presentations   53
The Public Television Marketplace • Proposal Writing
for Non-Commercial Television • How Projects Are
Evaluated • What Happens if Your Project Is Funded?

Part Two: Story and Character Development   75

5   Developing the Story or Treatment   77
The Importance of Plot • How to Develop the Story •
Adaptations

6   Developing the Character and Dialogue   97
Character Development and "The Method" Writer •
Dialogue: Problems and Solutions

Part Three: The Script   113

7   Developing the Film Script   115
How to Structure an Act • How to Structure a Scene •
Scene Descriptions • Common Problems in Scene
Descriptions

8   Film Script Format   123
Sample Film Script Format • How to Write Camera
Angles • The Master Scene Script • Special Problems
and How to Handle Them: Intercuts, Montages,
Dreams, Flashbacks

9   The Videotape Script Format   149
The Wide Margin Format • The Variety Show
Format • The Double–Column Format

10   A Check-List for Script Revision   169

Part Four: Marketing   173

11   The Cable and Pay TV Marketplace   175
Background on Cable and Pay TV • Marketing Your
Projects for Cable and Pay TV • What You Can Expect
in Negotiations • Other Avenues for Marketing: MSOs,
DBS, STV, Home Video, Access, LPTV

12   The Network and Studio Marketplace   185
What You Should Know before Marketing • Where to
Submit Your Project • How to Submit Your Project •
How to Get an Agent

13   Writers' Fees and Contracts   195
How Do You Join the Writers Guild? • Options,
Contracts, and Pay Scales: What Happens if a Producer
Is Interested?

Appendixes: Where to Go Next   209

A   Networks, Studios, and Production Companies   211

B   Cable and Satellite TV Companies   219

**C   National Funding Sources: Agencies, Resource
       Groups, Foundations**   227

D   Regional and State Funding Contacts   231

E   Professional Guilds, Unions, and Associations   249

F   Agents for Television and Film Writers   251

G   Trade Publications and Periodicals   265

Annotated Bibliography for the TV Writer   267

Index   277

Acknowledgments

I was pleased to learn that the first edition of this book was one of the fastest sellers in the field. It has been used widely at universities and colleges, professional workshops, studio story conferences, and by writers who labor at home with a handbook in one hand and a typewriter or computer keyboard in the other. I am grateful to all the readers, writers, teachers, and users of this book, and it is due to their interest and enthusiasm that this revised edition is possible. There have been some significant changes in the industry, and I have tried to incorporate them into this volume. It is my intention to provide you, the reader, with the latest formats, techniques, and marketplace trends.

One of the prime movers behind this edition is Arlyn Powell, publisher of Focal Press, who single handedly prodded for the right to publish this edition, and who supported and encouraged my efforts at every turn. His respect for readers and authors is commendable, and his sense of the literary marketplace is refined.

While wading through the maze of networks, studios, cable and pay TV companies, federal agencies, and state and regional associations, I encountered many people who gave freely of their time and offered practical suggestions for this book. There are too many people to thank individually, but let me offer a collective thanks to you all.

I would like to thank my family for bearing with me, once again, in the preparation of this book. I am particularly grateful to my children, Jason and Jennifer, for their understanding and patience during the closed-door marathon writing sessions. Eve Blum showed constant interest in the progress of this book, and I appreciate that support.

Friends and colleagues offered a strong network of support. Frank Tavares, Dan Wilcox, Larry Frank, among many others, have shared their professional insights and values. My gratitude to you all.

My writing students served as the initial impetus for this book. The questions asked, issues discussed, projects written, and experiences shared, helped codify the concerns of talented new writers. I hope this edition fulfills some of their needs, and yours, in the pursuit of many TV writing credits.

• • •

For permission to reprint excerpted materials, I would like to thank my writing partners and the following copyright owners:

"Agents List," reprinted with permission of Writers Guild of America, West, Inc.

"Compute-a-Quiz," co-written with Larry Frank, president, Laurence Frank & Co. 4605 Lankershim Blvd., North Hollywood, CA. All rights reserved.

"Death's Head," Episode #1 ("Circle of Fear" series) written by Rick Blum, reprinted with permission of Columbia Pictures Industries, Inc. All rights reserved.

"Disappearing Act," co-written with Robert Lovenheim, River City Productions, Los Angeles, CA. All rights reserved.

"Glues Company," Episode #2 ("The New Little Rascals" series) written by Dan Wilcox. © copyright TAT Communications Co. All rights reserved.

"Intercept," co-written with Hank Hamilton. All rights reserved.

"San Francisco Blues Festival," by Tim Curry. Reprinted with permission of Vince Casaleina, producer, Image Integration. All rights reserved.

"Susan Lennox," NEH Proposal, reprinted with permission of Charles Swartz and Stephanie Rothman, The Susan Lennox Project, Los Angeles, CA. All rights reserved.

"The Watchmaker," adapted for TV by Rick Blum, based on the novel, A Teaspoon of Honey (Aurora Publishers, Inc.) by Bert Kruger Smith. Reprinted with permission of the author, and Fred Miller, producer.© The Honey Production Company. All rights reserved.

"Wind Chill Factor," co-written with Dan Wilcox. All rights reserved.

"Writers Guild of America, Theatrical & Television Minimum Basic Agreement," excerpts reprinted with permission of Writers Guild of America, West, Inc.

"Ziggy's Gang," co-created with Rick Kaiser for Universal Studios. All rights reserved.

1

Introduction

Since the first edition of this book, some important changes have occurred in the television industry, most notably in the area of cable and satellite television. This edition takes into account the realities of the changing marketplace for writers, and examines the formats for presenting new ideas to cable and pay TV, as well as the networks, studios, and other commercial avenues.

Opportunities for writers have also undergone changes in public broadcasting, where grant opportunities have become more specialized. Material is presented here to offer a clear sense of funding resources available for new television projects. The entire spectrum of federal and private funding is covered, with an expanded look at national, state, and regional resources.

With all the expansion and changes in marketplace activities, one thing has not changed: the need for programmers to fill their schedules with new shows. As technology explodes and viewers have more programming options, they are more demanding about what they see. The need for new programming is the only constant in one of the most unpredictable fields. And that's where you, the writer, come into play.

The main objective of this book is to help you understand the practical needs of the industry, so your creative ideas stand a better chance of being read and considered. This book will show you how to create and develop projects in the right form and how to get them to the right place for consideration.

There is something very gratifying about developing new television projects. Perhaps it relates to the eternal fantasy of *doing* something about television. Just think of the average American TV viewer, staring at the set for almost seven hours a day. He or she is bombarded with network, cable, and satellite programming all out of the same mold, with only slight variations from season to season. In a very real way, this book is about how *you* can help change that picture, and upgrade the programming fare watched by millions of Americans every night. It's a worthy fantasy to pursue.

• • •

This book centers on the techniques and formats used by professionals to sell their ideas in the marketplace. *Part One* looks at the area of original program proposals and series presentations. Although this form of writing is one of the most consistent moneymakers, the series format is not generally made available to newcomers. There is no major conspiracy involved and I doubt if seasoned script writers are protecting themselves from outside competition. Rather, formats are simply never published and rarely handed down. This book offsets that problem by providing specific examples and guidelines for writing new dramatic and comedy series, as well as variety specials and quiz programs. The formats are designed with networks, studios, and cable TV companies in mind.

Part One also covers the marketplace needs and format requirements for non-commercial television, specifically public TV and federal agencies. The opportunities for funding new projects in these areas are very real, and the possibilities for script writing grants are substantial. This section looks at proposal writing requirements for federal, state, regional, and private sector support.

Part Two discusses the theory and practice of writing pilot stories and movies-of-the-week treatments. It deals with the problems of story and character development for dramatic shows, and details the most effective devices for developing plots and story outlines. Moreover, it shows how *Method* acting techniques can be used for developing characters in the story and script, and how dialogue problems can be identified and corrected in the script phase of writing.

Part Three concentrates on the specific formats involved in writing scripts for TV film and videotape. No producer, program executive, or agent will pick up a script unless it's in the proper form. All worthy projects won't be produced—in fact, most scripts won't even be read—but if the project is well written in concept, style, and form, it stands a much better chance of being evaluated. Technique and form are essential for writers who seriously intend to enter the mainstream of the profession. Just as an actor learns basic techniques to create effectively, so the television writer must learn techniques of writing, from the germination of an idea to the revision of a final draft. If the stress on form seems a bit dogmatic at times, please remember that competition is incredibly stiff and a professional-looking script can help you past that first major hurdle—getting the project read.

Part Four deals with the pragmatics of marketing the property—how, when, where, and to whom it should go. The odds against selling a new project are staggering, but without knowledge of the marketplace there's no glimmer of hope for success. This section answers key questions every writer should know: How do you break into cable and pay TV markets? How do you break into the network and studio marketplace? How do you get a producer to read the project? How and where do you submit it? What happens if a producer is interested? What contractual arrangements can be expected? How do you get an agent?

The *Appendix* offers a wide range of contacts and resources for you to explore, dealing with each major subject examined in the book. It also provides an Annotated Bibliography for further reference.

The writer who stands the best chance of making it is the one with industry awareness and contacts, coupled with talent, technique, and indomitable perseverance. If you're willing to confront incredible odds with highly imaginative program concepts, perseverance might eventually pay off. The industry consumes thousands of stories and scripts every television season. It requires a horde of able writers to keep those home lights burning. This book can provide you with certain writing techniques—from form to marketing—but only you can provide the essential ingredients of talent and creativity. Once you know the form, the demonstration of imagination and style is up to you. Why not put them to work and see what happens?

PROGRAM PROPOSALS AND SERIES PRESENTATIONS

2

Commercial TV Presentations: Drama and Comedy

If you're an aspiring television writer, you've probably tried your hand at writing some episodes for the latest series on TV. You may have sent one of the scripts to a series producer and waited anxiously for some career-changing response. That script was most likely returned, unopened, with a form letter attached: "Sorry, we don't read unsolicited material." Or, if you were lucky, a personal note: "We already have something similar in work." Or any variant thereof. Sound familiar?

Then you've discovered the reality of script submission—the producer of a current series is the *wrong* person to send an original script, and the unsolicited TV episode is the *least* likely to be sold. A series producer is concerned about Nielsen ratings, deadline pressures, and network paranoia. He or she has no time to nurture an unsold writer or to develop an unassigned script. Moreover, a series producer usually assigns scripts to "heavyweights" early in the development season. These are writers who have worked successfully in the genre, who are adaptive in story conferences, who are fast and reliable in meeting script deadlines.

Other variables come into play as well. While you've written a hilarious episode taking place in a country schoolhouse, the network has already decreed that the series must be less slapstick, more urban, more relevant, more romantic, etc. There may also be shifts in character emphasis with less stress on the lead, and greater emphasis on two minor characters in the series. There is no way for you, sitting at home

7

with your typewriter, to know the gist of story conferences, phone calls, and daily exchanges of memos. Once you've seen the format changes on the screen, new series modifications are already being discussed and implemented at the studio.

There is another reason why speculative writing for an on-going series is a futile route for the beginner. It's virtually impossible to know the premises of all stories in development at the studio. Given the range of series episodes, it's not unlikely that your story idea comes pretty close to another that was aired, discussed with other writers, or turned down in some other form. And that raises another reality. Producers are concerned that a freelancer may sue for plagiarism if a show looks similar to the unsolicited script. That's another reason "unsolicited" material is returned to the author without being read.

If a television script for an on-going series is the wrong way to break in, how does a writer show his or her potential for the medium? The same way professional writers do—by creating *original* shows for television. Specifically, this means developing original TV series presentations, or developing treatments and scripts for pilots, movies-of-the-week, or mini-series. The original project is unfettered by the dictates of another author's characters, formula situations, or pre-established conflicts that have been aired for two years. When you create a new television series or long-form drama, you're developing ideas directly for the medium. You're competing in the mainstream of new ideas.

A well-written television project shows you can effectively bring to life your own characters and formats, dramatic situations, and visual action. It shows your knowledge of the marketplace, as well as your grasp on writing technique. And that puts you in an enviable position compared to the beginning writer who is still turning out speculative scripts for a series that has just been cancelled.

The Networks and Program Development

A program development executive receives hundreds of submissions each week—sometimes over the phone, sometimes in skeletal proposals, sometimes in fully detailed presentations. He or she is responsible for bringing new ideas into the network. Once the show actually gets on the air, another department takes over—current programming or prime-time programming. That department is concerned with time slots, competition, demographic appeal, lead-in and lead-out programs, and other factors that will affect the ratings performance of a series on the air. The goal is always the same: to reach the largest number of television homes in the country.

Job security in programming is about as secure as the changing decimals on the overnight Nielsen ratings. So, understandably, some executives view innovative program concepts as a threat rather than a challenge. Jobs are literally dependent upon ideas that are greeted with enthusiasm by superiors, advertisers, and the whimsical public.

If an executive pushes for an innovative show and it fails, the Want Ads will soon be top priority reading. If the show is based on a proven formula (i.e., modeled after a highly successful show), the personal risk is somewhat lessened. The executive can always point to the unpredictable tastes of the viewing public.

Does this mean you have to create the same kind of formula programs you see every night? In one sense, yes; in another sense, no. Let me explain. Television is an imitative medium. It thrives on successes, and spits out a slew of carbon copies, spin-offs, and character duplicates in an effort to reach the same wide audiences as the original. We've all experienced the glut of sitcoms, medical shows, police shows, and prime-time soaps. If television is out for the greatest possible audience, why doesn't it break away from the trends rather than imitate them? A classic theory of LOP was proposed by former network executive Paul Klein. LOP stands for Least Objectionable Programming. The idea is simple: if a show doesn't offend anyone, it will appeal to the widest possible audience. If ABC comes out with a new show about a group of singing fleas—and if that show goes through the roof of Nielsen homes—you can be assured that NBC and CBS will have similar shows in development faster than you can call an exterminator.

This doesn't mean that new ideas or innovative concepts won't make it to the screen. Each television season brings too many examples of daring shows that break new ground. The fact is, once the ground is broken, the imitation syndrome runs rampant, and we quickly forget that one show was the forerunner of the current trend.

If a writer has a new idea with substantive content and characters, it can be presented in a professional format that will be accepted by any production company. A well-written series presentation might convince the reader that the concept has merit, longevity, and the magic ingredient of wide audience appeal. That last element is the most important for the networks. A good television writer learns how to work within those parameters, and does it with genuine creativity and style.

TV Series Formats

When writers come up with a premise for a new show, they generally test the idea in a brief proposal, and then flesh it out into a complete, fully detailed presentation called a *format*. The format describes the premise of the show, introduces the characters, and sets the blueprint for action in the series. (The term "format" also refers to the generic style of the show; more on that later.)

Once you have the basic idea for a new show, it helps to identify the type of series that will be developed. The most common is the *episodic series* which features the same characters weekly; those characters face different obstacles and conflicts in each episode. A writer who creates the presentation for a new episodic series, whether drama or comedy, must identify the main premise of the show, the leading characters, the pilot story, and future storylines which suggest the limitless potential for characters in conflict and action.

Unlike the episodic series, an *anthology series* (also called a *unit series*) does *not* have the same characters appearing in each show. The only common thread might be an unusual premise, or the umbrella title of the series itself. The written format for an anthology series might consist of an elaboration of the premise and a detailed outline of the first few shows. In reality, a series may have elements of both episodic and anthology shows, but your overarching premise can help dictate a singular direction for your series format.

Mini-series (or *multi-part series*) can also be written in presentation form. This format focuses on the larger saga of major characters and dramatically significant events. It provides a historical sweep of the subject matter and the lives of the leading characters. If a book adaptation is the basis for the series, the presentation must show how the work can be effectively translated to television. It offers a sense of the storytelling context for the screen. The presentation for a multi-part series is very lengthy and detailed, sometimes 100-200 pages in length. In that form, it is known as a *bible*. The bible is a thoroughly fleshed-out treatment of characters, dramatic narrative, and multi-part story lines.

Industry jargon is rife with terminology for proposals, formats, series outlines, presentations, and bibles, but the terms are often used interchangeably and can be confusing. For our own purposes, let's distinguish between a short proposal and a lengthy presentation. We'll refer to the *proposal* as the skeletal premise for the show, providing the general blueprint for the series; it can be 2-5 pages in length, and serves as the foundation for the more detailed presentation. The *series presentation* is the entire description of the show, with fully fleshed-out stories and characters; it can be 20-200 pages, depending on the length and content of the series. It is, indeed, the bible for the evolution of your characters and stories, and the compelling and fascinating events which will make your show the ultimate in programming entertainment.

Let's look at the process of creating a new show, and see how proposals and presentations are developed. At the beginning, you siphon through all the creative ideas filtering around in your mind, and ask some pivotal questions: Which of those ideas has an interesting *hook*, i.e., what is the show's unique premise, the very reason viewers will be unable to pull themselves away from the TV set? Is it a premise that lends itself to longevity as a series? Will the characters and situations easily center around evolving conflicts? Are the characters identifiable and likeable? Are they easily "castable?" Is the show manageable in terms of production requirements? What is the mood and atmosphere of the series—warm drama, outrageous comedy, action and suspense, horror and scare? Is it "high concept" programming? (That's network jargon for glitzy and appealing.) Only you can determine the flair and style of the series concept and format.

Let's go back to the first question, and probably the most fundamental. What is the "hook" of the series? If you have an idea for a show, and it has an interesting hook, try to express it succinctly in a line or two. If you have difficulty in condensing it, the premise might be too nebulous. If you *can* focus it, the premise is more on target. Here are some examples of series premises:

- "Together" is a dramatic series about two people who hitchhike across the country and get involved in the lives of those they meet.
- "Ghosts" is an anthology series about supernatural forces that invade the lives of everyday people.
- "Ziggy's Gang" is a children's series about a group of kids who will do anything for each other, and get into plenty of trouble in the process.
- "Intercept" is an action series about an American girl and a Japanese guy who are forced into partnership to thwart international criminals.

The hook is inherent in the premise. Once you've identified the series premise, you're ready to work on the proposal.

Here is a sample proposal based on the dramatic series, "Together." It's brief, but it conveys a sense of the series, the main characters, the dramatic mood and atmosphere of the show.

TOGETHER

It starts as a coincidence. JEREMY WALTERS, 24, bearded and

pensive, sits on the steps of the Student Union, watching the rat race go by. RACHEL STONE, 19, fragile and pretty, climbs

the steps, and tacks a note on the cluttered bulletin board:

WANTED. RIDE TO EAST COAST.

''I'm going back,'' JEREMY's voice is friendly, ''but, I'm

hitching.'' The idea intrigues RACHEL. He's going cross-

country at his own pace. To experience change. Adventure. A

break from routine. A chance to meet new people in different

places. An opportunity to free his spirit.

He's most definitely on RACHEL's vibes.

The groundrules are carefully set up...

The whole thing is on the up and up, platonic and friendly,

without any ties. They can stay in one place for an hour, a

day, a week, a month, depending on their circumstances at

the time. They can split any time they want to--the place or

each other. And when they want to stay somewhere for awhile,

or money is low, they pick up odd jobs, to help support

themselves.

That's what our series is about. Two young people experienc-

ing life to the fullest.

By themselves.

But getting deeply involved in the lives of those around

them.

The sights they see...the places they pass through...the

people they meet...are all key elements of the series.

We deal with life as it really is...

in the desert...

on the farm...

in small rural towns...

in suburbia...

in the big city.

JEREMY and RACHEL experience it all, and profoundly effect

the lives of those whom they meet in the process...

- The teenage hitchhiker, running away from home.
- The old farmer, whose land is threatened by a drought.
- The middle-aged salesman who picks them up, and wants to
  join them.
- The Vicar, who asks RACHEL to tutor his blind son.
- The owner of the roadside cafe, who was robbed of his savings
  and accuses JEREMY and RACHEL.
- The alienated little girl whom RACHEL counsels at a small
  rural summer camp.
- The elderly, frightened woman in a redevelopment project,
  whose home will be torn down.

In short...

JEREMY AND RACHEL ARE TWO PEOPLE TOGETHER, WHO PROVIDE A
RICH SOURCE OF WEEKLY DRAMA, AS THEY BECOME INVOLVED IN A
VARIETY OF HUMAN CONFLICTS... WITH DIFFERENT PEOPLE... IN
DIFFERENT PLACES... WITH WARM AND SENSITIVE OUTCOMES.

· · ·

You can see that the proposal supplies enough information to convey the basic concept and dramatic potential of the series idea. It uses a combination of narrative techniques and soft-sell approaches (suggesting the reasons why the show might be successful). The brief format offers a sense of the storylines and characters, but it does not provide a detailed visual treatment of the pilot or the leading characters.

The same technique can be used to write the premise for any show, including anthology series. Since the basic premise of an anthology piece centers around a unifying theme, it's important to stress the use of that theme. The proposal might not have any running characters, but it can describe the hook, and it can relate the premise to viewer interest.

As an example, here is the proposal for an anthology series, "Ghosts," which is based on the premise described earlier—identifiable people thrust into supernatural situations. This proposal has a more hard-sell approach than "Together":

GHOSTS!

A Proposal for an Hour Anthology Series

Ghosts. Vampires. Werewolves. Witches. Ghouls. The very words send ripples up the spine. There is a deep fascination for the unknown in each of us. It is an ancient interest--as ancient as the human race. Therein lies its power. It is stronger than our intellect, stronger than our fears. It goes down to the primitive core of our being.

But the special intrigue of the supernatural is even more terrifying and fascinating when it is spiced with recognizable, identifiable people and places. That is where our series differs from all others; that is where our series is totally unique.

''GHOSTS!'' is an hour television series that deals with

ordinary people from everyday life--confronted with sudden

extraordinary events. Some of the events can be explained

away. Most cannot!

The unexpected can happen anywhere--under the hair dryer

at home; walking down the street in Beverly Hills; eating

lunch at Denny's; shopping for gifts at Gimbel's; stopping

at the butcher shop in Flatbush; at the grocery store in

Austin; riding to work on the Capital Beltway; picking up a

date down the block; going to visit your mother-in-law in

Maine...

And the unexpected can happen to anyone you know--the

young man who walks the dog on your lawn; the old man playing

chess in a Greenwich Village park; the woman who goes to a

sale at Sear's; the girl you see in the laundromat; the boy

who delivers your paper; your blind date for Saturday

night...

In fact, it could happen to you. At any place. At any

time...

. . .

You can see that the proposal conveys the atmosphere of the potential show and promotes its dramatic *hook*. In "Ghosts!" the hook is the
intrusion of the supernatural into the lives of identifiable people. In

"Together," the hook is less formidable; it is the experience of a young couple hitching cross-country.

The proposal is a useful device to interest the reader in wanting to see more. The purpose of writing a proposal is really twofold: it provides you with a working sample of the series concept; and it provides the reader with material for evaluating that series concept.

Don't expect to have a sale on the basis of a proposal alone. Writers who have tons of "created by" credits may elicit interest on the basis of a premise, but unestablished writers face incredibly frustrating obstacles along the way. It's not worth the bother. Instead of shopping the idea for a sale, use it as the basis for getting feedback on the series premise. Let colleagues read the proposal and talk out format weaknesses, story problems, characterizations, setting, the pilot. And then, with a better sense of the series potential, you can sit down and write the series presentation (also called the *format*). *That* is your ultimate selling device.

How to Write a Series Presentation

A detailed series presentation reflects the writer's clear grasp of the show's content. It's a much better selling device than the skeletal proposal. Generally, the written presentation for a dramatic or comedy series consists of four separate parts:

1. A *format* section, which describes the premise, hook, and appeal of the show:
2. A *character* section, which introduces the featured players;
3. A *pilot story*, which outlines all the visual sequences for the first episode;
4. A section on *future storylines*, which relates story possibilities for additional episodes.

Let's examine the structure and format for each part of the series presentation:

1. The Format Section

The format section is just like the skeletal proposal. It outlines the basic premise of the series, briefly and cogently. The style of writing generally reflects the mood and pacing of the genre. If the show is a comedy, the format might be warm or slapstick; a drama, poignant and sensitive; action-adventure, fast-paced and action-packed. In short the format whets the reader's appetite for wanting to know more about the series, itself.

The format section usually appears at the beginning of a series presentation and is about one or two pages in length. It's simple and straight forward. This is the opening segment from a series presentation called "Ziggy's Gang," based on the premise described earlier.

ZIGGY'S GANG

FORMAT

ZIGGY'S GANG is a lively half-hour videotape series for

children.

The Gang is made up of five lovable, laughable, totally

identifiable kids. They are rich, poor, black, and white,

representing all shades of personality and character.

The featured characters in ZIGGY'S GANG are a group of

friends who go to the same school--a school that cuts across

the classes of a medium-sized city, in a neighborhood where

extremes live within blocks of one another. The racial and

economic mix of the group is never mentioned in the show; it

is treated as a simple, natural fact of life. As it should be

in real life.

It is ZIGGY's gang, but ZIGGY is the little human magnet who

draws the group together. He is the catalyst that brings out

the best in his friends. They care for him, and he cares for them. In fact, they are <u>all</u> inexplicably bound together, and

they intend to <u>stay</u> that way, no matter what.

• • •

The format is easy to read and describes the fundamental elements of the premise, approach, and character—in a few short paragraphs. Some writers will use separate pages for each paragraph or two, making the presentation appear even more spacious and easy to read. That's simply a matter of style and preference.

A format can also be written in less than a page. Here's the format for an action-adventure series called "Intercept," based on the last premise discussed earlier.

<u>INTERCEPT</u>

<u>FORMAT</u>

INTERCEPT IS A NEW TWIST ON AN ACTION-ADVENTURE IDEA.

IT TEAMS AN AMERICAN GIRL WITH A JAPANESE GUY, IN AN ATTEMPT

TO THWART INTERNATIONAL CRIMINALS.

THE MOOD OF THE SERIES?--TONGUE IN CHEEK ADVENTURE.

THE TWIST?

OUR TWO LEADS ARE EXPERTS IN THE MARTIAL ARTS. AND THE ARTS

ARE DEPICTED IN MORE DETAIL THAN EVER BEFORE. KARATE.

AIKIDO. BATON TECHNIQUE. THEY ARE USED IN HIGHLY STYLIZED

SEQUENCES EACH WEEK--<u>WITHOUT</u> GRATUITOUS VIOLENCE. AND <u>WITH</u>

A SENSE OF EXCITEMENT AND ENTERTAINMENT.

• • •

The information in the "Intercept" format is basically the same as "Ziggy's Gang." The concept of the series is presented, the atmosphere suggested, and the hook briefly delineated. However, the style of writing is different, and the form of presentation is different—all the information is double-spaced and capitalized in this presentation. In writing program formats, there is plenty of room for diversity and experimentation. The most important objective is to lay the dramatic groundwork, and evoke interest in the series idea.

2. Characters

Leading characters are described on the pages following the format. They can be described simply—looks, age, key character traits, potential interrelationships in the series. The characters can be developed more fully in the pilot story.

The number of leading characters should be relatively small. Some producers instinctively translate a long list of characters into a massive price tag for casting. In "Ziggy's Gang" there are five characters—an unusually large number for this section of the presentation—but each one is considered integral to the premise and pilot story. This is. how they are described:

CHARACTERS

ZIGGY

You can't help but love ZIGGY. He's an eleven year old

chubby kid with big, wire-rimmed glasses, floppy blonde

hair, and a cherubic baby face. He's the eternal optimist

who is momentarily crushed when things don't work out his

way. But he latches onto a new hope, and his enthusiasm waxes incredibly high again. ZIGGY's warm-heartedness and

undaunted spirit spark his friends to want to help set

things right; no matter how outlandish the scheme. ZIGGY's

the son of a college professor, and he gets his share of

jibes about it at school. He's idealistic, enthusiastic, and

adventuresome; he's sensitive, too, with a heart of pure

gold.

DUDE

DUDE dazzles you. He is a with-it ten year old hustler

who talks cool and moves cool. DUDE knows all the angles and

uses them to help his friends at all costs. He is a loyal

friend, with a sincerity that outlasts his con-man

exterior. His impetuous cons are responsible for

getting the gang into trouble and sometimes are the cause of

disharmony and misunderstanding within the gang itself.

DUDE is the flamboyant son of a blue collar worker; he lives

several blocks away from ZIGGY.

SAMSON

SAMSON's got to make you laugh. He's a short, wiry eleven

year old, with a tremendous sense of humor and an outlandish

laugh. Smaller than the others, he prides himself on being a tremendous athlete. His speed, agility and strength helped

earn him a tough boy reputation. (The reputation was

aided and abetted by DUDE, who has everyone convinced that

SAMSON is a karate expert.) SAMSON has one major flaw--a hot

temper that occasionally clouds his sense of humor.

Inevitably, it gets the gang into trouble when it surfaces.

SAMSON is forced to take trombone lessons in which he has no

interest or talent. He's utterly embarrassed on those days

he has to lug his oversized instrument to school.

BUCKS

You have to feel sorry for BUCKS. He's a tall, lanky

thirteen year old rich kid. He's prone to day-dreaming and

fantasy, which gives him an affinity for his younger

friends. BUCKS is the bumbler of the group. The son of a

corporation president, he lives in an expensive high-rise

apartment and refuses to take a large allowance from his

parents. BUCKS yearns to be ''poor,'' like the rest of the

kids.

LADY

LADY makes you stop, look, and listen. She's the only one

with both feet on the ground. She may be only twelve years

old, but she's got more than her share of common-sense and

book-sense. (She's brilliant in the sciences, and can do

wonders with anything mechanical). LADY is Latin American

with long jet black hair, big brown eyes, and a full, rich,

happy smile. She finds herself caught between the good times

she has as a tomboy, and the good times she's beginning to

have as a full-fledged, female, feminine girl. LADY is often

razzed by the others since she represents the lone, stable,

level-headed point of view. She is the daughter of a

neighborhood grocery store owner.

• • •

3. Pilot Stories and Treatments

Once you've described the format and the lead characters, you'll have to show how they work in the pilot story. It's the litmus test for your show. The pilot is written as a *treatment*, i.e., a narrative version of the dramatic story in your proposed script. It is supposed to give the reader a full sense of characters, place, and action. The characters and conflicts are usually introduced as early as possible, and the dramatic builds are carefully orchestrated from beginning to end. In Part Two there is a discussion of dramatic theory and story plotting techniques, essential to effective development. At this point, however, let's just look at the technical requirements and formal structure of an original treatment.

A pilot story can be segmented into several acts. A half-hour program usually has a brief "teaser" followed by two acts of equal length. A sixty-minute show might have a teaser and four acts. A two-hour project might have six acts—or none at all. These are general guidelines, rather than formal requisites.

As for professional jargon, relatively little is called for. These are some of the recurring terms or directions that might appear in a pilot story or treatment:

FADE IN. This means that the picture gradually appears onto the screen. Conversely, at the end of a story or script, the picture FADES OUT and the screen goes to black.

EXT. PARK-DAY. This is called a "slug line" or "scene identification line" because it spells out the different scene locations in the story.
It identifies the location as exterior (EXT.) or interior (INT.), specifies
the place of the action (PARK), and the lighting requirements (DAY or
NIGHT). Scripts are broken down this way to help identify production
elements in the show. In the story phase there is some variance about
the use of slug lines. Some writers will omit them altogether, preferring
a more narrative style.

O.S. This is a shorthand way of saying "Off Screen." If a character
sees something off screen, it means the viewer can't see what he or she
is looking at.

HIS P.O.V. This means we are now looking from the character's
"point of view." We see exactly what that person sees.

CU. This means "Close Up." The close up is a camera shot that
features a large image on screen.

On the following pages you'll find the pilot treatment for "Ziggy's
Gang." Let's examine the technical structure of the first act:

Stories and Scripts usually begin with this direction

PILOT STORY   *The Title of the pilot goes here*

FADE IN: *The "slugline" (or scene identification) may be used in the treatment or may be discarded*

EXT. PARK-DAY

The Gang is involved in a hot game of basketball at the park.
Characters are often capitalized throughout
ZIGGY, jaunting down the side of the court, has a clear path

to the basket, but suddenly stops short as he sees something
off screen
O.S. SAMSON passes the ball, but ZIGGY is oblivious, and the

ball bounces off him. SAMSON groans with exasperation, but

ZIGGY continues to stare O.S.

HIS P.O.V.   *a new angle from his point of view*

He's staring at the new girl in his class, SANDY HOLLANDER,

blonde and pretty, who is talking and joking with thirteen

year old Adonis, BILLY MATLICK. They're sitting on the grass

together.

> *double spacing suggests new angles or scenes*

BILLY sees the ball bounce off the court, and he gets up to

retrieve it. He gets the ball and tries a shot from way off

the court... He swishes it through the hoop. SANDY is

delighted and impressed, BILLY smiles proudly, and ZIGGY

doesn't react at all. From the sidelines, LADY is the only

one who seems to take stock of the situation.

> *The action in the sequence is described without using specific camera angles*

EXT. STREET-DAY

> *This sets a new place, a new scene*

DUDE, SAMSON, and BUCKS are entering the garage, but ZIGGY

sees someone coming down the street, and purposely lags

behind. It's SANDY, with BILLY in tow. ZIGGY greets them

awkwardly, and sees that she's carrying a new album...It's

by her favorite rock star, and BILLY just bought it

for her...She goes on about how unexpected the gift was, how

> *In a treatment dialogue is merely suggested*

unnecessary it was for BILLY to spend four dollars like

that, for no reason at all...BILLY smiles. It was nothing,

he says. And they exit, leaving ZIGGY gawking after them.

Almost instinctively, he digs into his pocket and pulls out

some change. He doesn't have nearly enough to compete.

LADY arrives on her bike, stands it up by the garage, and

apologizes for being late. She quizzically notes ZIGGY's

tormented look as he heads quietly for the garage. She looks

after him for a (beat) then glances down the street, where she

sees SANDY walking with BILLY. So that's it, she guesses.

A "beat" is a dramatic pause

INT. GARAGE-DAY

Inside the garage, BUCKS asks ZIGGY what's wrong, why is he

so down? It's so unlike him...It's nothing, ZIGGY says. But

LADY enters, and offers another theory...It's nothing to be

ashamed of...ZIGGY is taken with that new girl in

class...SANDY HOLLANDER...The guys break into hoots,

catcalls, general razzing...ZIGGY gets red-faced denies it,

and begins to storm out.

Once again, dialogue is implied without using actual dialogue structure

LADY shouts for the others to lay off...They stop. DUDE says

the new girl is BILLY MATLICK's, and there ain't nobody, no

how, gonna gel the li'l fox from BILLY-THE-KID...The others

agree wholeheartedly...LADY again chimes in, tells them

that instead of razzing ZIGGY, or telling him how hopeless

it is, they ought to think of something that might help...It

would take a lot to help, ZIGGY says half-resignedly, that

BILLY kid is even rich. He just bought her a new album.

The pilot story should be detailed enough to give a complete sense of time, place, action, and character development in each major sequence

All eyes turn at once to BUCKS--who looks horror-stricken.

But ZIGGY jumps in immediately, says no to the idea...You

know how BUCKS hates to take money from his dad. There <u>must</u>

be another way...BUCKS looks like a ten ton weight was just

removed from his shoulders.

Then SAMSON's eyes light up. He has an idea...What about

getting back at BILLY on the court, and impressing the

lady?...SAMSON can teach him everything he has to know. He

doesn't have to be big, or handsome, or tall, or strong to

beat BILLY in basketball...It's all in the moves, man, and

ZIGGY can take him in a one-on-one game...ZIGGY becomes

enthused. ZIGGY, the enternal optimist, agrees to give it a

try. The others cheer him on.

> *Instead of using the slugline, the writer may opt for a narrative style, e.g., "We are outside the garage and see that SAMSON is teaching ZIGGY...." etc.*

EXT. GARAGE-DAY

SAMSON is teaching ZIGGY the moves and the shots, using a

meg-shift hoop the gang set up in front of the garage. SAMSON

purposely lets ZIGGY get by him, and ZIGGY, after two

misses, finally hits a bucket. The gang cheers wildly, and

SAMSON smiles...You're ready, ZIGGY-boy. You'll beat him so

bad, she'll be begging for an autograph...ZIGGY beams, as

SAMSON runs out to arrange the match.

EXT. PARK-DAY

In the pilot story, a writer can use either of these approaches to (and/or) indicate a new scene

In the park, we see the kids gathering around the basketball

court, filtering in, jabbering about the match. Finally, the

crowd quiets down as BILLY strolls calmly out on the court in

his school team sweatshirt, and his brand new thirty dollar

All-pro basketball shoes. Two shots for warm-up; two

swishes.

New Angle is implied through double-spacing

ZIGGY strolls out onto the court now. His chunky belly and

short frame seem to belie his sense of calm and confidence.

BILLY hands him the ball for his warm-up shots, but ZIGGY

declines. BILLY asks ZIGGY to take the ball out, but again

ZIGGY gives him the advantage. Some buzzing from the crowd.

SANDY, on the grass, watches.

New Angle implied

The game is on, and cheers from the rooting sections

accompany the action. BILLY dribbles behind his back, and

ZIGGY looks momentarily confused. BILLY drives in, and ZIGGY

falls down. An easy lay-up for two.

ZIGGY tries to dribble behind the back, but trips over the

ball. Laughter, cheers, and groans from the crowd. SAMSON

and the others in the gang pass worried looks back and forth.

We can see that SANDY feels sorry for ZIGGY, but she roots

for BILLY.

This is the viewer's point of view

The scene description can define continuous action or compressed action

The game continues...BILLY looking like Pistol Pete, and

ZIGGY looking like Oliver Hardy. As the game draws to an end,

the Gang knows it's a totally lost cause. BILLY tosses in the

last bucket, and steps over the exhausted, nearly prone body

of ZIGGY. As the Gang forlornly moves in to see ZIGGY, BILLY

moves back toward the sidelines to see SANDY.

his point of view can be specified where necessary

From ZIGGY's P.O.V. we see the triumphant BILLY being

greeted with a hero's welcome. He puts his arm around

SANDY's shoulder, and they walk off.

Close-ups are one of the few shots called in a treatment. They can help establish a character's reaction to emotional crises or specific events unfolding.

CU ZIGGY's reaction. We see how crushed he is.

This slugline establishes a new scene and location

EXT. STREET-DAY

ZIGGY walks despondently back toward the garage, with a

silent Gang following along. Then DUDE thrusts his arm

around ZIGGY, and says as only DUDE can say...Hey, Man, he

may be a sportin' dude, and he may be richer and taller and

better lookin' than you, but nobody say that dude's cool.

And that's what you gonna be, ZIG, Man, you gonna be
cool...ZIGGY looks curiously up at DUDE's smiling face, and
the light of optimism begins to cross his features again.

Implied dialogue is sprinkled in the treatment

INT. GARAGE-DAY

and so are reactions

This is the final dress rehearsal. ZIGGY wears some far-out
clothes, and is finishing up his jive-talk speech to DUDE,
who plays the part of SANDY. DUDE smiles and says in high-
pitched feminine voice...Oh, you so cool, ZIGGY, you be my
new sweetie-man...ZIGGY beams from ear to ear. And just then
we hear the distant sound of SANDY's (O.S.) *off screen* laughter. She's
going to pass by the garage on her way home from school. DUDE
looks at ZIGGY and gives him the power sign...You ready,
Man...ZIGGY rushes out of the garage to meet her.

EXT. STREET-DAY

ZIGGY stands in front of the open garage, trying to look
inconspicuous. We see SANDY and BILLY walking down the
street towards him. ZIGGY whispers out loud to DUDE, hidden
in the shadows of the garage...She's with BILLY..DUDE
reinforces his friend's confidence...Don't worry, Man. When
you get through, the li'l fox'll be like ice cream in summer,
in your hands.

As SANDY and BILLY approaches, ZIGGY struts out and lays his

line on them. The words are right, but they sound like   *Implied dialogue*

they're being read from a textbook. The strut, the moves,

and the dress, make ZIGGY look more like a stand up comic

than a cool ladies' man. BILLY starts cracking up, becomes

hysterical. SANDY tries hard not to laugh, asks ZIGGY why

he's acting so funny...Laughing, BILLY tugs SANDY's arm, and

they continue on their way.

an EXTREME CLOSE-UP

In (an ECU,) we see how totally crushed and embarrassed ZIGGY

is.

This direction generally ends each act and concludes each film

FADE OUT

*   *   *

The Narrative Style Treatment

As mentioned earlier; a writer doesn't have to conform to that particular style of writing the treatment. A looser, more narrative style
omits the need for formal scene identifications. All the information is
given in visual description, and new scenes are suggested by setting up
new paragraphs.

Here is an example of the more narrative approach. It is an excerpt
from the "Intercept" pilot. The action picks up as Kubota, a martial arts
expert, escapes from his captors.

PILOT STORY EXCERPT

INTERCEPT

KUBOTA bolts down the darkened hallway toward a SECOND

GUARD, who turns clumsily with his shot gun.. But KUBOTA

does a flying leap kick, knocks the gun out of the man's

hands.

In the narrative format a paragraph establishes the place of a scene. There is no need for a slugline

Now he races down the courthouse hallway, toward the

elevator. He frantically forces the doors open.

The writer can still use a specific point of view

His P.O.V.--The elevator shaft is a black empty abyss. Far

below him a light seeps through one of the lower floors.

This is a new scene

KUBOTA has no choice. He leaps into the elevator shaft,

grabbing the cable, and descends rapidly hand over

hand...SUDDENLY we HEAR the SOUND of the elevator motor

Special effects are capitalized

starting up, echoing, pulsating below him. The elevator

starts to rise...Above him he sees the GUARD with the

Point of view is suggested

shotgun prying open the doors. He's caught in the middle.

Using the elevator as a swinging vine, he leaps over to the

side of the shaft, bumping against the second floor exit

door. He reaches for the metal handle of the exit and forces

the door open--just as the elevator itself is about to trap

him.   *This is actually a new scene— "INT. OFFICE-*
              DAY" But it is not necessary to
              identify it in the narrative format

He lets himself out.. <u>into a big office</u> filled with desks and

secretaries, other clerical types. They pay no attention to

him as he casually walks from the elevator exit to the front

entrance...nodding amicably to a person or two...as he

disappears out the front door.

                    •   •   •

Whatever style you use, more narrative or more visual (with slug lines), the general code word is consistency. Choose one style for the pilot story, and maintain it from the beginning to middle to end. As for the length of the story, here is a general guideline for page counts:

Length of Show	Pages in Treatment (approximate page count)
30 minutes	10–15 pp.
60 minutes	15–25 pp.
90 minutes	25–40 pp.
120 minutes	40–60 pp.

4. Future Storylines

Even with a strong pilot story, producers are inclined to ask: "Where does it go from here? They have an inordinate fear that pilot stories are one shots; that series longevity can't be achieved. That's what this section—Future Storylines—is about.

In no more than a few paragraphs you'll have to convince the producer that the potential for series episodes is virtually unlimited. You can provide a number of different storylines (6–13 on the average) showing the built-in diversity of the concept and character interaction. Each story area can reflect the potential for dramatic conflict.

The following storylines show how the "Ziggy's Gang" series might be developed in future episodes. The storylines are brief—a single paragraph with a beginning, middle, and end. Since the featured characters were already described in the presentation, and the pilot story showed them in action, the producer already has an idea of how they might act and react in these types of stories.

Future Storylines

1. ZIGGY is running for a school office, and the gang converts the garage into temporary campaign headquarters. The opponent is a fast-talking charmer who looks like a shoo-in. DUDE tries to teach ZIGGY how to out-talk his opponent, but ZIGGY knows he can't do it. As the campaign gets underway, he decides to be himself and suffer the consequences--but the gang plays up his honesty and down home sincerity, and ZIGGY wins in an upset victory.

2. There's a talent show at the park, and the gang wants to win the trophy. They enter SAMSON as a trombone player, who, of course, wants nothing to do with it. But he acquiesces for the gang's sake. He's terrible and loses. The gang realizes he did his best, and sacrificed his own desires on their behalf--so they build a trophy of their own, and present it to him in their own garage.

3. LADY is being pursued by a boy at school. She tells

everyone she wants to get rid of him, he's a pest, a

nuisance. Her reaction is so strong, the gang tries to

discourage the boy--until they realize LADY really likes

him. They recognize that LADY is not only one of the guys,

she's one of the girls, too. They do their best to set things

right.

. . .

The storylines can be written in separate paragraphs as they appear above, or on separate pages for each story. Once all the storylines are written, the writer can take time to embellish some, delete others, or add additional stories for the sake of series longevity and dramatic diversity.

The Completed Series Presentation

Once you've outlined the format, characters, pilot story, and projected storylines, you've laid the groundwork for the sale of your series idea, which brings us to an interesting point about your reader. The presentation is written for a very special person: a producer or program executive who reads new projects routinely. That person knows acceptable formats, is familiar with series hyperbole, and casts a jaundiced eye on rehashed ideas. Your project can shine above the rest if it addresses practical needs as well as creative ones. If it's in the correct form, if the premise is "high concept," if the characters are likeable and "castable," the pilot story well-crafted and produceable, you may raise an eyebrow. And if it's written with style and creative flair, you may raise two eyebrows.

The presentation itself is typed on 8-1/2" × 11" paper, double-spaced, and sequentially numbered from the first page to the last. Each section begins a new page, and is identified by the appropriate heading: "FORMAT"; "CHARACTERS"; "PILOT STORY"; "ADDITIONAL STORYLINES." The pilot story is the heart of your proposal, and is the most detailed part of the presentation. The story should be solidly designed and constructed for television, allowing for natural act breaks, and building credibly from beginning to middle to end. The characters should be fully integrated into the story conflicts, builds, and resolution.

Once the presentation is completely written, have some colleagues, knowledgeable friends, or professional contacts read the material and offer some suggestions for strengthening it. You may find useful ideas emerging about formats, characters, and plots. Listen objectively; constructive criticism may help sharpen the edges of the presentation. Then, with a strong and clearly written presentation, you'll be ready to hit the marketplace.

Whether you're writing high concept drama or slapstick comedy, the most polished work is the one that will win attention. And that brings you one step closer toward your ultimate goal in this business: a sale.

Series presentations can be marketed to networks, studios, production companies, cable TV-companies, syndicators, independent stations, and the list goes on. A detailed analysis of the market place is presented in *Part Four*.

3

The Variety Special and Quiz Show

The Variety Special

A television special requires a totally different approach from the weekly series presentation. The appeal of the show is generally based on the event itself—designed to be a one shot entry for the networks, syndicated market, or cable TV marketplace.

A proposal for a variety special generally centers around the star and the package. A *package* is a strong line-up of creative talent committed to the show (actors, singers, musicians, dancers, directors, producers). At this stage of the development, it may be too early to seek actual commitments, but it is possible to assess individual intents and interest. Even with that, every variable under the sun may affect the producer's ability to deliver a package—from availability dates and conflicts, to negotiations over salaries and screen credits.

As a perceptive writer, you might take note of all upcoming events in your local area, and see if they have relevance for the television marketplace. One or two events might be a natural for cable TV, local TV, or the larger national scene. Evaluate the schedules for night clubs, cafes, college concerts, jazz festivals, dance festivals, theatre performances, comedy clubs, even sports competitions. If an idea is particularly worth pursuing, contact the people who are in charge of the event, and see if broadcast rights are still available. If big stars are involved, chances are slim that you'll get the rights. But if the event is targeted to smaller audiences and the talent is amenable to being taped or filmed, you can develop an intriguing proposal. Work with the people in charge of the event, offering your services to write the proposal for the broadcast marketplace.

As an example of the success of this kind of technique, let's look at the proposal developed for a cable TV special on the San Francisco Blues Festival. Impressed by the possibilities of this annual event, the producer contacted the people who ran the Festival, and obtained rights to develop the project for television.

THE TENTH ANNUAL SAN FRANCISCO BLUES FESTIVAL

A Television Special

The blues is back! After a decade of being relegated, for

the most part, to obscure beer joints and roadhouses, blues

artists are returning to the spotlight. An international

blues revival, similar to that which occurred in the late

sixties, is well under way. Large and enthusiastic audiences

are rediscovering the musical roots of popular music as

evidenced by the growing number of clubs around the country

that are regularly featuring blues and the many successful

annual festivals such as those in Ann Arbor, Chicago and
Memphis.

The biggest audience for today's blues artists seems to be
coming from the members of the so-called baby boom although
a number of their younger brothers, sisters and friends seem
to be picking up on the sound, too. Some appreciate the
simple honesty and gut feeling of the blues as opposed to
overproduced, over-commercialized rock and pop music.
Others want music that's danceable without being mechanical
and formularized like disco. Some are interested in the
blues for its historical significance–blues is, after all,
the basis for the rock, jazz and soul music which has emerged
in the last three decades. Still others appreciate the blues
as a celebration of life and survival in hard times. In its
simple, basic eloquence, the blues can hit you where you
live like no other form of music.

The Bay Area Blues Scene

The San Francisco-Oakland area has been in the forefront of
this most recent blues revival. Over a dozen clubs in the
area are currently catering to the blues crowd. Blues

programs, including weekly live concerts, are being broadcast by several Bay Area radio stations. Arhoolie Records, a major independent blues and folk label is located here, as is Flower Films, home of noted ethnic documentarian, Les Blank. Tying these various blues circles together is the annual San Francisco Blues Festival, now in its tenth year, which has emerged as one of the premiere blues events in the country.

The Bay Area blues tradition goes back to the days of World War II when a number of blacks migrated to the area to work in the shipyards. Many came from Texas and brought with them a distinctive jazz and boogie-based sound. In the late sixties, there was another influx of bluesmen—only this time, the performers were mostly young, white, and from Chicago. Musicians such as Paul Butterfield, Elvin Bishop, and the late Mike Bloomfield, brought with them a love and respect for the old blues masters that had a strong impact on the music scene here. Rock palaces such as the Filmore and Avalon Ballroom began to book the likes of B.B. King, James Cotton, and Junior Wells, to the delight of the rock audiences. One of those most affected was Tom Mazzolini, who went on to create the first San Francisco Flues Festival ten years ago and has produced every one of them since.

The Tenth Annual San Francisco Blues Festival

This year's festival will take place on a specially con-
structed stage at Fort Mason overlooking San Francisco Bay.
In addition to some of the best talent in the area, this
year's festival is importing a host of major blues figures
from around the country, giving this event national stature.
Among the artists who will appear are Albert Collins,
Clarence ''Gatemouth'' Brown, John Hammond, and Clifton
Chenier. Each came out of blues scenes such as Texas,
Chicago and New York, which have been major influences on
the scene here. Joining them will be some of the best talent
the Bay Area has to offer, such as the Blues Survivors, the
Charles Ford Band, Robert Cray, and Cool Papa.

As producers, we intend to capture the essence of this
year's San Francisco Blues Festival in a one-hour special
that will exceed any previous efforts to bring the blues to
television. We begin, of course, with highlights of the best
performances. Interspersed with the music, we will also profile five of the featured artists, taking our audience
behind the scenes for insights into the lives and times of a
modern day bluesman, through interviews and historical
footage. The result should be a memorable show for die-hard
fans and casual listeners alike.

To capture all the action, we propose to use a five-camera

remote truck and three one-inch videotape recorders. We will

also utilize an experienced sound crew to record a stereo

mix of each performance suitable for simulcast. Once a per-

formance is shot, the editing process will incorporate the

best of the new technologies. Each program will be mastered

on the CMX 340, using a full range of visual effects.

Artist Profiles

CLIFTON CHENIER: Known as the King of Zydeco, Clifton has

been playing his distinctive brand of Louisiana-Texas Cajun

rhythm & blues since the 1950s. Rubboards and funky accor-

dians dominate this blend of r&b, boogie, and what Jelly

Roll Morton used to call stomps and shouts.

CLARENCE ''GATEMOUTH'' BROWN: Black men just didn't play

country music back in Texas in the 1950s but Gatemouth did,

even if it meant slipping away from his regular gigs to jam

with the likes of Willie Nelson and Roy Clark in the white

honky tonks. His blend of blues, jazz, Cajun, bluegrass, and

calypso has made him a favorite in the American southwest

and in Europe for years now, and this versatile performer is finally becoming known to a wider audience.

ALBERT COLLINS: Albert is another product of the Texas blues scene with Gatemouth one of his major influences, as well as T-Bone Walker, and everybody's favorite, B.B. King. His album Frostbite gave his career a big boost in 1981 and his icepick style of playing is guaranteed to cut through anybody's cool.

JOHN HAMMOND: Son of the famous talent scout, executive, producer, and entrepreneur of blues and folk artists, young John had a chance to hear and meet most of the great names as he was growing up. Considered the foremost white interpreter of the blues, Hammond has led blues audiences into a deeper understanding and appreciation of the works of people like Robert Johnson, Muddy Waters, and Blind Lemon Jefferson.

CHARLES FORD BAND: One of the most famous blues bands to come out of California in the early seventies, the three Ford brothers, Robben, Pat, and Mark, are reforming their late father's namesake band especially for this year's festival. Robben Ford is particularly well known in mainstream music circles, having cofounded the L.A. Express with Tom Scott, as well as backing up many name performers such as Joni Mitchell, George Harrison, and blues great Jimmy Witherspoon.

ROBERT CRAY & CURTIS SALGADO: Here's the real-life inspiration for John Belushi's and Dan Akroyd's ''Blues Brothers.'' As the story goes, Curtis met Belushi during the filming of Animal House in his native Eugene, Oregon. In fact, the first Blues Brothers album is dedicated to him.

JOHNNY LITTLEJOHN: Like many blues performers, Johnny taught himself guitar while still a child. After years of working at fish fries and house parties throughout the Delta, Johnny headed for Chicago in the 1950s where he's been a mainstay of that area's blues scene.

LLOYD GLENN: Now in his seventees, Lloyd provides one of the genuine links between the blues and jazz. His unique piano stylings have influenced a number of major jazz-blues artists including Ray Charles.

LITTLE CHARLIE & THE NIGHTCATS: This group, hailing from nearby Sacramento, is a Bay Area favorite. Their fifties style of Chicago blues was one of the surprise hits of the 1980 festival.

BLUES SURVIVORS: Another hit from previous festivals, the

Blues Survivors, and harp player Mark Hummel in particular,

represent the best of the up and coming blues groups in the

Bay Area.

.   .   .

The San Francisco Blues Festival was produced for cable TV and for the syndicated marketplace. The production closely adhered to the style and mood of the proposal. To keep costs down, the producer arranged for a production facility to coventure with him. Under that arrangement, the production facility provided services at cost, and shared in the profits from the sale of the show.

Another way for a writer to create a special is to fashion it after the packaging needs of stars and networks. The network may have a commitment with certain stars, or may want to attract those artists to the network with a packaged project. In that case, the writer puts together the outline for the show and the star segments. It's unlikely that an unestablished writer will be called on to write the special, but it's helpful to know the way a special is developed.

Let's assume the network is looking for a new Sinatra special, and you happen to have strong contacts among Sinatra friends and colleagues. Since specials sell on the basis of concepts and packages, here is a sample proposal that might start the ball rolling.

HOLLYWOOD IN VEGAS

A Music Special With Nancy and Frank Sinatra, Jr.

OUR TOUR GUIDES...NANCY AND FRANK SINATRA, JR.

THEY TAKE US ALL OVER HOLLYWOOD AND VEGAS, SINGING AND

MINGLING WITH THE BEST...

HELEN REDDY IN VEGAS...THE ROLLING STONES AT A HOLLYWOOD

RECORDING SESSION...LIZA MINELLI IN CONCERT...HENRY WINKLER

ON A PROMO TOUR...

THEY GO TOGETHER, SING TOGETHER, PLAY TOGETHER, EVEN AT A

MEN'S ONLY CLUB, WHERE DON RICKLES IS THE ROAST MASTER.

THIS SPECIAL IS ONE THAT WILL BE REMEMBERED. EVEN BY PAPA

FRANK SINATRA, SR., WHO PAYS A SURPRISE VISIT AT THE END.

THIS SPECIAL IS A FAMILY AFFAIR IN EVERY SENSE OF THE WORD!

                            •   •   •

If the stars agree to the premise, the creator needs to line up some
other heavyweights, including a strong producer-director. The creator
also needs to provide a *Rundown Sheet* which delineates show segments and the expected timing for each segment. The timing is generally broken down into Seg Time (segment time) and Run Time. *Seg Time*
refers to the length of individual segments in the show; whereas *Run
Time* is the accumulated timing for the entire program. Once the project actually goes into rehearsals, the timing is modified to fit the actual
production requirements of the show.

This is what a sample rundown sheet looks like:

"HOLLYWOOD IN VEGAS" RUNDOWN

Seg.			Seg. Time	Run Time
I.				
	A.	Frank and Nancy at home, opening patter and intro. (:50)		
	B.	First Song: Nancy & Frank (2:24)	3:14	3:14
		COMMERCIAL	1:04	4:18
II.				
	A.	Frank & Nancy prep for concert with Helen Reddy (:17)		
	B.	Helen Reddy sings in concert (3:14)		

/

"HOLLYWOOD IN VEGAS" RUNDOWN
(Continued)

Seg.			Seg. Time	Run Time
	C.	Frank & Nancy joke in concert (1:00)		
	D.	Helen joins Frank & Nancy for medley (4:34)	9:05	13:23
		COMMERCIAL	1:04	14:27
III.				
	A.	Prep for joining Henry Winkler on promo tour (:07)		
	B.	Henry's patter on tour, comedy bit (2:14)		
	C.	Nancy & Frank intro Henry doing Shakespeare (:42)		
	D.	Henry Winkler does Shakespeare (3:29)		
	E.	Henry joins Nancy & Frank for song (2:34)	9:06	23:33
		COMMERCIAL	1:04	24:37
IV.				
	A.	Frank & Nancy patter, heading toward recording session (:20)		
	B.	Intro Rolling Stones, who have the studio before them (:13)		
	C.	The Stones do medley in studio (6:40)		
	D.	Nancy & Frank record their songs (3:32)	10:45	35:22
		COMMERCIAL	1:04	36:26
V.				
	A.	Frank & Nancy patter; Don Rickles invites them to appear with him at unnamed club (:30)		
	B.	Nancy arrives at club: A Men's Only (:10)		
	C.	Rickles does comedy routine (4:03)		
	D.	Nancy & Frank join in comedy bit (2:23)	7:06	43:32
		COMMERCIAL	1:04	44:36
VI.				
	A.	Prep for night's concert with Liza Minelli (:11)		
	B.	Liza sings medley in concert (3:43)		
	C.	Liza, Frank, and Nancy sing (2:40)	6:34	51:10
		COMMERCIAL	1:04	52:14

"HOLLYWOOD IN VEGAS" RUNDOWN
(Continued)

Seg.			Seg. Time	Run Time
VII.				
	A.	Nancy's solo number (2:10)		
	B.	Frank's solo number (2:30)		
	C.	Frank & Nancy at home, surprise appearance, Frank Sinatra, Sr. (:45)		
	D.	Frank & Nancy's Goodnights to audience (:20)		
	E.	Credits (:38)	6:23	58:37

If a production company or a network wants a more detailed presentation, they might set a deal to put the project together. (For sample Writers Guild Minimums on Variety Shows, see p. 203.) Variety proposals are usually short and sketchy, to test the waters for a nibble. Until you have strong connections and a good track record, it will be a hard sale to make.

The Quiz Program Proposal

The proposal for a quiz show is an entity unto itself. The narrative is a combination of hard-sell and practical description. It conveys the excitement of the show, while it answers questions about the format, set design, and production values.

Here's the program proposal for a quiz show called "Compute-a-Quiz." It describes the format and production requirements, while it offers an on-going sense of the show and it's pacing. The first page sets the premise:

COMPUTE-A-QUIZ

COMPUTE-A-QUIZ IS AN EXCITING HALF-HOUR GAME SHOW FOR

CHILDREN, WHICH STIMULATES THE MIND AND CHALLENGES THE

REFLEXES. IT'S AS FAST-PACED AS A MODERN DAY COMPUTER.

IN EACH SHOW, THE CONTESTANTS--AGES 6-12--VIE FOR A WIDE

RANGE OF PRIZES, FROM CREATIVE PLAYTHINGS TO EXPENSE-PAID

TRIPS TO DISNEYLAND. THE FINAL GRAND PRIZE OF THE DAY IS

AWARDED IN THE SHOPPING-HALL-OF-THE-FUTURE, WHERE THE TOTAL

PRIZE POINTS ARE COMPUTED.

• • •

That first page just denotes a general idea or premise of the series, and tries to elicit interest. The following pages provide a more visual sense of the show. The format section details how the game is played, what the set looks like, where the players are, and so on. This is what that section looks like:

COMPUTE-A-QUIZ

THE FORMAT

Our M. C. introduces two contestants to the audience, asks

them about their background, their age, school, and

interests. Now the game begins.

The contestants are seated on futuristic podiums, facing a

giant, stylized computer screen. They have ''compute-a-

control boards'' which activate a circle of flashing lights

on the screen. The contestant who first flashes the lights,

answers the question.

If the answer is right, the computer counts out the prize

points. If the answer is wrong, the computer fizzles.

Our M. C. gives the right answer, then it's on to the next

question.

Our program is keyed to a lightning fast inquiry of general

knowledge, and is climaxed by the Compute-a-Point

Shopping Spree. Once the points are accumulated, the

contestants enter the shopping hall of the future, where

they can select any number of prizes--so long as they stay

within range of their computer prize points.

.   .   .

Now that the reader has some sense of the format, sets, and game rules, you can be even *more* specific about the content of the pilot show. The next section of the proposal is rife with a sampling of questions and answers. It's a good idea to provide different kinds of questions and answers, so the producer is reassured that the possibilities are endless for upcoming programs. This section appears right after the format. It can be titled anything from *Sample Game Show* to *Sample Q & A*.

COMPUTE-A-QUIZ

SAMPLE QUESTIONS

COMPUTE-A-QUIZ questions are designed to test general

knowledge as well as academic prowess. And they come in any

form...

VISUAL. On the computer screen, itself...

AURAL. Heard through the computer speaker...

TOSS-UP. Direct from the M. C.

The questions appear in haphazard combinations, keeping
contestants and viewers on their toes.

On the computer screen we see a horse, a chicken, a cow. The
M. C. asks: Which is a member of the fowl family?

Two voices are heard through the computer speaker. The M. C.
asks: Which of those voices is the President of the United
States?

On the screen, we see a rectangle, a triangle, a square, and
a circle. The screen goes blank, and the M. C. asks: Which
shape came before the triangle?

On the screen, we see an apple, a pear, and a lemon. The
M. C. asks: Which of these are fruit? The contestant
must name all in order to win.

We hear a train whistle, a coach's whistle, a clarinet, and a
tug boat. The M. C. asks: Which is used by a football
coach?

On the screen, we see the numbers: 0,2,4,5. The M. C. asks:
Which can be divided by two?

We hear the computer whirr, and see the lights flash. From
the speaker we hear a lion's roar, a dog's bark, a cat's

meow. The M. C. asks: Which belong to the feline family?

The respondent has to name the cat and the lion to win.

*   *   *

The look of proposals for quiz shows vary considerably, but the general formula remains the same—quick format, fast tempo, and a visual sense of the game in play. Proposals build an enthusiastic and "live" sense of the show.

Proposals can be submitted to any successful quiz show producer, videotape production house, or television packager. The fees for creating a new series, as well as for writing skits, sketches, questions and answers, are all covered by the Writers Guild Minimum Basic Agreement Sample Minimums for Quiz Shows and are listed on p. 204.

4

Public TV Presentations

The Public Television Marketplace

America's system of public television was originally inspired by a Carnegie Commission report, published as *Public Television: A Program for Action.** Twelve years later that system of program development, financing, production, and distribution underwent a probing reexamination. The Carnegie Commission on the Future of Public Broadcasting undertook an eighteen month study, hearing testimony from TV writers, producers, station managers, and others involved in public broadcasting. That report found the system fraught with weaknesses—from political in-fighting to lack of funds for significant creative development.‡

As a result, the Commission recommended the establishment of a new national entity—The Public Telecommunications Trust—which would replace the Corporation for Public Broadcasting (CPB). In essence, the Trust would be responsible for national leadership, planning, and development in the entire public television realm. One of its chief functions would be to house and protect a most important Division from outside pressures; a Program Services Endowment.

---

*Public Television: A Program for Action, New York: Harper & Row, 1967.
‡A Public Trust: The Report of the Carnegie Commission on the Future of Public Broadcasting. New York: Bantam Books, 1979.

The Program Services Endowment was conceived as the central agency for increasing public television's commitment to American writers and producers. According to the Carnegie Commission, this Endowment would have a single objective—to support the American creative community and the development of quality programs.

That report had enormous impact on the structure and management of CPB. The agency revamped itself and created a separate Program Fund, which is fully supportive of independent filmmakers, TV writers, and public TV producers. It is designed to be insulated from political pressure, and remains one of the most important single sources for funding in the public television marketplace.

The Corporation for Public Broadcasting (CPB)

The Program Fund of CPB is a major funder of public broadcasting programs. The congressional mandate of the agency is to develop public TV programs of high quality, diversity, creativity, excellence, and innovation. That's where you and your ideas fit in.

Independent producers, writers, and public TV stations can submit program proposals, and CPB encourages co-productions between independents and Public Broadcasting Service (PBS) stations (they also encourage submissions by women and minorities). If you have an idea for development, you can write to them directly, or, more practically, set up a meeting with the head of programming for your local PBS station. Local PBS stations are likely to know the program proposal requirements of CPB, and can help you put together a more competitive proposal if you mutually decide to pursue the idea.

CPB regularly publishes requests for proposals along with guidelines for submitting projects. Contact them for the latest guidelines and Program Fund announcements.

When you apply for funding, you'll need to fill out a *basic information sheet*, which is supplied with the program guidelines. That is the *Face Sheet* of the application, and describes the content of the show, costs, and key personnel involved. In addition, you'll need to write a 3–5 page synopsis which shows how you plan to handle the subject matter for television. It's written precisely the same way you would write a storyline for the networks. If you have completed a detailed treatment, that can be attached as well.

A budget is required for CPB applications, indicating how much money is needed for development or production of the television show. The budget *is* something a writer must deal with in grant applications. The funding agency needs to know where you plan to spend its money. For script development grants, the budget is usually very simple:

writer's fees (this can be based on Writers Guild minimums), research fees, travel, and administrative costs. Some helpful hints on budgeting appear later in this chapter, and a sample budget is available from CPB is you ask for it.

CPB is an approachable agency. If you are developing a cultural project or one that fits into a dramatic or special category, contact the Associate Director of Cultural Programs for some feedback. Similarly, if your project is public affairs oriented, contact the Associate Director of News and Public Affairs. In addition, you can submit your project to the Executive Producer of series funded by CPB. Dramatic projects have been funded through *American Playhouse* (WNET-TV, New York); documentaries through *Frontline* (WGBH-TV, Boston); children's and family through a consortium of stations (headed by WQED-TV, Pittsburgh).

Another interesting resource is the *Annenberg/CPB* project, which is separate and distinct from the Program Fund. The *Annenberg* project received $15 million over a ten-year period to support innovative projects that use new technologies—including television and film—to improve higher education. It's a very different and intriguing opportunity for writers and producers who want to collaborate with institutions of higher learning (and vice versa). For guidelines and more information about the program, write to the *Annenberg/CPB* project (same address as CPB, see *Appendix C*).

Public Broadcasting Service (PBS)

PBS is the representative national agency for public broadcasting stations. PBS functions primarily as a distributor of programs, although it does get involved, peripherally, in the development of new shows for the system.

The PBS Programming Department is primarily concerned with acquisition of programs already produced, but can be helpful in offering some backing for projects that might be of interest to their station membership. That support usually comes in the form of a letter of endorsement rather than a banker's check for writing and producing TV shows. They will, however, help secure interest from appropriate funding sources, and, in some rare cases, will put up some seed money for development. The reality is that PBS funds are scarce, and they are not considered a primary source for program funding.

Each year, PBS membership (stations, not viewers) gathers together in an annual rite known as the Program Fair. Independent producers and local PBS stations show off their wares, and the station managers vote on those projects which they are willing to buy. The Program Fair is comprised of a diversity of program offerings, from dramatic series to local cooking shows. Usually, those shows are available for screening by other station members. Those programs which pass the first round of scrutiny still have to be approved in other steps beyond the annual voting rite.

Although PBS is not the place to expect realistic funding for script development, there is a division that is active in developing new projects. The Station Independent Program Cooperative (SIP) seeks out television projects that might have special appeal to audiences during pledge week. They are looking for shows that appeal to the right demographic audience: those with hefty pocketbooks and wallets for station donations. SIP wants high-powered shows with big-name stars, and may put up some co-financing dollars for production or for program acquisition.

Regional Public TV Networks

Some public television station managers are not comfortable with the national programming role imposed by PBS. They believe that PBS can't possibly represent their local interests and needs. As a result, they joined together to form regional networks to develop, produce, acquire, and distribute programming.

The Eastern Educational Network (EEN) is the oldest of all the regional networks, founded in 1960, and is composed of 33 corporate member stations (including WGBH-TV, Boston, WNET-TV, New York). EEN is particularly active in the programming area, and administers a service called the Interregional Program Service (IPS). IPS has become a strong contender in the area of new programming and serves as a broker for independent producers, public broadcasting stations, and other distribution sources. They serve a clientele of licensees nationwide. EEN has initiated major programming efforts for national audiences, including development, co-production ventures, and program acquisition of new material.

The Southern Educational Communications Association (SECA) has been actively involved in helping producers and writers find funding for projects which might be produced through a station in their region and distributed nationally. SECA represents 91 public television stations in a 15-state range, including Virginia, Florida, and Texas. They have a strong track record in developing, co-producing, and acquiring projects for national distribution.

The Central Educational Network (CEN) represents 35 public TV stations in the heartland, and has been primarily involved in marketing educational programs to public TV stations and universities. They are interested in program acquisition, as well as developing original projects that might have appeal to their member stations. Like other regional networks, they have recognized the need for more original programming to help bolster their schedules, and to possibly earn profits in national distribution.

The Pacific Mountain Network (PMN) is the newest regional network formed by the merger of the Western Educational Network and the Rocky Mountain Public Broadcasting Network. They represent 32 stations in the west, and have been involved in a number of co-production efforts (including sports and public affairs programs). They have a program fund which supports projects from member stations and independents. For locations of the regional networks, see *Appendix D*.

National Endowment for the Arts (NEA)

The National Endowment for the Arts was created by Congress in 1965 to encourage and support the arts in America. Its fundamental role is to support creativity at the highest level, and to stimulate the enjoyment of the arts in our country. The agency fulfills its mission through various grant-making programs, including one called *Media Arts*, designed for individuals and organizations in television, film, and radio.

The Media Arts Program

This NEA program offers support for individuals and nonprofit organizations in TV, film, and radio. Projects that are eligible include narrative, experimental, and documentary works. This program also funds a small number of public television series that focus on the arts. Here are some of the categories of grant support *within* the Media Arts Program:

Film/Video Production offers grants for original productions that intrinsically deal with the arts. Individuals can apply for outright grants of up to $25,000, but should have significant experience in television or film. If you apply in this category, you'll need to fill out a Face Sheet that describes the project, and write a short treatment (2–3 page synopsis) showing how the project will be translated for television. You'll also need to include a brief biography, a detailed budget, and a superb sample of your previous work in film or tape.

Panelists for NEA give very serious consideration to the level of artistic and professional achievement exhibited in your sample project. Most of the film/video production grants are made to non profit organizations and are limited to $50,000 with a requirement for matching funds.

Programming in the Arts is a category for a limited number of PBS series, and requires substantial funding from other sources. Sample projects funded include *American Playhouse, Great Performances,* and *Live from the Met.* No single programs are funded under this category, but a small number of grants are available—up to $50,000—for documentaries on major living American artists. Prior to submitting application in this category, NEA requires consultation with their staff.

American Film Institute (AFI) Independent Filmmaker Program is designed for independent video and film artists. AFI administers this program for NEA, offering grants of up to $10,000 to individuals working in narrative, documentary, experimental, or animated projects. The Institute also runs a conservatory for the training of advanced students in film writing, directing, and producing. There is an excellent program for women directors, and related services for television and film fields.

The Regional Fellowship Program is an important one for writers and producers to know about. Independent film and video artists can apply for fellowships through a regional program set up by NEA, AFI, state arts agencies, private foundations and corporations. This program is administered by regional media arts centers throughout the country and is a good multi-state resource for funding projects in television and film. You can contact the regional media arts center closest to you to determine eligibility requirements. (A directory of media arts centers is listed in *Appendix D.*)

Short Film Showcase is a program for independent producers who have produced short films and want to distribute them to commercial movie theaters around the country. This program is administered by the Foundation for Independent Video and Film in New York.

Radio Production is a program that supports development and production of single programs and series, emphasizing creative use of the medium. Independent writer-producers can apply for non-matching grants of up to $15,000. Organizations can receive up to $50,000 on a matching basis.

Other Programs of Interest at NEA

Other divisions of NEA supports project of interest to professional writers. For example:

The Literature Program offers fellowships for $20,000 to creative writers. Applicants should be published authors, and must submit samples of their work. Although the guidelines don't specify TV and film writers, the fact is writers for television and film *are* eligible to apply. Contact the Literature Program at NEA for more information and guidelines.

The Theatre Program offers fellowships for professional playwrights to advance their careers. Applicants in this category should have had a play produced within five years prior to application. One year fellowships range up to $17,500. A small number of two-year fellowships are also granted.

For a comprehensive look at all the programs at NEA, write for a free copy of their *Guide to NEA*. You can also write to the individual programs that interest you for their guidelines and application forms. (For address, see *Appendix C*; for publications, see "Grants and Non-Commercial Funding" in the *Annotated Bibliography*.)

The National Endowment for the Humanities (NEH)

The National Endowment for the Humanities was created by Congress in 1965, along with its sister arts agency. The mission of NEH is to encourage and support important works in the humanities, and to disseminate that information to the widest possible audience. The Media Program at NEH has been one of the largest and most important funding sources for public television.

Humanities Projects in Media

Within the Division of General Programs, the awkwardly titled *Humanities Projects in Media* is particularly relevant to freelance writers and independent producers. The Media Program supports the development and production of new television, film, and radio projects, with grants ranging from $10,000 to several million dollars.

The Media Program of NEH has funded such television projects as *Vietnam: The Television History, Mark Twain Series, American Short Story, Middletown, For Us The Living, Odyssey, Rosie the Riveter, The Scarlet Letter, The Adams Chronicles, The Best of Families, To Be Young, Gifted and Black,* and many others of high merit.

The general themes that are relevant to NEH shift with the incumbent administration's interpretation of the humanities. In the past, NEH supported socially relevant projects tied to humanities themes, then shifted to a more conservative stance, supporting classical scholarly subjects, e.g., *Masterworks of Civilization.* You can keep up with the current trends by reading the Media guidelines carefully and contacting staff members to determine eligibility.

A project that is submitted to NEH for consideration should meet one or more of these basic NEH goals: provide an interpretation and appreciation of significant cultural works; help illuminate historical ideas, figures, and events; provide an understanding of the disciplines of the humanities. Those disciplines have been defined by Congress, and are listed by academic fields in the guidelines.

The NEH Media Program encourages professional writers and producers to work in cooperation with scholars in particular program areas. The meeting-of-the-minds between professionals and scholars creates a challenging atmosphere, and contributes to some mutually rewarding ideas about program development in the humanities.

NEH offers several types of grants:

1. *Planning grants* of $15,000 or less, support writers, producers, and scholars seeking to develop innovative media humanities projects.

2. *Script development grants* are the most relevant for television writers, since they are designed to support the writing of scripts and series outlines. They cover appropriate research costs for treatment and scripts (travel, consultants, etc.) as well as other development costs (writer's fees, story conferences, typing and duplicating, etc.). These grants might range from $20,000 to over $100,000, with no requirements for matching funds (i.e., it is an outright grant to the writer or project director).

3. *Production grants* can be for single programs, pilots, or series episodes. These can range from $100,000 to over $1 million or more, and can include the development of additional scripts. Since these grants are so costly, they usually require additional gifts and matching funds from other sources.

As for submission of proposals, NEH strongly recommends a preliminary inquiry at least six weeks before each deadline. The staff can help determine the appropriateness of the project and can help you to prepare a more competitive proposal for submission. In addition, the staff can guide your project through formal evaluation procedures.

A complete description of relevant grant programs, proposal requirements, and application deadlines are available in *Humanities Projects in Media,* published by NEH. Write for your free copy. (For address, see *Appendix C.*)

Other Funding Sources

The following chart outlines the funding sources available for independent writers and producers in public television. As you can see, there are a number of other resources for funding possibilities. In addition to CPB, NEA, and NEH, other federal agencies offer support for developing and producing certain kinds of TV and film projects. Independent projects can also be funded through state and regional associations, film funds and associations, and private and corporate foundations.

Funding Sources for Writers and Producers

Federal Agencies

Corporation for Public Broadcasting
National Endowment for the Arts
National Endowment for the Humanities
Agencies with Requests for Proposals
  (RFPs)

Networks

Public Broadcasting Service
Regional networks: EEN
                SECA
                CEN
                PMN

State Agencies

State arts agencies
State humanities agencies
State education agencies
Regional media arts centers
Film and TV commissions

Private Foundations

Guggenheim
Ford
Mellon
etc.

Corporations

Exxon
Mobil
Xerox
etc.

Independent Film Funds

American Film Institute
Film Fund
Independent Documentary Fund
Sundance Film Institute

Federal Agencies

Some federal agencies have a long history of awarding contracts for media projects, although the projects are often narrowly targeted to restricted needs. The Department of Defense (DOD), for example, has been a major contractor of film projects, but the content is heavily oriented toward informational and instructional requirements of DOD.

The U.S. Information Agency (USIA) has been a steady user of media. In addition to producing and managing *Voice of America*, they produce and acquire television programming for broadcast overseas. Most of these projects, however, are heavily politicized in terms of reaching USIA goals and missions.

The Department of Education (DOE) was one of the largest funders of children's programming for PBS. Some of their projects included *Spaces, Somebody Else's Place, Sesame Street, 3–2–1–Contact, Electric Company, Que Pasa, USA?, Villa Allegre, Rebop, Vegetable Soup*. With changes in administration and departmental policy, DOE no longer funds television programs. However, they have distributed *block grants* to the state education agencies for regranting purposes. The states are supposed to fulfill the same kind of mandate, and it is possible for state agencies to fund television projects. You can contact the state agency nearest you to discuss that possibility. (A directory of state education agencies is listed in *Appendix D*.)

The National Science Foundation (NSF) was an important supporter of television projects, especially those providing insight into the sciences, e.g., *Nova, 3–2–1 Contact*. However, that funding program has been discontinued and it is unlikely that NSF will have funding available for television projects in the near future.

As you can see from this brief look at some federal funding patterns, the needs and priorities of federal agencies undergo constant change. Those changes are announced through periodic Requests for Proposals (*RFPs*) which outline specific needs and requirements of agencies looking for contracts to award. RFPs list the mandate of the agency, the type of project sought, application deadlines and guidelines. All RFPs are published in *Commerce Business Daily*, the federal equivalent of *Daily Variety* and *Hollywood Reporter*. Unfortunately, there are scores of irrelevant RFPs published, and it is frustrating and time-consuming to find one that is pertinent to your interests. A combined listing of RFPs is published in the *Federal Domestic Assistance Catalogue*, which might be available through a federal section in your library.

State Arts and Humanities Agencies

One of the most practical places to explore seed money for the development of original scripts is the state arts and humanities agencies. Each state has money appropriated by the legislature for support of artistic and cultural work relevant to that state. NEA and NEH also contribute block grants for regranting purposes to the state agencies.

The arts and humanities agencies are separate and distinct from each other, operating within the same general mandate as their national counterparts. Since each agency has different guidelines, you can contact the staff to determine if script development grants are possible. (A directory of state arts agencies and state humanities agencies can be found in *Appendix D*.)

Regional media arts centers are another source of funding. As mentioned previously, these multi-state agencies are supported by grants from NEA, AFI, state arts agencies, and private corporations and foundations in the states. These centers offer fellowships and grants to independent creative artists. (See *Appendix D* for a list of media arts centers.)

State Film and Television Commissions

State Film and Television Commissions are another resource for discussing your ideas and projects. Although they have no funding capabilities, these agencies are committed to the idea of nurturing new productions, and they can be helpful in the pragmatics of pre-production contacts. They know who is doing what in your state, and can often provide interesting leads. (A directory of state film and television commissions is in *Appendix D*.)

Independent Film Funds

Some independent sources of funding are available through a number of film funds established by the private and public sector. Among them:

American Film Institute (AFI), as discussed earlier, is largely funded by the National Endowment for the Arts. In addition to the independent fellowship program, AFI supports the Regional Media Arts Fellowships, trains advanced students at its conservatory, and supports an array of television and film services. It offers training in screenwriting at the conservatory, and supports a director's apprenticeship program with the Academy of Motion Picture Arts & Sciences. You can get more information directly from AFI in Los Angeles.

The Film Fund is the only funding organization specifically encouraging projects on contemporary issues and controversial topics, e.g., nuclear policy, prison reform, racial injustice, sexual harassment, environmental abuse. The fund is supported by foundations and individuals, and offers grants for preproduction and script research, as well as for production, editing, and distribution. Grants are small ($1,000 to $10,000), but the staff also assists in finding additional grant money.

The Independent Documentary Fund (The Television Laboratory/WNET) is funded by the National Endowment for the Arts and the Ford Foundation. It's designed for producers seeking limited production or completion funds for documentaries. The application process is simple, involving a three-page proposal and submission of sample material from the program.

Foundation for Video & Film, also supported by NEA, administers the Short Film Showcase. It's one of the few places to turn for assistance with production and distribution of short films. The foundation selects projects for placement in commercial movie theatres nationwide.

The Sundance Institute for Film and Television was founded by Robert Redford and other professionals to provide a resource center for writers, directors, and producers interested in exploring film projects with strong humanistic content. The Institute conducts two programs. *Script Development* is the first, designed to offer selected screenwriters on-going collaborative input from professional story editors and film writers. The Institute provides funds for travel expenses to story conferences if the writers are separated geographically. The second program is a month-long residency fellowship for filmmakers at the Sundance Resort in Utah. The Institute looks for fictional feature-length projects, but not necessarily for the commercial marketplace; some have been selected for the *American Playhouse* series on PBS.

The Writers Guild of America Foundation is a foundation set up and administered by the Writers Guild of America, East, Inc. The foundation has periodically offered fellowships and stipends for new writers in television and film.

Private Foundations and Corporate Sources of Funding

Relatively few foundations are waiting to fund scriptwriters. However, several have been active in funding major television projects, including Guggenheim, Ford, Lilly, Mellon, Markle, Exxon, Xerox, Mobil, and others. Private foundations and corporations have established objectives and mandates which might fit into the project you propose.

One very helpful place to begin your search for appropriate funding is The Foundation Center, located in New York City, and Washington, D.C. (They have field offices and repository libraries in several parts of the country.) The Center is the only nonprofit organization in the country designed to analyze and disseminate information about foundations. One of its publications, *The Foundation Directory*, profiles thousands of foundations and can help identify those organizations that support projects similar to your own. The directory identifies foundations that have supported film and video projects, as well as those interested in a vast array of catalogued subjects.

After determining the most appropriate possible contacts, tailor a letter to the specific interests of each foundation. You can define how your project relates to the mission of that organization, how you plan to carry out the project, what the television project might look like, and how your background fits in to guarantee success of the project.

With respect to corporations, you can learn a great deal about their interests, objectives, and philosophies from their annual reports. You can also delve through a number of research directories available at your local library to determine which ones support similar kinds of projects.

A listing of selected foundations appears in *Appendix C* of this book, and a complete resource guide to important publications on funding appears in the *Annotated Bibliography* (pp. 268–271).

Proposal Writing for Non-Commercial Television

If you're planning to submit a project to any public agency, first write for the guidelines and application forms. The guidelines will give you a broad idea of the agency's needs, and your proposal will have to address those needs. A public television proposal is generally comprised of three parts: (1) the application form (called the *Face Sheet*); (2) the narrative proposal, which details your objectives and program format; and (3) the budget. In addition, a timetable is usually included, and the vitae (resumés) of all key personnel are included.

The Face Sheet

The first page of the application is called a face sheet. It asks for identifying information about the applicant and the proposal. Most face sheets require an abstract to be written in a paragraph or two, outlining the objectives and format of the show. It also asks for information about key personnel. A carefully worded synopsis is especially important when you consider the fact that some evaluators might only see that first page abstract.

A sample Face Sheet appears on the next page. There are *many* variations on the same theme, depending on the agency's individual forms.

NEH — APPLICATION COVER SHEET

Form OMB-128-R-0071

1. Individual.Applicant/Principal Project Director
a. Name and Mailing Address

(1) Swartz, Charles S.
(last,) (first,) (initial)

(2) Rothman, Stephanie

(city) (state) (zip)

Co-Project Directors
title/position

f. Telephone
-- -- ext.

g. Citizenship
1. ☒ USA 2. ☐ Other Specify:

b. Date of Birth
-- / -- / --
mo day year

c. Major Field of Study
(1) History
(2) Sociology

d. Highest Degree Attained
(1) B.A.
(2) B.A. _ / _ mo year

e. Education
(1) Yale U.
(2) UC Berkeley

(For NEH use ONLY)

Date Received
Application #
Initials

2. Type of Application
1. ☒ New   2. ☐ Revision
*3. ☐ Renewal *4. ☐ Supplement
*If 3 or 4 (above) enter previous grant #

4. Type of Applicant
1. ☐ Individual
*2. ☒ Institution/Organization

3. Program To Which Application Is Being Made

___ Media Program - Scripting

5. Requested Period
4/1/85 _ 3/31/86 __ 12 __
From: mo day yr To: mo day yr
Total Months

6. Audiences (Direct Beneficiaries)
a. General public
b. Out-of-school adults
c. Minorities - women

7. Requested Amount
Outright $ 68,877
Gift & Match $ -0-
NEH Total $ 68,877
Cost Sharing & Other Contributions $ 6,000
Total Project $ 74,877

Congressional District 23--

* If (2) above (inst./org.) enter -
Type: Public media
Status: Private non-profit

8. Field of Project
American history and literature

9. Location Where Project Will Be Completed
Los Angeles, California

10. Public Issues Of Project
gender equality; social costs of urbanization & industrialization

11. Topic (Title) of Project
''SUSAN LENOX: HER FALL AND RISE''

12. Description of Proposed Project (Do not exceed space provided)

This proposal is for funds to complete the research and development of a three-hour television script dramatizing the novel Susan Lenox: Her Fall and Rise, by David Graham Phillips. The humanities objective is to provide general audiences with insight into the critical issues raised by Phillips' work, including social problems of urbanization and industrialization, many of which are still with us today; the status of women in the period; and the role of individualism in American life. Project Directors: Stephanie Rothman (writer-director) and Charles S. Swartz (writer-producer). Advisory Board: Ronald Gottesman (Director, U.S.C. Center for Humanities & Prof. of English), Steven J. Ross (Asst. Prof. of History, U.S.C.), Daniel Aaron (Prof. Emeritus of English, Harvard & President Library of America), Nina Baym (Director, School of Humanities & Prof. of English, U. of Illinois at Urbana-Champaign), & Walter B. Rideout (Prof. of English, U. of Wisconsin). Media Consultant: Richard A. Blum.

13a. Have you submitted, or do you plan to submit a similar application to another NEH Program? If yes, provide name(s):[year(s) when applicable]

No

13b. Have you submitted, or do you plan to submit a similar application to another government or private entity? If yes, provide name(s): [year(s) when applicable]

C.P.B.

IMPORTANT — READ INSTRUCTIONS CAREFULLY BEFORE COMPLETING BLOCKS 14 & 15

14. Authorizing Official (name & mailing address)

Charles S. Swartz

15. Institution/Organization (name & mailing address)

The Susan Lenox Project
℅ Charles S. Swartz.

Certification: I certify the statements herein are true and correct to the best of my knowledge and belief:

Sig. _____ Date / /
authorizing official/applicant   mo day yr

Type Ins./Org.: Private non-profit

Let's examine the Face Sheet to identify some terms and to answer some questions you may have about filling it out.

Item #1 asks for the name of the individual applicant or project director. In non-commercial television, the project director is equivalent to an executive producer. This is the person (or persons) responsible for creating the show and overseeing the total creative and administrative activities.

Item #2 asks whether the proposal is new or was submitted in some other form earlier. The application is considered *new* if it was never submitted to the agency before. It is a *revision* if it was submitted and was rejected previously. It is a *renewal* if it is based on work done in an earlier grant (e.g., a request for production based on a script development grant). A *supplemental* request is one that is an extension of current grant activities.

Item #3 asks the name of the "Program." This refers to the name of the division within the agency, as it appears on the program announcement.

Item #4 asks if the applicant is an individual or an organization. If you are applying as a freelance writer or independent producer, you would specify *individual.* If you are applying as a production entity or joint venture, you would check *institution,* and specify the type of company (e.g., Television Production) as well as private or non-profit status. Unless an agency specifically requests evidence of non-profit status in advance, you can generally incorporate *after* a grant is awarded.

Item #5 asks for the grant period, i.e., when the project will start and finish. As a rule, the start date should be several weeks *after* you expect to hear about the award decision. That assures you that your time won't be wasted waiting for a letter of confirmation, while the grant period is already in effect. Similarly, the completion date ought to provide you ample time to finish the project. It is not unusual for script development requests to be six months long. That length of time serves as a contingency since federal agencies are reluctant to authorize extensions later on.

Item #6 asks you to define the intended audience. You can take your cue from the stated objectives of the agency. One might be primarily interested in reaching general adult audiences; others might be targeted for minority, handicapped, bilingual, aged, children, etc.

Item #7 asks for the amount of funds required to accomplish the project. The money requested directly from the agency is called an *outright* grant. The *gifts & matching* category refers to money that might be forthcoming from other sources. Some agencies require a gifts and matching situation, i.e., they will offer money contingent upon your ability to raise a matching sum from another source. *Cost-sharing* refers to the contributions received in the form of service, facilities, and similar donations from you own production company.

Item #8 asks for the field of the project. This refers to the specific subject category as it relates to the agency's announcement (e.g., history of the theatre; women's studies; American studies).

Item #9 asks for the chief location in which most of the work will be accomplished during the grant period. It is a curious category for freelance writers, and can generally be listed as your home state. The purpose of this type of question is to provide the agency with a broad base of data to determine how effectively they serve their constituencies.

Item #10 asks for the public issues of the project. This refers to the thematic issues of relevance to the agency.

Item #11 asks for the Topic/Title. This is the complete working title of the project.

Item #12 asks for a description of the proposed project. This is an extremely important item, since it defines the objectives and approach in a paragraph or two. The synopsis should clearly and succinctly define the intentions, the filmic approach, the proposed content, and the key personnel involved. You'll be able to flesh out all that information later in the attached narrative proposal.

The Narrative Proposal for Funding Agencies

The narrative is the body of your request; it functions as a series presentation, fully detailing the concept and filmic approach of the show. The narrative may run 20–100 pages or more, depending on the nature of the project. The narrative section expands upon the ideas proposed in the abstract. Objectives are clarified, approaches are defined, and sample visual treatments are provided. In a request for script development funds, a fully detailed pilot story or treatment may also be included. If a production grant is sought, the full script is needed, and a budget breakdown is required.

A well-written narrative generally covers each of these areas in depth:

1. the nature and scope of the project;
2. the importance of the project to target audiences and general audiences;
3. the selected format and visual approach for television;
4. the timetable for research, development and/or production;
5. the background and expertise of key personnel;
6. the budget.

Some applications, e.g., those for NEH, ask for a detailed synopsis of the project on a continuation sheet. This is the time to address the points above in a condensed version of the entire proposal. A continuation sheet provides significant background information on the nature and scope of the project, the personnel, and the relevancy of the project to specific agency goals.

As an example, see the synopsis of the grant proposal on p. 70. It is a one page synopsis of the *Susan Lennox* proposal, which requests $68,877 from NEH to develop a three-part television series based on the book by David Graham Phillips. The actual description of the book is minimal, compared to the larger discussion of issues and themes relevant to the humanities. The treatment itself would appear in the narrative section of the proposal.

If this project were designed for another agency, e.g., CPB, this page would offer a straightforward synopsis of the dramatic storyline, instead of focusing on the historical and cultural background exclusively.

The narrative section of the proposal begins after the application forms are completed. This is the heart of the grant proposal. Objectives need to be stated clearly and the program content should be relevant to those goals.

A well-written *treatment* is particularly important, since it gives the reader a specific sense of the program you have in mind. It's the basis for determining *how* you intend to script the show. Treatments for public television are written precisely the same as those for commercial television. The format and structure are the same, and so is the dramatic story-telling technique.

The Budget

A budget is an integral part of a public television proposal. It demonstrates the creator's ability to plan accurately, realistically, and professionally. Moreover, it assures the funding agency that the money will be spent reasonably.

"But wait!" you say, "I'm a writer! What do I know about budgets!" That's a reasonable, plaintive cry. The fact is, in non-commercial television, the creator must be equipped to think like a *hyphenate* (writer-producer).

The budgetary needs of projects differ considerably. However, certain elements do tend to appear regularly. For example, in script development the budget generally includes costs for scriptwriting, research, travel, consultant fees, typing and duplicating, administrative overhead, and so on. The actual cost for each item is dependent upon the development needs of a particular show.

16. Institution/Organization Name The Susan Lenox Project	NEH USE ONLY Application Number

17. Title of Project

''SUSAN LENOX: HER FALL AND RISE''

18. Category of Grant

Completion of research and script development

19. Additional Background Information

The Susan Lenox Project is a non-profit independent production group formed by writer-director Stephanie Rothman and writer-producer Charles S. Swartz for the express purpose of dramatizing David Graham Phillips' novel Susan Lenox: Her Fall and Rise. Rothman and Swartz bring to this project 17 years of professional writing, directing and producing experience, and a background and continuing interest in intellectual and cultural history.

David Graham Phillips (1867-1911) was a catalytic figure of his time. Originally a journalist and editorial writer, he wrote ''The Treason of the Senate,'' a series of articles which provoked Theodore Roosevelt's famous attack on ''the Man with the Muck-Rake.'' Phillips' articles were to a great degree responsible for the passage of the 17th Amendment, which provided for direct election of U.S. senators by popular vote. ''Muckraker'' became a term not of opprobrium but a label worn proudly by such figures as Upton Sinclair, Ida M. Tarbell, and Lincoln Steffens.

Phillips was assassinated by a deranged man who became convinced that an earlier Phillips novel had slandered his family. Only three weeks before, Phillips had finally completed Susan Lenox, which he regarded as the finest of his more than 20 novels written beginning in 1901. It was praised by Edith Wharton as ''a forgotten masterpiece'' and by H.G. Wells as ''the greatest novel in the American manner,'' and condemned by newspaper reviewers of the time, who were blind to its plea for reform, as ''repulsive'' and ''offensive.'' The book is a compelling realistic novel written by a journalist with a strong social conscience. By today's standards, it offers a serious and clear-eyed look at the issues it raises, and it contains nothing that exceeds what is fully acceptable on television.

Susan Lenox's story is a physical and psychological odyssey covering the period from 1895 to the first years of the 20th century, the so-called Gilded Age. The novel is about the tarnish on that gilt. Susan, born illegitimate and forced into marriage, rebels and runs away without skills or money. The story takes her from sweatshop to tenement and eventually to riches and lonely success, achieved by tenacity of purpose and force of character but at a great price. The book's thematic emphasis on the sexual and economic exploitation of women delayed its publication, and the New York Society for the Suppression of Vice coerced the publisher into cutting 100 of its 1065 pages, which have now been restored.

The value of this project to the humanities is: it will retrieve a piece of the usable past to illuminate problems of the novel's period which remain with us today; and it will recover a thought-provoking work of literature that explores the role of individualism in American life and the role of existential choice in shaping our lives, and that deserves new generations of readers.

20. Key Personnel

Project Directors:	Stephanie Rothman	Writer-director
	Charles S. Swartz	Writer-producer
Advisory Board:	Ronald Gottesman	Director U.S.C. Center for Humanities & Prof. English
	Steven J. Ross	Asst. Prof. History, U.S.C.
	Daniel Aaron	Prof. Emeritus English, Harvard & Pres. Library of America
	Nina Baym	Director School of Humanities, U. of Illinois & Prof. English
	Walter B. Rideout	Prof. English, U. of Wisconsin
Media Consultant:	Richard A. Blum	Pres. Richard A. Blum & Associates

• • •

This is not to suggest there are no budget guidelines for research and development. CPB will provide you with a sample budget on request, and you can refer to the Writer's Guild of America M.B.A. (Minimum Basic Agreement) for public television rates for writing. You'll find sample minimums for writing PBS series presentations, drama, documentary, and special interest programs on pp. 205–207 of this book.

You may need to budget *consultants* into your project. These are individual academic or technical advisors who are experts in their fields. You may find that one or two will be sufficient for the project, or that a full-fledged 15-member Advisory Board is necessary. Usually consultants for public television receive an honorarium of $150–$350 per day. The number of days must be clarified in the budget; their role responsibilities should be clarified in the narrative.

As for travel costs incurred in researching or developing a script, it's necessary to know who must travel where and for how long. Funding agencies will support travel, but the costs must be justified in the budget. Airplane trips should be coach fare, and per diem costs should be within standard federal guidelines. The funding agency, itself, can offer per diem guidelines for travel in both domestic and foreign cities.

Production budgets are much more difficult to determine than script costs. If you are seeking funds for production on the basis of a completed script it is essential to get some professional help. At the local television level, a production manager can supply you with Rate Sheets, i.e., the established costs for using station facilities and personnel. If the show is to be produced on a more complex level, an independent producer or production manager can help break down costs for *above-the-line* (talent and creative staff) and *below-the-line* items (technical services and facilities).

The Directors Guild of America might help you locate specific people for the purpose of budgeting the show. In addition, other key guilds and unions can provide you with up-to-date information concerning going-rates. (Those guilds are listed in *Appendix E*.) Make no mistake: production budgeting requires a professional and experienced hand.

How Projects Are Evaluated

Every agency has a different review system but the general process remains the same. PBS and CPB review projects in cooperation with each other and will try to find support and distribution for the projects of the highest merit. CPB usually preselects projects for review by an advisory panel of experts in broadcasting. They base their evaluation on the relevancy of the project to the priorities of CPB and PBS, the credentials of the production team, and the innovation and diversity the project offers to the PBS schedule.

Regional public television networks also review projects for development and prospective funding: EEN evaluates projects suitable for IPS with representatives from the station system. All the networks assess projects on the basis of relevancy to member stations, potential for outside funding, and potential for profits in national distribution.

Independent PBS stations also accept submissions. WNET—TV, New York, for example, evaluates each proposal submitted to the Program Planning Department. Their staff determines 1) if the proposal reflects priority needs of the station; 2) if the program is innovative and unique (i.e., not duplicating other projects in work); 3) if funding potential exists. Once they approve the project, negotiations take place between the station and the creator. It is likely that your local PBS station has a similar evaluation process or can initiate that process with your project ideas.

Some federal agencies who publish *RFPs* (requests for proposals) literally have a point system for ranking proposals. Various segments of the proposal are judged according to specified criteria in the guidelines. The proposal with the highest ranking receives the award. Unfortunately, some outstanding projects get left in the dust because they miss out by two-hundredths of a point on some technicality.

One of the most rigorous evaluation systems is set up by the National Endowment for the Humanities. NEH might select outside reviewers who are scholarly experts in various fields to look at the proposal and comment on its intellectual soundness. Whether or not the proposal receives this outside review, it is submitted to a specially convened panel of 10–15 people who represent a wide range of experience and interests in academic circles and in the media. The panel might be comprised of a Hollywood writer, network executive, philosopher, anthropologist, cultural historian, archaeologist, and documentary filmmaker. The panel meets for two days—much like a sequestered jury—discussing each proposal on its own merits and in comparison with other projects submitted in that cycle.

The NEH staff forwards the recommendations of reviewers and panelists to the National Council on the Humanities. The Council is comprised of 26 presidential appointees who generally endorse the recommendations of reviewers, panelists, and staff. The Council then recommends action to the Chairman of the Endowment, who has sole legislative authority to make final decisions about funding. Most often, those decisions are consistent with the advice received from the evaluation process.

The process sounds terribly cumbersome, but in fact the applicant gets a definitive word in 3–4 months from the submission deadline—a much faster turnaround time than at the networks. In addition, if you request the information, the staff will provide you with complete copies of the reviews, and a summary of the panelists' comments.

The National Endowment for the Arts has a similar, though less complicated review process. The staff reviews the applications and refers them to appropriate advisory panels. The panel's comments are reviewed by members of the National Council on the Arts, and they in turn recommend approval or disapproval to the Chairman of the Endowment. Once again, the Chairman has sole legislative authority to make final decisions, but will most often act on the advice and recommendations of the Council. The applicant is notified of acceptance or rejection by the Chairman's office.

What Happens if Your Project Is Funded?

If a project is funded, the creative rights in public television are usually retained by the writer or project director. However, the question of rights should be fully investigated—and negotiated—before the signing of any agreement. NEH, for example, gives the grantee *total control* over the project and *total ownership* of creative rights. That's a very critical and important right for any creative writer. The award stipulates that PBS should be offered free use of the show, but the grantee is also free to negotiate for commercial sales through network, syndication, cable TV, international, and theatrical marketplaces. Any distribution agreements, primary or secondary, should be cleared with the agency.

As for profits, NEH policy allows the first $50,000 in annual program income to go directly to the grantee (the writer or producer). Once a project earns more than $50,000 in any year, the excess is split 50–50 with NEH, up to the amount of the original grant award. From that point on, all program income can be retained by the grantee. In some cases, the grantee can retain all program income for five years, provided that any excess over $50,000 is used for continuous development of humanities programs.

Try to get complete information about a particular agency's stance on royalties, profits, and rights. If the policies seem carved in stone, there's probably no room for negotiation. However, if there *is* some latitude, it can't hurt to point to NEH's policy as a guideline to follow.

PART TWO

STORY AND CHARACTER DEVELOPMENT

Developing the Story
or Treatment

The Importance of Plot

Whether you write for the major networks or PBS, a dramatic presentation requires a solidly written story or treatment. It's the plot of the story that can make or break a show.

Dramatic critics have argued for centuries about the importance of plot. Aristotle called it the first and foremost principle in drama, the "soul" of tragedy. George Pierce Baker, the granddaddy of American playwriting teachers, argued in *Dramatic Technique* that characters are of prime importance; their very presence affects others in the scene, and therefore the action in the scene is bound to be affected. The French critic, Ferdinand Bruntiere, in *The Law of the Drama*, argued that drama is based on the conflict of wills among characters. In his excellent book, *The Art of Dramatic Writing*, Lajos Egri concurred that characters are of prime importance. And the arguments continue today with critics taking every possible side.

Obviously, it is difficult to separate plot from character in the well-developed treatment or script. However, the dictates of television almost require the predominance of plot as the "heart" of television drama or comedy. The television writer creates a story which inherently feeds on visual imagery to sustain viewer interest and appeal. If that appeal diminishes, or is absent, viewers will click their remote control to watch another program. The competitive and technological nature of the medium requires quick and effective plotting to sustain viewer interest.

As evidence of the heightened importance of plot, one might look at the basic conflict structure in most television drama. Generally, the conflict is external to the character. He or she must overcome some obstacle imposed by others to achieve some goal. On the other hand, a character drama is based on inner decisions and conflicts. If those conflicts are not externalized into action, the story becomes static and talky, rather than dramatic, visual, and emotionally compelling.

This is not to imply that character development is not important in the well-crafted treatment or script. The character *must* be integrally related to the plotting, and *must* be credibly motivated and dimensionally conceived. Otherwise the audience won't be able to identify, won't believe the developing action, and won't care about the outcome of the story.

And what about the importance of theme in a television script? If it's too heavy or predominant, it will stick out like a sore thumb. (Incidentally, the industry uses "theme" to identify the premise of a show, not the intellectual concept. The studio reader provides a thumbnail sketch of a writer's story; that's the story's theme.) Sometimes a writer consciously and deliberately pushes a message. When that happens, the entertainment value is lost and the personal or ideological statement overshadows the story appeal. Theme material is most effectively handled when it springs naturally from the integration of plot, character, and action.

How to Develop the Story

1. Finding the "Hook"

A story idea can be derived from any personal experience or observation, any music, poetry, or book that moved you, a newspaper article that intrigued you, any source under the sun that sparked your imagination. However, the selection of the story idea must be more rational. First and foremost, it must have a hook—a unique premise that will grip the audience immediately. If the hook is strong, the story has a much better chance of eventually reaching the screen and touching the lives of millions of viewers.

Here are a few headlines that appeared in the papers. They are good examples of story hooks.

"FIERY METEOR NEARLY MISSES U.S."

"CAMPERS LOST IN UNSEASONABLE BLIZZARD"

"F.B.I. AGENTS KILL WRONG MAN IN MISTAKEN IDENTITY
CHASE"

"SCIENTISTS BAFFLED BY PULSING BLOBS IN TEXAS"

"FANS ROBBED—BEFORE BUS GETS TO TRACK"

All the stories are true, and with some dramatic license each offers intriguing potential for story development. However, the premises are much too broad in this present form. Specific stories and conflicts need to be defined, lead characters need to be suggested, and particular points of view need to be established in the development process.

The first headline, for example, deals with a near catastrophe—a meteor slamming into the U.S. That story could be told from any number of vantage points. The first step in story development is to identify the approach, conflict, point of view, and character. For example, this might be one approach: *An aging scientist discovers a fiery meteor is about to hit the U.S.—but no one believes him.*

Now the story has a featured character who can evoke empathy. It has a point of view, told from the perspective of an aging scientist. It has a built-in dramatic conflict with a "time-bomb" situation (the scientist must find a way to convince others—and to act—before the meteor strikes). As the story develops, other characters and sub-plots might be incorporated, but the basic premise is fairly well defined at the outset, and the hook can be told in a nutshell (or in a *TV Guide* blurb).

Look at the second story idea ("CAMPERS LOST IN UNSEASON-ABLE BLIZZARD"), and try to define the best dramatic angle. You might choose the point of view of one camper or a number of them; or you might want to tell the story from the point of view of the rescuers. The basic conflict and plot pattern centers around a jeopardy situation, but *who* is in jeopardy, and how great is the sense of urgency for escape and survival? Those decisions dictate the direction and visual approach of the story.

2. Identifying Plot Patterns

Once you have an idea, it might be helpful to categorize the plot according to genre and situation. An early analysis of genre and plot patterns can help you keep a better handle on the story development. If the story was meant to be dramatic but comedy elements come into play, the plot might be enriched by the interweaving of genres.

However, once the comedy elements become dominant, the original intent is lost, and a different story is in the making.

The industry defines program types according to those listed by the Nielsen ratings company: general drama, suspense and mystery, situation comedy (or character comedy), variety, feature films (which means theatrical motion pictures, not films made for television), informational programs, quiz and audience participation, children's programs, and sports events.

Dramatic critics and writers identify plot patterns from a more contextual standpoint. Georges Polti compiled a catalogue of "Thirty Six Dramatic Situations," which identifies basic plot patterns that appear in all dramatic stories. Lewis Herman, in A Practical Manual of Screenplay Writing for Theatre and Television Films reduced those patterns to nine: (1) Love—boy-meets-girl, loses-girl, wins-her-back-again; (2) Success—the lead character wants to achieve and succeed at all costs; (3) Cinderella—an "ugly duckling" is changed into a perfect human being; (4) Triangle—three characters are in a romantic entanglement; (5) Return—a long-lost lover, wandering father, missing husband returns; (6) Vengeance—a character seeks revenge for some wrong-doing (this is the basic pattern for suspense and mystery shows); (7) Conversion—the bad guy turns good; (8) Sacrifice—the lead character sacrifices his or her own good to help someone else; and (9) Family—this pattern focuses on the interrelationship of characters in a single place and situation (on a plane, in a hotel, in a prison, on a farm). We might also add a tenth plot pattern, which is a favorite formula of the networks: (10) Jeopardy—a life and death situation, dealing with the survival instincts and prowess of the lead characters.

Plot patterns are not mutually exclusive, and any number of subplots can emerge within a given story. Still, this type of cataloguing provides the writer with a clearer overview of the dominant story elements, and the concurrent identification of background material. Once the dominant pattern is identified, there's a lesser chance of the writer being side-tracked by intriguing sub-plots or minor characters.

3. The Step Outline and Dramatic Action Points

One of the first problems in developing a story is knowing where to begin, i.e., establishing a point-of-attack. Why is this day, this moment, this situation critical to the lives of the leading characters? If the situation has great personal meaning for the characters, and helps establish the emerging plot, you'll have a much better chance of holding the audience throughout the progression of the story.

A common technique for plotting the progression of the story is a

Step Outline, i.e., a condensed scene-by-scene version of the narrative action. Careful selection and placement of sequences can heighten the storytelling effect, and makes it much easier to move directly into script form. The question is, how do you select the most effective combination of scenes? Which scenes go where? Which characters are needed at what points? Which scenes build the conflict? Which scenes are extraneous?

Aristotle talked about the importance of the proper arrangement of incidents in a plot to have the greatest impact on the audience. Twentieth century critics still agree. Elder Olson, in *Tragedy and the Theory of Drama*, argued that story elements should be selected by a writer only to heighten dramatic credibility and the emotional impact on an audience. Similarly, Eric Bently, in *Life of the Drama*, contended that a carefully arranged sequence of action is essential for achieving maximum effect. He called it a "rearrangement" of incidents as opposed to a simple chronological arrangement. In short, *dramatic* action rather than literal action.

I've found that the use of *dramatic action points* is an effective way to select and arrange key incidents in the story. I call them dramatic action points in deference to Aristotle's concept of a forward thrust in drama. These are the basic dramatic units and events which advance the story. Once action points are identified, they can be placed in different contexts (much like the restructuring of a puzzle) to strengthen the plot structure. They can be used to orchestrate the pacing and balance in the story.

The use of dramatic action points is an on-going process in the story development phase. As an example of how it might work, let's look at one of the premises mentioned earlier in the headlines:

"CAMPERS LOST IN UNSEASONABLE BLIZZARD"

We might try to outline these points for the opening sequences:

1. A family is en route to the Berkshires for a camping weekend.
2. They arrive and find the campgrounds in disarray, but decide to stay.
3. They get snowed in.

Even in this sketchy form, it becomes apparent that the point-of-attack is not strong. There is no suggestion of conflict or character. The action points can be revised accordingly:

1. A couple's marriage is shaky. The husband works too hard and they need a vacation.

2. They head up to the Berkshires for a camping weekend. He brought along work, anyway, and they argue.
3. They arrive at the campground, which is in disarray. It's late at night, and they decide to stay.
4. It snows.

But even here there are some problems. The points are too choppy, and are not really comprised of individual dramatic sequences. The action needs to be clarified and the characters need more definition. It might be possible to merge the first two action points for the sake of pacing and add other people to the story—their children, other campers, perhaps even a pet that is lost in the storm.

This is what the revised outline might look like:

1. BARRY, SHARON, and KIDS ride to the campsite. We learn they have marriage problems.
2. They arrive at the campgrounds and find it in disarray. It's late, they're tired, they decide to stay.
3. Setting up camp, we meet other campers, and follow-up marriage conflict.
4. It snows as they sleep.
5. An expensive trailer reaches camp, finds no power. The irate owner blames Barry.
6. In morning, Barry's kids play in the snow. Their dog gets swept away in the river.

And so on. Dramatic action points provide a very bare—but specific—blueprint for the structure of the story. There are roughly 21–26 major action points in a 90-minute film, which translates to four or five pages for each sequence in the script. Those are, of course, very general figures, but they do provide some guidance in assessing the time count for an eventual script.

Here's how the action points might eventually translate into the treatment itself. The following act is derived from these action points outlined above.

THE WIND CHILL FACTOR

April. A bright, spring day.

We follow BARRY and SHARON RUTLEDGE, and their SON and

DAUGHTER, riding in a new, but small camper from New York

City to the Berkshire Mountains. Throughout the trip, we

This derives from Action Point #1

hear innocuous commentary from the radio about a cold front

moving in from Canada. But the noise is lost in the sounds of

the children at play, and the dog barking.

The marriage is rocky. BARRY is a lawyer who works too hard

and is constantly afraid he won't be advanced. This family

weekend was arranged to save the marriage; but BARRY has

brought along a legal brief, anyway.

They reach the Berkshires just at dusk, and follow the signs

Action point #2

to the campground. They drive down a steep dirt road, into a

valley nestled among the mountains. But when they arrive,

they find the campgrounds in disarray. A sign that reads

''OFFICE'' points to some prefabricated walls lying

unassembled on the ground. Another car is parked nearby--a

VW. The young couple inside, STEPHEN and MARIAN, commiserate

with the RUTLEDGE's; they, too, made reservations, but the

campground obviously went bankrupt before it could open.

They're all undecided about what to do. They should find

another campground. But it's getting dark, and there's a

storm brewing. Besides, this place can shelter them--the

campsites are cleared, there are picnic tables, fireplaces,

there's a centrally-located water pipe, and there are two

outhouses, one male, one female. The two couples decide to

stay until morning, when the storm will be over.

Action point #3

BARRY struggles through the unfamiliar tasks of setting up a

campsite, and he is forced to finish in the rain. Thunder and

lightning follow him as he returns to the camper, drenched

to the bone. The KIDS think it's outrageously funny.

Another car arrives, drawn by the light from the lanterns. It's

a group of FRIENDS, two boys and a girl, who set up a

rudimentary tent in a nearby campsite.

Inside the RUTLEDGE camper, after dinner, the family goes to

bed, accompanied by the sound of rain on the roof. SHARON

bickers with BARRY, who refuses to go to bed without reading

over his brief. Angry, SHARON gets into bed. BARRY reads.

The sound of the rain peters out. BARRY offers his wife some

minimal consolation--at least it's stopped raining.

Action point #4

But in a WIDE SHOT of the campground, we see that it's begun

snowing.

. . .

During the night, a sleek, flashy, expensive-looking silver

trailer arrives in the snow, driven by CHARLES EVANS who is

Action point # 5 camping with his wife, MAGGIE, and their teenage daughter,

BETH. The family is dismayed to see the condition of the

campground, and an irate CHARLES follows the only visible

light--BARRY's--to register his complaint.

BARRY is surprised to see it snowing, but he suggests that

CHARLES do what everyone else has done; camp here for the

night. After all, how long can a snowstorm last in April?

CHARLES tries to connect his electrical system to the power

outlet at the campsite, but finds that the power has not been

turned on. He's furious; now he has no heat. And, like

everyone else, he has no cold-weather clothing.

Disgruntled, he bundles up his family into the silver

trailer for the night. Gradually, the campground lights go

out, first in the EVANS camper, then in BARRY's.

In the morning, it is still snowing heavily. The RUTLEDGE

Action point # 6 KIDS, eager to build a springtime snowman, find make-shift

winter clothing--dishrags for their ears, pinned-up

blankets for sweaters, plastic bags for galoshes. And they

rush out into the snow, with their dog, to play.

When SHARON calls them to breakfast, the dog (a city dog,

used to a leash) bolts and races along the edge of a small

river. The pup loses its footing in the snow, falls into the

water, and is swept downstream.

This is all derived from Action point #6

The KIDS race along the riverbank, following their pet,

plodding through the snow, calling to him. STEPHEN spots

them, races over, and restrains them from following the dog.

He tries to explain they can't save their pet. It couldn't

see the footing in the snow; neither can they. But the

children are unheeding; they scream and cry as they watch

their pet sweep out of sight...

• • •

4. Plotting Audience Interest

It helps to visualize the plot in terms of a graph which measures intended audience interest. Many television programs go through the process of audience testing to provide studios and networks with some idea of the program's effectiveness. By means of electronic testing, a graph is generated and instantaneous viewer response is recorded. Producers can literally see how every joke, line, car chase, action sequence, or romantic intrigue holds audience interest. Writers can apply that same principle to the plotting of the story; they can creatively "manipulate" audience interest levels.

For example, a two-hour television film might be charted as shown on page 87.

If you read from left to right, you can see that the short teaser was very effective as a hook, and that each act break was designed to maximize audience interest up until the commercial breaks. Interest picks

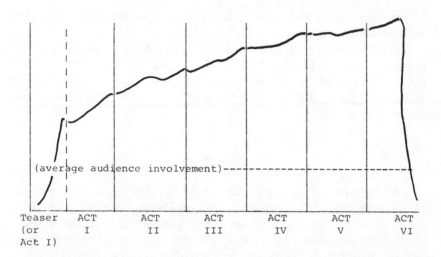

up, with a snowballing effect throughout the entire show, and sustains until the end of Act VI.

If we were dealing with motion pictures, the chart might look a little different. The writer has more time to develop characters and can build a slower pace that increases throughout the film. The result is a skewed bell-shaped curve:

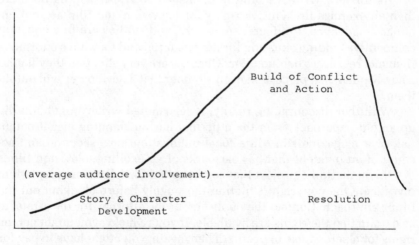

The plot interest curve, or audience interest curve, is just one more conceptual device to help visualize the story in development. It helps set the pacing of the story as it unfolds, and suggests the intensity of action sequences and dramatic interrelationships that can sustain—and build—audience interest.

The treatment serves as the foundation for the entire script. With the right amount of visualization, character development, suspense builds, and comedy relief, the reader will get an accurate picture of the show. Conceptual devices for story development can help sharpen that impact and appeal.

Adaptations

With an increased marketplace for TV films based on previously published stories, the process of adapting literary works for television has become an important concern for many writers. In the novel or short story, an author can spend a great deal of time on character development, exposition, the free association of time and place and so on. In television, that same story must be told in a 90-minute or 120-minute structure. That means streamlining the plot and characters. The writer must be an artistic surgeon, with a very fine and sensitive touch, knowing what must go and what must stay. Ideally, the television adaptation should remain faithful to the original work, conveying the same feeling, atmosphere, plot, and characterization—even though scenes, characters, and conflicts have been modified.

As for new writers adapting published works, it will be no more than an exercise if exclusive rights for television and film are not obtained in advance. Producers, networks, and studios are in a constant competitive bidding situation for new material and they have enormous financial resources behind them. Chances are very slim that they'll miss a newly published piece, and even slimmer that a newcomer will outbid them.

With that discouraging reality, a determined writer might still dig up an old paperback from the attic that has outstanding visual potential, or a magazine story in a local publication, or a second-hand account of an incident that has earmarks of an exciting television film.

If you do find a project that seems suited for television adaptation, investigate the copyright situation thoroughly before blocking out the filmic approach. Contact the publisher, or the attorney for the estate, to be certain that the rights are available. If you're lucky, you might get the rights for a percentage of profits. Then, again, you might have to pay for it dearly.

The actual form of adapted works is precisely the same as an original treatment. It must convey the appropriate atmosphere, characterization, and dramatic integrity of the published novel or story. The use of dramatic action points and audience interest curves can help define the best plotting structure.

On the following pages you'll find the opening segment from a fifty page treatment, "The Watchmaker," based on the book, *A Teaspoon of Honey*. Although you may not be familiar with the book, you might still sense the character orientation of the original piece and the integrity of the adaptation to a specific style. In this particular format—which is both narrative and visual—the scene identification headings are kept to an absolute minimum.

FADE IN.

Sochi, Russia - 1902.

A brisk autumn air blows through the open door of the

Malinsky Brothers Watch Shop, as HERSCHEL MALINSKY, 20 years

old, impatiently straightens the magnifying loupe over his

eye. Outside the shop, the boardwalk is almost deserted; the

lodges on the hillside are virtually empty. His older

brother JACOB glances up from his work, almost reading his

thoughts. ''It would be nice if you were here when the

tourists come again.'' HERSCHEL nods. He'll try not to think

of his impending term in the army, or how the Czar's soldiers

declare free reign on Jews. ''At least I'll get to see momma

and poppa in Schershov before I leave.'' JACOB will worry

about his brother, even though HERSCHEL seems blessed with

the survival instinct...He survived near death as an infant,

so weak on the day of his circumcision...He outwitted AUNTIE

TAUBE, who tried to enslave him and humiliate him when he

lived there as a teenager...He emerged safe from the

massacre of the Jews in Kishenev last year...And now he'll

be a Jewish soldier in the Russian Army. With God's help,

he'll survive that, too.

HERSCHEL and his friend LEE are celebrating his last few

weeks in Sochi. They're on a forest trail, warmed by a

pitcher of vodka, lying sprawled out in the grass. A tin of

tobacco lies nearby, a gift from LEE, a gentile friend who

treats him like a brother. This is the way it should be...And

then, wobbling to his horse, he responds to a challenge:

''Let's race!'' HERSCHEL climbs into the saddle, breaks into

a grin, and takes off. LEE's horse falls behind, HERSCHEL's

horse sprints ahead. But soon the animal stumbles, throwing

its rider helplessly to the ground. LEE dismounts quickly

and rushes to his friend's aid. HERSCHEL sits himself up,

and feels for any broken bones. Instead, he finds a ragged

piece of cloth hanging from his trouser leg. ''I tore my

pants!'' LEE laughs, ''You're lucky that's all you tore.''

HERSCHEL bemoans his fate; his tailor is out of town. But LEE

has heard of a seamstress on Minskovoy Street. She just

moved into the area. ''A seamstress!'' HERSCHEL looks as if

he'll fall from his horse again. ''I need a suit mended, not
a petticoat hemmed!'' LEE smiles, ''Maybe she'll mend your
knee with satin, my friend?''

On Minskovoy Street, LEE rides the horses back to the stable
as HERSCHEL, newly changed, stands in front of a brown
cottage, his trousers slung over his shoulder like a shawl.
Feeling uncomfortable, he knocks. He's certainly in no mood
for this kind of thing. A man should not have to rely on a
woman to fix his pants. Besides, the woman is probably an old
hag...The door opens, and we see HERSCHEL's P.O.V.--MIRIAM
stands before him, an astonishing looking eighteen year old
girl, red hair piled high on her head, eyes green and wide.
After a beat, she moves back into the house, replaced by
MR. PELTZMAN, a smallish man with a yarmulke on his head, a
prayer book in his hand. He looks quizzically at HERSCHEL,
who seems immobilized. Finally, HERSHEL holds out the pants
in his hand and stumbles out the words: ''Is this the
dressmaker's...?'' The man ushers him in and introduces him
to his daughter MIRIAM. She watches, from the front of the
fireplace, stroking her cat, smiling slowly. ''I think I'll
stay until these are mended,'' HERSCHEL says.

The next night, as crazy as it seems, HERSCHEL scrambles

through his dresser drawers, finding a shirt which needs

mending. JACOB, watching from the bed, sees his brother pop

off a shirt button and lay it aside. After the expected

inquiry, HERSCHEL explains too casually that the seamstress

can work wonders. Besides, since when can't a grown man have

his clothes repaired if he wants. JACOB shrugs knowingly.

HERSCHEL is like a new man with a new life blood. In his

watch shop, he works diligently and happily until a customer

happens to mention that a marriage is being arranged between

SCHMUEL RAZNIKOFF and that new seamstress in town. But he's

heard that the dowry isn't enough. Good gossip, isn't it?

That night, HERSCHEL bolsters himself, and heads back to the

PELTZMAN house with a shirt held tight in hand. He knocks on

the door of the brown cottage, and MR. PELTZMAN greets him.

With the door open, HERSCHEL can see SCHMUEL RAZNIKOFF on

the sofa beside MIRIAM. He drops his shirt to the floor and

MR. PELTZMAN picks it up. Seeing MIRIAM's imploring face, he

says, ''Nu, Herschel? You come every night with something to

be mended. The others bring only themselves. If you'll come

by tomorrow, Miriam will see you at 8:00 by yourself.'' An
open-mouthed HERSCHEL stumbles out, ''Thank you...''

HERSCHEL manages to see MIRIAM for two weeks, in the
synagogue and in the house, but always MR. PELTZMAN sits
with the Talmud in hand, not leaving them alone. Maybe
tonight will be different. It's his last night in Sochi. As
he walks to the brown cottage on Minskovoy Street, he turns
up the collar of his warm raincoat; it's cold outside, it's
drizzling. He silently curses the army as he looks up at
MIRIAM's house. The lights are on. He tries to see if
MR. PELTZMAN is in his customary chair, but he can't make out
the figures in the window. He knocks. MIRIAM answers the
door, dressed beautifully in a long, full dress with white
lace. He would love to sweep her into his arms, but he can
only follow her to the warm fire inside. MR. PELTZMAN closes
his prayer book and rises awkwardly, excusing himself for a
glass of tea. They're alone! The fire crackles in the
fireplace, the rain splatters against the windows, and
HERSCHEL can only fumble with his cigarette papers and
tobacco. MIRIAM sits close beside him, and they talk
quietly. Then HERSCHEL touches her face and slowly presses

his lips to hers. She responds hesitantly at first, then

kisses him with erratic passion. She draws away now, lifts

her hand, and slaps him hard across the cheek: ''You

shouldn't kiss me like that, Herschel. No girl should be

kissed like that except by her husband.'' ''I want to be your

husband,'' he says. ''Let's ask your poppa.'' MIRIAM

responds warmly, but MR. PELTZMAN is already shuffling back

into the room. ''You think I should let my daughter sit until

her curls turn gray?'' HERSCHEL rises. ''After the army,

we'll have the rest of our lives together.'' HERSCHEL and

MIRIAM look expectantly toward the old man, who adjusts the

yarmulke on his head. The silence seems to last forever.

''Herschel, already I like you. Come back on furlough and

we can talk then.'' HERSCHEL breaks into a smile and shakes

his hand. ''A chance is all I ask.'' And now he turns to

MIRIAM, addressing her quietly. ''Just wait for me. I'll be

back for you, I promise.''

At his apartment, he undresses quietly, trying not to wake

JACOB. But JACOB was hardly asleep, worrying about his

brother's trip in the morning. HERSCHEL packs his things

carefully--MIRIAM's gift of cakes, LEE's gift of tobaccos,

and all the things he bought for his family: the gray wool

shawl for MOMMA; the heavy union suit for POPPA; the scarf

for ESTHER. And now he carefully packs his watchmaking

tools, wrapped in a piece of flannel cloth. JACOB watches

his brother sadly. ''You'll send my love to momma and poppa

and Esther?'' His younger brother nods dutifully. ''And,

Herschel,'' JACOB continues, ''You'll take care in the

army?''

HERSCHEL turns to him with a forced smile. ''Don't worry,

Jacob. I'll take such care, they'll make me a Captain.''

JACOB frowns. ''A Jew a Captain? Never! You'd make jokes at

your own funeral.'' HERSCHEL finishes packing in the

darkness.

MIRIAM sits quietly by the fire, trying to concentrate on

her sewing. But all she can think about his HERSCHEL

MALINSKY. No man has ever stirred her the way HERSCHEL has.

She puts down her sewing, crosses to her father who is busy

reading in his chair. She leans over and kisses his

forehead, thanking him. If any man is worth waiting for,

HERSCHEL is that man. She goes back to the fire and prays

silently for his safekeeping and quick return.

•   •   •

As you can see, the form of this adaptation is the same as any treatment. What you may notice is that the opening sequences seem to emphasize character development and interrelationships, rather than the traditional action or "tease" emphasis of episodic TV. Since this adaptation is for a two-part film (4 hours), it is structured more like a film epic than a television episode. As a result, it's possible to *slowly* develop the characters and build toward the conflicts and tensions that will hold an audience throughout the multi-part story.

6

Developing the Character and Dialogue

Character Development and "The Method" Writer

Characters move a story forward through credible motivations, actions, reactions, and interrelationships. They must be totally identifiable—whether good, bad, or indifferent. They must be real people, with a consistent pattern of behavior, and a complete psycho-social-physical frame-of-reference.

It may be difficult to develop the complex innuendoes of character in the treatment stage where dialogue is limited. Nonetheless, the writer can paint intricate portraits of the character through behavioral action and reaction. Let's take, for example, the character of a boss who can no longer employ his secretary; he is impelled to find her another job. If the literal route is taken, the scene opens in his office where the two confront each other, and he picks up the phone to find her work. That literal approach waters down the potential of the character and the depth of intentions and attitudes. It would be more effective if the audience sees the boss alone, clearly upset at the impending task. When the secretary comes in, he puts on a supervisory air, informs her that she's fired. The secretary may resist, fight, or storm out in anger, but the boss remains resolute, maintaining his composure throughout the ordeal. Only after she leaves does he let down his defenses. He can take a *Beat* (a "Beat" is a dramatic moment in which the character makes internal transitions in thought or attitude). Then he picks up the phone, calls a colleague, and recommends a damn good employee. That action, in the privacy of his office, makes him a more sympathetic character in the eyes of the audience. He's not out to gain anything or prove anything. He's acting in the best interest of a sacrifice pattern.

Such private moments are very important for establishing the true inner nature of characters. The audience can see how genuinely concerned they are, how brutal, how comic, how gentle, how disturbed. It helps to build in a sense of vulnerability or susceptibility for each character. That makes them more identifiable and provides a more interesting dimension to their behavior. Even the traditional bad guy should be justifiably motivated. Perhaps he's driven by anguish, frustration, deprivation, jealousy. The audience can understand that kind of motivation, although the action might not be condoned.

Knowing the character's inner life is a crucial part of story development and scripting. You might not be able to define inner realities at the conceptual stage, but in the process of development, the character's personality emerges. The writer must know who the character is, how the character thinks, reacts, interrelates, behaves in any given situation. One of the best ways to accomplish this is through an analytical technique similar to The Method approach used by actors trained in a modified American version of the Stanislavski system of acting. Constantin Stanislavski was a Russian director whose acting principles reshaped the twentieth century stage; he provided new "tools" for achieving realism.*

The Method actor approaches his or her craft with a disciplined sense of creativity and spontaneity. In this sense, "disciplined" means using the tools at one's disposal to create a sense of inner life for the characters in every scene of the script, from beginning to end. The Method writer can flesh out the text and sub-text in every scene. He or she is sensitive to the motivations of characters, the consistency of attitudes, the justifiable actions and reactions in the plot structure. The writer gets to play every part, and if a behavioral problem is discovered, there's still time to fix it in a rewrite.

Here are some of the analytical questions a Method writer might ask to keep a firm hold on the behavioral realities in story and character development:

---

*The Stanislavski system of acting was adapted by Lee Strasberg, among others, at the Group Theatre in New York in the 1930s. Strasberg put new emphasis on inner technique and psychological realism, which became the cornerstone for training at the Actors Studio. That interpretation of Stanislavski's work became known as The Method, and was at the heart of artistic controversy in the 1950s. It remains the staple for acting realism in film, TV, and theatre today. For more on The Method, see Annotated Bibliography at the back of this book (pp. 272–273).

1. What Is the Super-Objective of the Story?

The "super-objective" is the writer's main purpose for developing a story. The aim may be to build suspense, offer new insights, make an audience laugh, grip them in terror. When you define that objective it's easier to gauge the effectiveness of character development, visual action, dramatic mood, plot sequence, and filmic pacing.

2. What Is the Through-Line-of-Action for Each Character?

The "through-line-of-action" is a conceptual thread which shows how each character fits into your main objective. Each character serves a very specific function in relation to the plot development and the realization of your thematic goals. Each scene should bring you closer to those goals.

3. What Is the Character's Intention?

The "intention" is a character's planned action. It can usually be stated as an infinitive—to relax, to rob a bank, to go shopping, to keep a secret, etc. A character's intention may change from scene to scene, and may even change within the scene itself (given the properly motivated transitions).

4. What Is the Character's Motivation?

The "motivation" explains *why* a character wants to achieve a specific intention. It is the *inner need* for the action. For example, if a character wants to leave her husband, there might be any number of emotional factors contributing to that decision. However, one motivation may be dominant; she may be in love with someone else; she may be frustrated, unfulfilled, afraid, bored. The motivation imprints a uniqueness to the character, and provides a psychological framework for action and reaction throughout the treatment and script.

5. What Is the Character's Sense of Urgency?

A "sense of urgency" tells the viewer how *badly* your character wants to fulfill his or her intention. A rule of thumb here: *the greater the sense of urgency, the greater the dramatic conflict.* The character needs to adjust, adapt, or overcome the situation to achieve a state of harmony (or to achieve consonance).

6. What Is the Character's State of Being?

The "state of being" is a character's total psychological and physical frame of reference in a scene. A writer creates more realistic dimensions by incorporating given circumstances into the character's thoughts, behavior, and attitudes. Let's create a scene with these given circumstances as an example. Steve is frantic to see Marian. He runs over to her apartment and finds it empty. It's been raining, it's late at night. What behavioral reality needs to be conveyed? Steve is wet, cold, out of breath, concerned, anguished. The writer may have to convey all that without a line of dialogue. The stage directions might suggest this: *"Steve slams open the door, glances anxiously around the room, sees no one. Breathing hard, he wipes the rain from his face."* And so the stage directions can paint reality through description, keeping alive all the elements in the given circumstances of the scene.

7. Are the Moment-to-Moment Realities Established in the Scene?

The "moment-to-moment" reality is a character's reaction to each and every dramatic unit in the scene. A character needs ample time to build attitudes and to shift thoughts in order to be credible to an audience. Once again, let's create a scene to show how the concept works.

Suppose we're in Berta's apartment when a power failure hits Los Angeles. When the lights go out, she would never think the whole city is powerless. She would have to build logically to that moment of discovery. First, she might try the light switch, or test the bulb in a lamp. Then she might discover that the light is out in the next room. She might search for a flashlight to take to the circuit breaker. And that's where she discovers that the apartment building went dark. She still has no idea of the scope of the blackout. She goes out into the street and finds the whole block is out. And then, through a neighbor, she learns the momentous reality—the whole city is dark.

Meanwhile, what are her moment-to-moment *attitudes?* This depends on Berta's state of being, her intention in the scene when it opened, her motivations and sense of urgency. If she were dressing for an important night out, the power loss would be frustrating, but she would go through each moment credibly to *build* that frustration. At first, she would simply be annoyed. That motivates her to correct the situation by finding another light bulb. However, the power is out in the other room. Her reaction? Greater annoyance. She can't complete her intention. Now she learns the whole apartment building is dark. Her attitude: Frustration! She'll *never* be able to get ready on time. When she learns the whole city is dark, her attitude is coupled with anxiety and curiosity. Each moment can be played out credibly, and each reaction conveyed effectively to the viewer. With the proper builds and reactions, the writer can avoid inconsistent or "manipulated" action which forces an incident or telegraphs the story. A viewer may know the lights went out in L.A., but there is no way for the character to know it until she experiences the actual moment of discovery.

That same moment-to-moment technique can be used for building tensions in a scene. Suppose an escaped convict is hiding in the closet of Berta's room. The viewers may know the danger, but Berta doesn't. You can play up those realities in the story, and orchestrate the pacing of the drama. Once the audience knows that danger lurks in the closet, you can take your time bringing Berta to that confrontation scene—and heighten suspense in the process. She may come inside the room, take off her coat, and head to the closet—then spot a newspaper on the table. She tosses her coat on the chair, glances at the paper, reads about the convict at large, and instinctively locks her front door. Now she heads to the closet with her coat—and the phone rings. She answers, but no one is on the line. She hangs up, reaches for a cigarette, and goes to the closet once more. This time she opens it, and—*nothing*. She gets a hanger, puts her coat away and turns to go. Then, suddenly, a hand reaches out, and *grabs* her—

You can play all those realities in the plot to heighten the eventual confrontation. Hold the audience, surprise them, play out all the moment-to-moment tensions. But now the story needs a *twist* (i.e., a surprise element in the plotline) to help Berta escape. Perhaps she breaks away through some ingenious action or special skill. If she has some special skill, it should be *planted* earlier in the story, so it won't appear to be contrived. A story *plant* provides a logical and proper buildup for action on the screen.

"What if—?" Technique

A good suspense story is usually brimming with unusual twists— sudden switches in the plot, "red herrings," the unexpected. If a character gets into a hopeless situation, and the audience is totally caught up in the action, it would be absolutely anticlimactic for the police to burst in suddenly and save her. The audience has seen that a hundred times before; the action becomes predictable and cliche.

One of the most useful devices for finding innovative twists is the

"*What if—*" technique. As the story develops, ask a steady stream of "*What if—*" questions, until you find a number of different possibilities. "What if this happens? What would she do?" Try to go beyond the first immediate response. Give yourself a number of alternatives; try any combination of thoughts that are consistent with the credibility of the piece. The more you ask, "*What if—*", the greater the possibility of keeping the story and characters alive and interesting. The reverse was aptly illustrated by a cartoon I remember seeing. A frustrated TV writer sits by his typewriter, completed pages strewn all over the room. The caption went something like this: "Oh, to hell with it! 'Suddenly a lot of shots rang out, and everyone fell dead. The End.'"

Dialogue: Problems and Solutions

Dialogue is an integral part of scripting, and is intricately bound up with character development. Inner values and motivations are communicated by the uniqueness of dialogue. What a character says—or doesn't say—tells us about that character's state of being.

Ideally, dialogue should be motivated by the given circumstances in the scene, and should be consistent with the character development already established. Just as the writer has an "inner eye" for visualization, he or she must have an "inner ear" for dialogue that makes the character come to life, adding a dimension of spontaneity and realism to the roles.

Sometimes writers have difficulty with dialogue. Lines may tend to be choppy, staccato, unrealistic, or, perhaps over-theatricalized. The script might be peopled with characters transposed from an English drawing room comedy ("quite grammatically correct, but evuh so boring, dahling"), or with characters misplaced from a 1950's version of *A Streetcar Named Desire* ("Well . . . uh . . . I . . . um . . . uh . . . well, y'know what I mean, huh? Don'cha? Hmm. . . ?).

To help identify and overcome those problems, here is a list of *The Ten Most Common Dialogue Problems and Solutions.*

1. Too Head-On

This is dialogue that is much too literal and embarrasingly obvious. It sounds very contrived. For example:

```
            MARIAN comes in the door and STEVE smiles.

                        STEVE
               Marian, I'm so glad to see
               you. I love you so much. I've
               been waiting to see you for so
               long.
```

That kind of dialogue is pretty embarrassing. No subtlety at all. It would be more effective if he were too overtaken to speak. Or, he might grab her close and say nothing. Then, after a *Beat,* he might say:

```
                        STEVE
               Y'know, I can't stand to see
               you.
     And they hug.
```

Well, of course, actions speak louder than words, and you've built a nice counter-point to the action. Marian knows what he means, and so does the audience. Subtlety can be achieved through understatement, "playing against" the expected material, and playing out the character sub-texts and inner attitudes.

2. Too Choppy

This is dialogue that is staccato. Filled with one liners. A word or two. When you thumb through the script it looks like a Pinter play rather than a realistic and cinematic vehicle. This is an example of dialogue that is too choppy:

```
                        MARSHALL
               I'm hungry.

                        SANDY
               Me too.

                        MARSHALL
               Let's go out to eat.
```

> SANDY
> O.k.

> MARSHALL
> Is the deli o.k.?

> SANDY
> Yes, it's o.k.

One solution to the problem is providing credible motivation for dialogue. The characters need a motivation and intention for speaking. They need a pre-established pattern of thought and behavior. Marshall, for example, might be checking out the refrigerator through an earlier piece of action, then:

> MARSHALL
> Hey, there's nothing in the
> fridge. Wanna go out for a
> bite?

> SANDY
> Mmm. I'm famished.

> MARSHALL
> How does the deli sound?

> SANDY
> Like chicken soup in heaven.

And they get ready to go.

In essence, the dialogue is the building block for moment-to-moment realities in the scene. It should spark behavioral action and reaction to be most effective.

3. Too Repetitious

Dialogue becomes repetitious when a character repeats himself or herself in a number of different ways. The character offers redundant information, or repetitive phrases:

```
                    RONNIE
          I had such a good time on the
          trip. It was one of the best
          trips I ever had.


                    ARNIE
          I'm glad you enjoyed the trip.


                    RONNIE
          It was so good to be away. It
          was a terrific trip.
```

If the problem of repetition is examined, it might stem from one or two problems: the writer doesn't know what the character should say next, so relies on earlier dialogue; the writer is afraid the audience won't "get" a specific point unless the character emphasizes it in dialogue. One solution to redundancy in dialogue is to go back into the script and clearly motivate each speech—or delete the speech altogether. This is how the dialogue above might be handled in revision:

```
                    ARNIE
          You must have had some time. I
          never saw you so excited about
          anything.


                    RONNIE
          It was fantastic. I'm just
          sorry it's over.
```

The simple character interchange affects the whole point of the dialogue exchange. One character is reacting to the other's emotional and physical state-of-being in the scene.

As for points the viewer should get, it's helpful to put in some preliminary plants in the scene. Then a casual line of dialogue by a character is sufficient to trigger the "Aha!"-syndrome for the audience.

4. Too Long

Dialogue that is too long reads like an editorial speech or a philosophical diatribe. It creates static action in the script and often includes related problems of redundancy and preachiness. Let's examine this speech:

```
                    RITA
                  (to Anne)
          They fired you because you're
          a woman, not for any other
          reason. If you were a man you
          would have been promoted.
          Don't let them do that to you.
          Go back and fight for what you
          believe in. They wouldn't get
          away with that on me, I can
          assure you that. I remember
          when I was growing up, my
          mother always told me to look
          out for bigots like that.
          You've got to stand up and let
          them know you're not going to
          take that kind of treatment.
```

The speech tends to dominate visual action and incorporates too many different thoughts, without essential breaks for transitions or reactions. It would be helpful to intersperse reactions and stage directions at the end of each major unit of thought. That makes the speech seem less formidable, and its impact more immediate. Here's what it might look like:

```
                    RITA
                  (to Anne)
          They fired you because you're
          a woman, not for any other
          reason. If you were a man you
          would have been promoted.
```

Anne tries not to pay attention. She's in no mood for Rita's harangue.

```
                RITA (cont'g)
          Don't let them do that to you.
          Go back and fight for what you
          believe in.
```

Anne says nothing. Rita sees she's getting nowhere, crosses over to her friend and speaks softly but urgently.

```
                RITA (cont'g)
          I was always warned to look
          out for bigots like that.
```

```
                    RITA (cont'g)
        You've got to stand up and let
        them know you're not going to
        take that kind of treatment.
```

```
    A BEAT, then Anne turns to look at her friend. The conviction
    is sinking in.
```

The idea is to integrate reactions and dialogue in a long pattern of speech, and to trim "the excesses" wherever possible. Long speeches are not always a problem. It might be possible, for example, that Rita blurts out her dialogue in anger and frustration. That reaction might be dramatically imperative and germane to the character's state-of-being. If so, the speech can stand on its own merits.

5. Too Similar

Sometimes characters sound the same; their dialogue patterns are indistinguishable from each other. Once that happens the character's individuality has been lost. Can you distinguish between these two characters:

```
                    MARILYN
        Hey, did you see the race?
```

```
                    EDDIE
        Yeah, I saw the race. They
        were fast, weren't they?
```

```
                    MARILYN
        Yeah, they were fast. Did ya
        win?
```

```
                    EDDIE
        Nah, not when I needed it.
```

The characters sound precisely the same, and they're redundant on top of it. One way to counter the problem is to provide some psychological richness to the scene. The characters need to be re-examined in terms of motivations, intentions, and sense of urgency. Psychological dimensions might provide a greater dimensional canvas for the creation of dialogue. Since Marilyn and Eddie are two different human beings, their inner thoughts and attitudes might be expressed in totally different dialogue structure. Here's how the scene might play:

```
                    MARILYN
                 (tentatively)
            You saw the race?


Eddie shrugs off the question.


                     EDDIE
            Sure. They were fast, Ran neck
            and neck--

                    MARILYN
                 (interrupting)
            Never mind that. Did you win?
            Eddie?


No response. Then:


                     EDDIE
            Not this time. Not when I
            needed it.
```

When creating dialogue remember that your characters are unique human beings, with ability to interact at the highest levels of subtlety and complexity. One producer told me he covers the names of characters during the first pass at a script, to see if they're drawn dimensionally. If he can't distinguish between the blocks of dialogue, he discards the script as "characterless."

6. Too Stilted

This is dialogue that sounds as if it came from a history book, a poem, a newspaper, a grammar text, but not from a person. This is an example of stilted dialogue:

```
                     ALLEN
            It is my responsibility to
            provide you with my
            interpretation of the event.
            You are the only person that
            might accept that
            perspective. You must hear me
            out.
```

Unless Allen has a particularly pedantic problem it would be more effective for him to colloquialize and get to the bottom line quickly:

                              ALLEN
                    You gotta listen to me!

And that says it all. Don't be afraid to use contractions in dialogue;
that's the way real people speak. It helps to read dialogue aloud, if
necessary, to hear the character in action. If the speech pattern is
stilted, you can improvise the scene. That might provide a more spon-
taneous feel to the character's actions and reactions. If you improvise,
try putting the same characters into different conflicts. You'll be surprised how much you learn about them.

7. Too Preachy

   This is a problem related to being "head on," "redundant," "too
long," and "too stilted." The character tends to sound very formal, and
espouses thematic ideas or philosophical notions. He or she becomes
an ideological mouthpiece for the writer rather than a dimensional being. This speech, for example, borders on the preachy side:

                              MARK
                    Do you see what happens when
                    criminals run free? They
                    belong in jail or they
                    threaten the very fibre of
                    society. This sort of thing
                    would never happen if we had
                    stronger lawmakers and laws.

If a character must speak with strong convictions, it doesn't have to
sound like an editorial. Mark can get the same point across by growl-
ing:

                              MARK
                    The creep belongs in a cage
                    for everyone's protection. I
                    don't care what the law says.

The exact nature of the dialogue is, of course, dependent on the unfolding action in the scene, and the consistency of motivations and behavior of the character throughout the story and script.

8. Too Introspective

   This problem deals specifically with the character who is alone,
and speaks out loud. This cliché is typical:

```
                    JUDY
                 (to herself)
             Oh, how I long to be with him
             now.
```

That's enough to make any writer cringe. How often does a person actually talk to himself or herself? Not very. And when we do, it's not in complete, logical sentences. Logic is antithetical to the emotion of the moment. The dramatic conventions of a Shakespearean soliloquy are very different from the cinematic expectations of television realism. It makes more sense for the character to take advantage of the private moment on screen through visual convention. She might glance at her fiance's picture, close her eyes, and try to gain back her composure. Once again, actions speak louder than words.

9. Too Inconsistent

This means a character is saying something that doesn't "fit" the personality already created. The dialogue is incongruous with character. In some cases, that inconsistency is due to lack of proper transitions in the scene. This is an example of erratic dialogue or attitudes that change too quickly to be believed.

```
                    DEBBIE
             I wish you would both listen
             to me.


                    HOWIE
             No! David and I have better
             things to do.


                    DEBBIE
             I'm telling you this for your
             own good--


                    HOWIE
             O.k., we'll do it.
```

The thought transitions are simply too quick to be credible. It might work better if the proper actions and reactions are built into the scene through suggested transitions. This is one way of handling that problem:

<pre>
                    DEBBIE
          I wish you would both listen
          to me.

                    HOWIE
          No!
</pre>

He glances up at his sister, and sees the hurt in her eyes.
Then, softer, he tries to explain.

<pre>
                    HOWIE (cont'g)
          David and I have important
          things to do...
</pre>

That obviously has no impact. She tries to control the
urgency in her voice.

<pre>
                    DEBBIE
          I'm telling you this for your
          own good--
</pre>

A long BEAT, then Howie turns away, heading toward the
couch. He mulls it over. Finally:

<pre>
                    HOWIE
          O.k., we'll do it.
</pre>

Debbie breathes a sigh of relief.

Sometimes the problem of inconsistent dialogue can be helped by
analyzing the character's inner drives and attitudes on a moment-to-
moment basis in the scene. The solution might simply lie in the need for
more transitional time; or there might be a need for more thorough
character development in the script.

10. Too Unbelievable

This is a catch-all category that implies a character doesn't sound
real—for any number of reasons. A writer can test the credibility of dialogue by speaking it aloud, seeing if it rings true. It should sound like a
real person responding to the immediate circumstances we've just
seen. If there is a problem, try this exercise: put the same characters

into a different conflict situation. That kind of written exercise provides a direct conflict of wills, with totally opposing intentions. The two characters might thrash out the conflict in two or three pages. One may give in, one may walk out, both may compromise; the outcome is strictly up to you. However, the dialogue and reactions must integrate, the motivations and behavior must be logical and consistent. Once you know how the individual characters interact, the integrity of the character is assured. The original dialogue can be tested against your heightened insight into motivations, intentions, and attitudes.

PART THREE

THE SCRIPT

7

Developing the
Film Script

How to Structure an Act

The development of an Act rests on the established principles of story plotting and scene construction—hook the audience early, and build the action and conflict at a steady pace. The entire story has to be told within the parameters of a given number of acts and a limited number of script pages.

The audience interest curve is especially helpful in conceptualizing the story needs for each act. A writer can block out the major crisis point in each act and build the story conflict accordingly.

With the interest curve in mind, the writer can examine the function of each act and determine its effectiveness in the total plot structure. You can see whether an act sustains or builds audience interest, and whether it makes effective use of dramatic action points throughout the show. Many shows begin with a short "teaser" which hooks audience interest in 3–4 minutes. Then the script builds the story with 12–14 minutes of plotting for each act, at an increased intensity throughout the script. The end of an act usually peaks audience interest (to hold viewers throughout the commercial) and reflects a natural break in the story line.

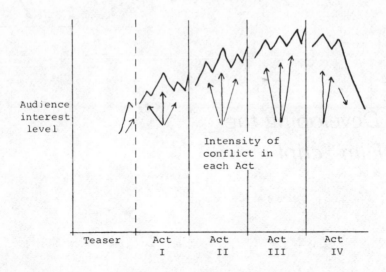

Here's a chart of the act structure, based loosely on Jerome Coopersmith's informative "script table" in *Professional Writer's Teleplay/Screenplay Format* (available from Writers Guild of America, East). Keep in mind that these are just rough guidelines to provide a sense of the act structure and length in a television show.

LENGTH OF SHOW:	TEASER:	ACTS:
30 min. (about 30 pp.)	(*optional*) (3–6 pp.)	I, II (about 13–15 pp. each)
60 min. (about 60 pp.)	(*optional*) (4–8 pp.)	I, II, III, IV (about 14–15 pp. each)
90 min. (about 90–110 pp.)	(*optional*) (4–8 pp.)	I, II, III, IV, V, VI (about 14–18 pp. each)

In the case of a 120-minute film, the script is generally written without any Teasers or Act structure. It's structured like a feature film with an open-ended story approach and can run from 120–140 pages.

How to Structure a Scene

Scenes are plotted carefully to provide full impact of an unfolding story. They are both visual and dramatic structures to help build the effectiveness of the larger acts.

A scene is one link in a dramatic sequence of events. It is comprised of action and dialogue that occurs in a single place and time. Once the location changes, so does the scene. The dictates of the story determine how long each scene will be, but many writers try to economize. Some scenes may run a few sentences, others as long as a few pages.

Here is a dramatic sequence which takes place at the airport. It is actually comprised of three separate scenes:

1. outside the airport
2. inside the terminal
3. inside the baggage compartment

Within each scene, a number of different camera angles and shots may be required to put the sequence together. But the general location remains the same, and the production crew will not have to move elsewhere.

① EXT. AIRPORT–DAY

We're at L. A. Airport, clogged with traffic, the lines of cars backed up as far as we can see. A large 707 sits waiting for take-off at one of the terminals.

② INT. TERMINAL–DAY

As busy inside as it was outside. Lots of people milling around waiting for the word to board the plane to Washington. A small coterie of FIRST CLASS PASSENGERS make their way into the plane, obviously important. They're government V.I.P.'s.

In another section of the terminal, watching the action, are THREE MEN near a food stand. One wears a suit and tie, the others wear baggage handling outfits. The MAN IN THE SUIT slips open his attache and manages to pass some writing to the BAGGAGE HANDLER. A quick glance around. No one has seen them. We HEAR the call over the P.A. system for all

passengers to board the flight. The MAN IN THE SUIT, attache
firmly in hand, waits on line for the security check. He
passes through the gates without a problem.

INT. PLANE'S BAGGAGE COMPARTMENT—DAY

The two BAGGAGE HANDLERS work furiously to attach wires to
the wall of the compartment. One HANDLER opens a plaid piece
of luggage, exposing some kind of electronic device. Time is
pressing, but they complete their mission. One of them
reaches down into the luggage and snaps a switch. The
countdown has begun. They scramble out of the compartment
and slam the door shut, leaving us in darkness.

The *first* scene—outside the airport—is an *establishing shot,* which
provides a visual orientation to the viewer. When the scene is shot, the
director may use a number of different angles (a HIGH ANGLE of the
Airport, VARIOUS ANGLES of the traffic, a CLOSE UP of the large
707, etc.), but the actual scene location does not change (EXT. AIR-
PORT—DAY).

The *second* scene takes place inside the terminal. It identifies and
focuses the action on some key characters. The director may use a
number of different *set-ups* (camera angles and lighting changes) to
achieve the total effect of passengers waiting, men interacting,
passengers boarding, and so on.

The *third* scene takes place in the baggage compartment, and com-
pletes the dramatic action in the chain of events. The scene's action is
specifically related to the previous scenes in the sequence.

Scenes can be viewed as links in the dramatic action chain, holding
your story sequences together with a clear purpose—transitional, ex-
pository, build up of conflict, or final resolution (among others). They
move the story forward with skill and maintain a tempo and rhythm
for the entire script.

Scene Descriptions

Every scene needs to be richly described, locales defined from the
camera's perspective, stage actions and reactions visually presented,

and characters dimensionally drawn. The script's imagery and atmosphere are derived directly from the scene descriptions and stage
directions.

Some writers are concerned about including too much—or too little—information in scene descriptions. Each scene requires its own
analysis in the context of the larger act. Visual descriptions can be long
enough to establish the full flavor of the place and action; short enough
to keep the pacing alive and the reader interested in the story flow.

As for the description of locale, if the scene requires a special
environment, by all means create it and embellish the surroundings.
But there is nothing wrong with using recognizable locales in the
script, and building from that point. If a character waits under the arch
of MacDonald's restaurant, or is trying to find parking near the White
House, real images are conjured up. The locations have a built-in value
for immediate identification.

A different problem arises if you want to incorporate recognizable
names or contemporary songs in the scene description. Aside from the
issue of rights and clearances, that person or song might fade into obli-
vion by the time the script is ready to be produced. As for music, unless
a particular song is *critical* to the needs of a script, you can simply suggest a song style rather than provide someone else's lyrics. For example:

```
In the b.g. (background) we hear the strains of a blues song,
and the husky voice of a nightclub vocalist. Over the song,
we hear the din of the supper club crowd, ignoring the music
behind them.
```

This scene description sets atmosphere, without defining the song
or the lyrics. On the other hand, some writers deliberately choose a
dated reference to establish the period atmosphere of a piece. The
appropriateness is determined by the needs of a specific project, and
the artistic style of the individual writer.

A writer's style is partially determined by the images used in scene
descriptions. Two writers can approach the same idea with dramatically different results. One may have the viewer on the edge of his seat in
suspense; another may have him rolling in the aisles with laughter.
Both may be telling the same story. A writer who is adept at visual
description greatly enhances the mood and atmospheric values of a
script.

Common Problems in Scene Descriptions

Just as there are problems in dialogue, so there are predictable pit-falls in scene descriptions. These are some of the more common stylistic problems.

1. Too Choppy

Some scene descriptions are written too *choppily*, presumably to account for each piece of state business. Here's an example of that problem:

```
Marsha picks up the garbage. She stops to feed the dog. She
goes to the back door.
```

The writing style can be smoothed out by avoiding separate sentence units and excessive use of pronouns. The action can be described more comprehensively:

```
Marsha picks up the garbage, stops to feed the dog, then
continues on her way out the back door.
```

2. Too Confusing

A similar problem occurs when a number of different characters are in a scene, and the writer wants to keep them alive. The tendency for *pronoun confusion* increases with the number of characters interacting in the sequence. For example:

```
The dog barks. Steve enters. Marsha sees him and tries to
calm him. She gets him a drink from the bar and he barks
louder.
```

Confusing to say the least. The problems can be corrected by addressing the specific characters and compressing the action:

As Steve enters, Marsha tries to calm the barking dog.
Unsuccessful, she heads toward the bar and gets Steve a
drink. The dog barks louder.

3. Too Redundant

A related problem is *redundancy* in visual description. A number of
key words might be repeated needlessly. It helps to "flag" those words.
You can literally circle them to see if they intrude on the reading flow:

Marsha smiles and he smiles back. Steve crosses to the
fireplace and he starts the fire and lights the wood. He
pokes the fire with brass tongs and the fire begins to
crackle.

The stage directions need to be smoothed out. The phrasing can be
modified and polished:

They exchange smiles as Steve crosses to the fireplace. He
lights the wood, pokes the brass tongs into the flames. The
fire begins to crackle.

Limiting the amount of repetition—in both words and phrases—cleans
up the description and makes the script more readable. Clean and well-
written scene descriptions help keep the tempo of the script alive, and
the rhythm flowing naturally from scene to scene.

8

Film Script Format

Sample Film Script Format

Most dramatic series and long-form TV projects (mini-series, movies-of-the-week, 120 minute pilots) are shot on film, and use a script format similar to a motion picture screenplay: each scene is broken down and described in visual detail; the stage directions and dialogue are single-spaced; the visualization is described in paragraph form.

The more scripts you read, the more familiar you'll become with various styles, forms, and techniques. TV and film scripts are available from special holdings such as the Charles K. Feldman Library at the A.F.I. Center for Advanced Film Studies in Los Angeles, California (they have thousands of scripts on file), or the Academy of TV Arts & Sciences Library at UCLA. Scripts might also be available from independent production companies, or special collections at libraries and universities. If you read a published version of a screenplay, be sure it's not subject to modifications by a publisher who might alter the format for editorial spacing and economy requirements.

On the following pages, you'll find a film script model which analyzes the structure and format of a television script.

SAMPLE FILM SCRIPT FORMAT ←

The title goes here, Capitalized and underlined

The Type of Project is in Small Letters, e.g.,

A Series Presentation--or--a 120 Feature for TV

A brief description of the nature of the project

by

Writer is named here

The Writer's Name

You can indicate first or final draft here, sometimes adding the date of completion

FIRST DRAFT

Contact Address

This can be your address, production company, agent, or business manager

WGAW Reg.

This means: "Registered with Writers Guild of America, West"

SAMPLE FILM SCRIPT FORMAT ← *The title goes here*

FADE IN: ← *This is the first written direction in every script*

EXT. CITY STREET-DAY ← *This is a "slugline" which identifies each new scene*

|| *double-spaced* ||

This is the way you start a film script, with a succinct
designation in the slug line of Exterior or Interior (use
EXT. or INT.), the location of the scene (HOSPITAL PARKING
LOT; MACDONALD'S RESTAURANT; DAVID'S BEDROOM; THE HOTEL
BAR; etc.), and the time of day, i.e., DAY or NIGHT. That
information is necessary for the production unit manager to
determine the set requirements, location requirements, and
lighting requirements of your show.

Locations, actions, and characters are described here

|| *double-space implies new angle* ||

Sometimes you can simply skip a paragraph to describe
another angle in the scene, without actually having to label
it above. This is particularly true if you are thinking of a
related piece of stage action in a master shot, or wide shot.
This saves you from over-directing your script, ·and permits
ease of reading.

ANGLE ON PARKED CAR ← *You can specify an angle this way*

You should use specific angles when you want to focus our
attention on a specific visual item--objects, people,
P.O.V.'s (Points of View). This helps move your plot forward
in a linear fashion. Note that the above angle does not have
to include any other slug-line references (e.g., DAY/
NIGHT), because it is still part of the same scene (EXT. CITY
STREET-DAY). You are merely calling for a different angle
within that scene.

INT. CAR-DAY ← *This indicates a different scene and location*

If you change the physical locale of the scene, you must
provide a new slug line. You'll note that it isn't necessary

(CONTINUED)

CONTINUED: ← *(This indicates continuation of scene.)*

to put CUT TO from the previous scene, because it is still
part of a related visual sequence, occurring at the same
time and place.

When you describe your CHARACTERS or any information
pertaining to CAMERA SHOTS, be sure to cap that information.

Try to be as visual as you can in your description of the
CHARACTERS--who they are, what they look like, what they're
doing at the moment we see them. Don't forget the setting in
the scene. You'll have to describe it in vivid detail, to
give a rich and clear picture of the mood, atmosphere, and
dramatic action.

(This is how to set up dialogue)

                    JANET
        Let's move on to something else, O.K.? How
        about the shot numbering system?

(parenthetical directions can be used to clarify an attitude or interpretation)

                    TOM
        (mock disgust)
        You mean numbering all of the camera shots?
        Forget it! That's done by the production
        secretary after the final shooting script is
        turned in. Writers don't have to be concerned
        with that. Directors will want to change it,
        anyway.

(This is one way to indicate reactions)

(JANET shrugs,) starts the car, and pulls away.

EXT. STREET-DAY ← *(A new location and scene)*

We see the car pulling away from the curb, and disappearing
down the street in light traffic. Notice that it is necessary to
provide a new slug-line, because we are now shooting outside
again. If we CUT back to JANET and TOM in their car, we
would have to designate another INT. CAR-DAY description.
But we can use another technique to keep the dialogue alive,

                                        (CONTINUED)

CONTINUED:

and the visuals wide open. That's the use of V.O. (VOICE
OVER) or O.S. (OFF SCREEN).

                    JANET (V.O.) [*here's how to indicate "voice over"*]
So, while you see the car pulling down the
street, you can still hear me talking.

                    TOM (V.O.)
Incidentally, there is a technical
difference between the voice over and the off-
screen voice. The V.O. is generally used like
this or sometimes by a Narrator. The O.S. is
used when one of the characters isn't seen in
the shot but we know he or she is in the
scene, perhaps on the other side of the room.

                    JANET (V.O.)
That's confusing. No wonder a lot of writers
are just using V.O.'s all the time.

HIGH ANGLE [*a new angle in the same scene (EXT. STREET-DAY)*]

From an AERIAL SHOT, we see the car blend into the light
maze of traffic on the city streets.

[*here is the same description*]

EXT. BEACH-DAY [*here's the new scene*]   CUT TO [*This indicates the end of one sequence of action, and for a new scene and location*]

We're in a totally different location now, so the first thing
you must do is describe it. Try to set the right visual and
emotional atmosphere with your description. If we see TOM
and JANET, do they look tired after driving all day? Are they
wearing different clothes? Are they tense? bored? anxious?
happy?

CLOSE UP-TOM [*One way of indicating CLOSE-UP*]   [*reactions are described here*]

The CLOSE UP can be called in a number of ways, e.g., CU

                                        (CONTINUED)

CONTINUED:

TOM, CLOSE ON TOM, or simply: TOM. Now you describe
what the CU reveals. Perhaps it is a look of concern.

TOM'S P.O.V.-DOWN THE BEACH ← *One way of indicating "point of view"*

In the distance, he sees the light of a bonfire. Several
FIGURES are huddled nearby. Note that the point-of-view
shot clearly describes what the character sees.

here's what the charac-ter sees

                          JANET (O.S.)
            Tom? What's the matter?

This is how to indicate "off screen" dialogue

BACK TO SHOT ← *One way of returning to a previous shot*

This designation simply calls the scene's prior establishing
shot. You might also use ANGLE ON TOM AND JANET,
which calls for a shot featuring both characters.

                          TOM
                        (tense)
            Nothing's the matter.

parenthetical directions under character's name should be short

The parenthetical information should be used if the attitude
of the character is not clear by dialogue alone. It wouldn't be
necessary for you to say TOM speaks angrily if he shouts, Get
out of here! You might also include some relevant stage
business for the character, if this can be done succinctly. For
the most part, however, try to let the dialogue speak for itself.
Stage directions can generally be incorporated in this space.
For example: JANET glances down the beach, squints to see
the bonfire O.S. (off screen), and looks back at TOM. A
BEAT, then she packs their belongings hurriedly.

                          JANET
            Let's go.

A "BEAT" is described here

The Beat that was used above is a filmic version of the
dramatic pause, or the Chekovian pause. It implies a second
or two for the character to digest the information, before he
or she acts on it.

                                              (CONTINUED)

CONTINUED:

NEW ANGLE ⟵ ⟮ *Another way of calling a shot in the scene* ⟯

This is a legitimate angle designation, which implies a
different camera angle from the previous one. You don't have
to specify the shot, but you should describe the action taking
place. Note, too, that if some background action is occurring,
you identify it as b.g. (not spelled out); similarly, if camera is
focused on foreground action, you would say ⟮f.g.⟯ ⟮*"foreground"*⟯

ANGLE ON THE CAR

JANET and TOM trot through the beach to their car, and
hastily climb in. She starts it up, but the engine won't start.
In the ⟮b.g.⟯ we can make out the FIGURES by the bonfire,
moving toward them. ⟵ ⟮*"background"*⟯

                    TOM
          Hurry!

A BEAT before the ignition catches, then the car starts up
and skids away. Note that the character doesn't have to
repeat any visual information, i.e., he wouldn't say, Hurry,
the figures are coming toward us! We can assume that
JANET sees the same thing he does.

When you have special sound effects, e.g., the waves
crashing, the fire crackling, etc., you can place those directly
in the scene description to add atmosphere and mood to the
piece. Keep the action moving from scene to scene, and be
sure your characters act and react like real people. Each one
is unique, and must sound and behave like a credible,
identifiable person. Once the script is finished, be sure to:

all effects- visual and sound- are incorpo- rated into the scene description

                                        FADE OUT.

⟮*This is the last direction in the script. The screen image fades to black*⟯

Capitalizing in the Script

Words are generally capitalized to identify NEW SCENES, NEW CAMERA ANGLES or SHOTS, SPECIAL EFFECTS (camera or sound effects) and scene transitions like CUT TO or DISSOLVE.

The names of CHARACTERS are also capitalized to indicate who is performing in the scene, and who is speaking at the moment. If a character is simply mentioned by another, there is no need for capitalizing. There is some latitude about capitalizing a character's name throughout the script. Some writers will only capitalize it the first time the character appears in the script. Others will capitalize the name throughout each scene in the script. Both ways are considered acceptable.

If a scene is continued on a new page, that is indicated by a "(CONTINUED)" at the bottom right hand page of the script, and "CONTINUED" at the top left of the following page.

If dialogue is broken at the end of a page, it should end with a full sentence. Then "(MORE)" is added under the broken dialogue, and "(CONT'D)" is typed on the following page, after the character's name.

Typewriter Settings for a Film Script

Margins for a film script are generally set according to these guidelines. Most scripts are typed in standard (*Pica*) type on 8½" × 11" manuscript paper.

	Pica	*Elite*
Script Margins	19–73	22–88
Dialogue	30–65	35–79
Name above dialogue	43	52

For writers with word processors, margins can be easily set using a good word processing package. Some systems allow you to set tabs and margins with the format displayed on screen, which is a useful and time-saving device. Once you have the basic software for text editing, you can even select software packages that will aid in revising your draft. These can be especially helpful in adjusting for margin changes, page changes, and intelligent page breaks. (For more on word processing, see the *Annotated Bibliography*.

How to Write Camera Angles

Most television scripts are written *without* complicated, extensive camera directions.

There is no need to clutter scripts with OVER-THE-SHOULDER SHOTS, REVERSE ANGLES, MEDIUM SHOTS, or TWO SHOTS. The director will make all those decisions in pre-production planning. It's the writer's responsibility to merely suggest the *potential* for camera coverage without complicating or over-directing the script.

Here are a few angles which are particularly helpful in scripting:

WIDE ANGLE. This provides full screen coverage of all the ensuing action. It's also called a FULL SHOT.

NEW ANGLE. This suggests that some other perspective is needed, but does not necessarily pinpoint that coverage.

CLOSE UP. This is the magnified coverage of a person's face or a specific object on the screen.

BACK TO SHOT. This is a way of suggesting that a previous angle is called for.

ANGLE ON. This might focus attention on a specific place or person (e.g., ANGLE ON HALLWAY or ANGLE ON HARRIET).

The following is from a television film called "Death's Head." You can see how simply the angles are set up for the opening sequence in the script.

FADE IN:

INT. CAROL'S BEDROOM-NIGHT

It's late at night, and we can barely make out the figure of
a woman sleeping alone in a king-size bed. She's cuddled up
under the covers, the other half of the bed remains
untouched. A shaft of light seeps in from the hall
highlighting her face as she stirs...CAROL MADDEN is a
striking woman...early 30's, long blonde hair, soft
compelling features.

(CONTINUED)

CONTINUED:

Over the STEADY RHYTHM of the air conditioner, we hear a
SLIGHT RUSTLE. It doesn't seem to disturb her...But then,
after a Beat, we hear another RUSTLING SOUND. Tired, CAROL
opens her eyes...inquisitive at first, not really sure if
she's heard anything.

CLOSE ANGLE ON BED

A huge black spider is crawling across the covers, gliding
slowly and methodically toward her.

CLOSE-UP CAROL

She sees it, recoils in fear.

                                                         CUT TO:

INT. DOWNSTAIR'S DEN-NIGHT

CLOSE ANGLE ON CRATE

The black furry legs of a spider can be seen trying to climb
the ledge of the crate. A hand gently cups the insect, and
adroitly puts it back into the crate, closing the cover.

NEW ANGLE

We see CAROL's husband, STEVE, in the brightly lit room
downstairs. The wood-panelled Den sports a good many insect
displays on walls and table...exotic butterflies, beetles,
moths, all artfully pinned and exhibited under glass.
There's a peculiar beauty about the whole collection. STEVE,
a slightly built, but good-looking man in his late 40's, is
straightening up from the small wooden crate beside him. He
glances around, looking for something. One of the spiders is
missing.

                                   •   •   •

If you analyze the script structure and camera angles, here's what
you'll find:

1. The "slug-line" identifies individual scenes (INT. CAROL'S BEDROOM—NIGHT; INT. DEN—NIGHT).
2. Each scene is comprised of different shots or camera angles. So when we describe Carol's bedroom, then cut to a close-up of the spider on the bed, we are still in the same scene. We simply changed the viewing perspective.
3. Camera angles are suggested clearly. The description of CAROL'S BEDROOM is an implied WIDE ANGLE which establishes all the action in the scene. CLOSE ANGLES are used for special dramatic emphasis and impact. NEW ANGLES imply different perspectives within the same scene. Sometimes NEW ANGLES are implied by simply skipping a paragraph in the scene description.
4. The scene descriptions provide exact visual information about the set, character, and stage action. The descriptions tell us exactly what the camera sees.
5. The camera coverage and special effects are capitalized; so are the characters' names. Capitalizing is not mandatory, but it does help in pre-production breakdown of the script.

The Master Scene Script

Most original television scripts are submitted in the Master Scene form as opposed to shooting script form. A Master Scene script is one that offers a vivid description of action within each scene, but does not break down specific camera angles or shots; nor does it number the shots in the margins.

In the Master Scene script, the visual descriptions are particularly important. The script allows latitude for the integration of character and action, without the encumbrance of complex camera coverage.

The following script serves as a good example of the readability and visual effectiveness of a Master Scene script. The excerpt is from a television film called "Disappearing Act." In the script, CAPT. DAN is an old retired cop, AL SILVERMAN is a young clerk from Missing Persons Bureau, and JOYCE KESSLER is his partner. They are determined to find out what happened to a missing subway train full of people. In the process, they are stalked by adversaries as well as police.

The excerpt opens in a SUBWAY TUNNEL at night where the three featured characters are searching for the missing subway. We are picking up the action in the middle of a scene as indicated by the CONTINUED on top of the page. Note the relative scarcity of camera shots and the strong visualization in the scene descriptions.

CONTINUED:

They begin crossing through the maze of tracks.

                    CAPT. DAN
          Careful now. Watch the wooden rail, that's
          the live one.

                    SILVERMAN
          Are you sure this is right? Let's see the map.

                    JOYCE
          If we get run over by an A-Train, we went
          wrong.

Capt. Dan takes the map out of his pocket and Silverman holds
the flashlight. It is a normal Transit Riders Map and shows
almost no significant detail. As they stand in the maze of
tracks a rumble is heard growing rapidly louder.

                    JOYCE
                  (frightened)
          Which way is it coming from?

                    SILVERMAN
                  (panicking)
          I don't know.

                    CAPT. DAN
          Get the lead out!

Capt. Dan hop-scotches across the rails towards a small
depression in the tunnel wall. Silverman follows, dragging
Joyce by the hand. Before he has made it a headlight flashes

                                        (CONTINUED)

CONTINUED:

around the bend and a train roars straight toward them.
Joyce screams and grabs Silverman as they both flatten
themselves against the wall, trying to squeeze into the too
small alcove. The train roars straight for them and the
last instant veers left, passing within twelve inches of their
bodies as it negotiates a sharp curve.

                         JOYCE
                 (panting uncontrollably)
         Oh my God...

                         SILVERMAN
         Shhh, it's all right, calm down.

He strokes her to calm her down.

                         CAPT. DAN
         At least we know they can't sneak up on us.
         We'll always have enough warnin'.

INT. DARK TUNNEL-NIGHT

Illuminated only by an occasional low wattage lightbulb,
this tunnel is smaller, darker, danker than the one before.
We can barely make out our three heroes as they approach.
Capt. Dan's limp is becoming more pronounced. Silverman shines
his light ahead.

                         SILVERMAN
         I can see another set of switches up there,
         must be where the Far Rockaway line cuts off.

                                              (CONTINUED)

CONTINUED:

                              CAPT. DAN
              Let me set a minute, this damp air has got me
              winded.

He leans against the tool box next to the wall. Joyce looks
around, notices water dripping from above, mud all over her
shoes. Another rumble is heard.

                              SILVERMAN
              Behind the tool box!

They run to where Capt. Dan is sitting and hunch down in the
shadow of the large wooden bin. We see the flashlight drop
from Silverman's pocket and fall between the rails.

                              JOYCE
              Al, the light...

Before he can retrieve it the train comes roaring through.
In the small tunnel wind howls by their ears and the noise is
deafening. They close their eyes as whirlwinds of grit,
soot, and dirt pockmark their faces.

CLOSE-UP JOYCE

She opens her eyes and tries to adjust to the near blackness,
her eyes widening in terror.

P.O.V. JOYCE

Dozens of luminous, close-set pink eyes stare back at her.

                                                    (CONTINUED)

CONTINUED:

CLOSE-UP JOYCE

She screams at the top of her lungs.

Silverman lunges for the flashlight, turns it on in time to
see a pack of white albino cats glide noiselessly across the
rails and disappear.

                    CAPT. DAN
          Just cats, thousands of em live in the tun-
          nels and never see the light of day.

INT. CONVERGENCE OF TUNNELS AT SWITCHING POINT-NIGHT

Here the passageway widens as two other lines feed in and
exit from a common point. Silverman, Joyce and Capt. Dan
gingerly begin picking their way across the rails.

                    JOYCE
          My shoes are so muddy it's like walking on
          suction cups.

                    SILVERMAN
          I don't ever remember walking on suction
          cups.

                    CAPT. DAN
          Shhh. Hear that clanking?

They stop and listen. Suddenly it stops. Then it begins again.

                                        (CONTINUED)

CONTINUED:

                          SILVERMAN
          What is it?

                          CAPT. DAN
          Shhhh.

Now we hear it again, this time more distinctly. It sounds
like canteens banging against the paraphenalia that soldiers
always wear. Before they can answer the question they see
several flashlight beams approaching from two different
tunnels. Now we see uniformed policemen running towards
them from the distance.

                          COPS
                        (distant)
          There they are.

                          COP
                    (through bullhorn)
          Okay, stay where you are.

Silverman, Joyce, Capt. Dan stand in shock.

                          SILVERMAN
          Come on!

                          CAPT. DAN
                    (gasping for breath)
          I can't make it. You two go ahead and I'll
          turn myself in.

                                              (CONTINUED)

CONTINUED:

                              JOYCE
          No!

                           CAPT. DAN
               No time for sentiment, get going.

Silverman turns to run but hesitates.

                           CAPT. DAN
          GO!!!

Silverman grabs Joyce and they run. A flare goes off showing
a line of cops closing in from all directions.

                              COP
                           (bullhorn)
               There's no way out. Put your hands up and re-
               main where you are.

A rumble reverberates through the tunnel. Capt. Dan raises
his hands and walks toward them.

                           CAPT. DAN
                           (gasping)
               Hold it boys, I'm coming out.

At this a train roars through from behind Capt. Dan heading
for the cops. It is on the opposite rail but has the effect
of splitting the body of men in two and adding to the
confusion.

                                              (CONTINUED)

CONTINUED:

A particularly hefty cop in full battle dress runs forward
into the light caused by the flare. He wears a huge cartridge
belt hung with every conceivable kind of weapon plus a
helmet with face shield. He reaches Capt. Dan and brutally
knocks the old man aside with the butt of his gas gun, kneels
in firing position and fires a shell at CAMERA. Though we
don't see his face too clearly, his shape is that of Sgt.
Santucci.

It explodes behind Silverman and Joyce and they turn to face
him, choking in the fumes.

                        JOYCE
                      (coughing)
              My shoe! I lost my shoe!

The hefty cop charges forward, his gas rifle dangling down
from one hand, and a raised club over his head. His fat
bounces and his teeth are clenched in eager anticipation of
striking a blow at Silverman and Joyce.

Silverman steps in front of Joyce to protect her. The hefty
cop is about to bring his club crashing into Silverman's
skull when he trips over Joyce's shoe, losing his balance.

He falls forward but quickly regains his balance. In the
process the metal barrel of his gas gun strikes the third
rail, causing a bright blue spark. An instant later another
flare bathes him in brilliant white light. He stand frozen.

Under the sound of the roaring train comes the faint, short
beginnings of a strangulated scream that is never finished.

                                        (CONTINUED)

CONTINUED:

Santucci's whole body begins convulsing in spasms. Smoke
rises from his clothes.

Joyce looks on in horror, begins screaming. Silverman grabs
her and drags her, screaming and hysterical, back into the
tunnel.

The train passes and the disorganized force begins to
regroup.

                         COP ONE (O.S.)
          What smells?

                         COP TWO (O.S.)
          Get an ambulance. Get an ambulance!

The smoke clears. Silverman and Joyce have disappeared.

INT. ANOTHER TUNNEL, SMALLER AND DARKER-NIGHT

Joyce leans against the wall, shaking and sobbing. Silverman
stands beside her, pale and weak.

                         SILVERMAN
          We've got to keep going. We're bound to come
          to a station where we can get out.

                         JOYCE
                    (uncontrollably)
          I want to go home, please get me out of here.
          Please, I want to go home. I want to go home.

                    •   •   •

The visual style of the writer can come through in a Master Scene script, which relies on *few* camera directions and on a *great deal* of scene description. Most scripts submitted in the marketplace are in the Master Scene form.

Once the first draft of a Master Scene script is written, the writer faces the arduous, intensive task of rewriting. The pacing and atmosphere are analyzed and the story and character development are probed. However, before we talk about the rewriting process, let's look at some special problems you may encounter in writing certain types of sequences in your script.

Special Problems and How to Handle Them:
Intercuts, Montages, Dreams, Flashbacks

1. Intercuts

Intercutting is switching back and forth between two or more scenes consecutively. For example, a script may call for parallel action and dialogue during a phone conversation. If the writer plays the scene in one location, it could result in static dramatic action. If the script cuts back and forth between characters, it might result in awkward repetition of scene descriptions.

The most common solution to this kind of problem is to identify the on-going scenes in advance by calling for an INTERCUT SEQUENCE. The appropriate scenes are defined while action and dialogue are written as usual. The last scene concludes with: END INTERCUT SEQUENCE. This is what it looks like:

```
NOTE: INTERCUT SEQUENCE:


INT. LAURA'S APT-DAY


She's on the phone in the den, pictures scattered all over
the floor.
```

EXT. PHONE BOOTH-DAY

It's raining cats and dogs as we see MIKE, drenched to the
bone, talking to Laura.

                        LAURA
                   (into phone)
            Hello?

                        MIKE
                   (into phone)
        Hi, Laura, It's me. You o.k.?

                        LAURA
                   (into phone)
        Fine, but I miss you somethin'
        awful. When will you come
        back?

He takes a deep breath. Then, trying to sound casual:

                        MIKE
                   (into phone)
        Not for a long time.

LAURA's eyes widen. She didn't want to hear that.

END INTERCUT SEQUENCE.

    The need for an intercut sequence is dictated by the length of the re-
quired scene and the importance of seeing consecutive dramatic action
on the screen. The sequence allows the director to edit as he or she sees
fit.

2. Montages

A *montage* is a succession of different shots that seem to condense time, emotions, and action in just a few short scenes. The story may call for a quickly established romance, or an historical progression of images leading to the present time.

As with intercuts, the montage is identified in advance of the sequence and at its conclusion. The individual scenes are sometimes listed by number (although this is not always the case).

If a writer needs to show a character undertaking different activities in a progression of time, the montage sequence is ideal. This is one way it would be set up:

MONTAGE SEQUENCE:

1. INT. CAROL'S ROOM-DAY

She's cleaning it up, carefully straightening the sheets on the bed.

2. EXT. SUPERMARKET-DAY

She wheels a basket down the aisles, quickly pulling food from the counter, and piling it into the basket.

3. INT. CAROL'S KITCHEN-DAY

A bandana over her head, she's polishing the oven fast and furiously.

4. EXT. CAROL'S PORCH-NIGHT

She's in her jeans collapsed on the swinging porch bench, tired and weary.

END MONTAGE

There's no need to show Carol cleaning up everything in the room, or conversing with the cashier at the supermarket. The visual information in a montage implicitly gives the viewer that sense of completed action.

3. Dreams and Fantasies

In scriptwriting, *dreams* and *fantasies* are used interchangeably. They permit the viewer to enter the character's mind, to literally see imagination, daydreams, fantasies, nightmares.

If a dream sequence is short and fleeting, it can be distinguished from "real time" by inserting specific parenthetical information. For example:

```
CU CAROL


She's fast asleep, a look of anxiety twists her face.
Clearly disturbed, restless...


CU SPIDER (DREAM SEQUENCE)


It crawls toward her at an inscrutably slow pace...


CU CAROL (BACK TO REALITY)


She snaps her eyes open and looks around. There's nothing
there.
```

In this case, the dream sequence shot is almost a *flashcut*, i.e., it is a very fast insert into the "real" world—Carol sleeping.

If a dream or fantasy is longer, the entire sequence might be distinguished from "real time." That practice minimizes the chance of confusing the reader. A longer sequence is generally identified in advance, and the first "real" scene is also identified.

Here's what a longer dream sequence—or fantasy sequence—looks like:

CU CAROL

She's fast asleep, a look of anxiety twists her face.
Clearly disturbed, restless...

                                             DISSOLVE TO:

DREAM SEQUENCE

EXT. MARINA VILLAGE-TWILIGHT

We hear an eerie, toneless quality to the b.g. music from the
village shops...This is a distorted, nightmarish replay of
her first visit...

ANGLE ON GIRL

A young GIRL beckons to her from one of the shops. The GIRL
is hawking something, we're not sure what. CAROL moves
curiously toward her, in SLOW MOTION...

INT. SHOP-TWILIGHT

CAROL enters the shop, looks around, sees the young GIRL
behind the counter, back to camera. She turns to face
CAROL...

CLOSE UP-CAROL

Her face reflects shock, her eyes widen in horror as she
sees...

HER P.O.V.-EXTREME CLOSEUP-GIRL

The GIRL has become a TOOTHLESS OLD HAG. We're on a DISTORTED
FISH EYE LENS...the HAG beckons to CAROL, smiling
bizarrely...We see the sign of a hexagon dangling from her
neck, shimmering...THE OLD HAG continues to beckon, drawing
her closer...

EXTREME CLOSEUP-CAROL

She shrieks in fear.

END DREAM SEQUENCE

                                                          CUT TO:

INT. CAROL'S BEDROOM-NIGHT (REALITY)

She is sitting up in bed, screaming, frightened...stops.
Looks around the room...silence...

The entire dream sequence is played out in two scenes: EXT.
MARINA VILLAGE and INT. SHOP. The various angles and visual
descriptions help set the mood and atmosphere. Once the sequence is
over, the "real time" sequence picks up the pace and helps sustain the
mood.

4. Flashbacks

A *flashback* distinguishes "time remembered" from real time and is
set up like the dream sequence. If a memory is very brief, the writer can
parenthetically identify the FLASHBACK. For example:

CU RONALD

He remembers something, the memory plagues him.

INT. ATTIC-NIGHT (FLASHBACK)

It's a dingy place, no air, no light. In the corner,
something moves...We can't make it out, but it's alive.

ANGLE ON RONALD (FLASHBACK)

He's on his knees, a flashlight in hand. He tries to switch
it on, but the batteries are dead. He throws it toward the
moving object, and races toward the attic steps.

CU RONALD (REALITY)

Jarred by the memory.

If a FLASHBACK SEQUENCE is much longer, it would be written just
like the longer Dream Sequence.

This might be the time to caution against the unnecessary use of
flashbacks. The technique is helpful to provide some exposition about
characters or to establish a "backstory" to the plot. However, if it's used
too often, the effect can be detrimental to the story. The more a writer
relies on Flashbacks, the more he or she intrudes on the forward thrust
of the plot. If a story begins in the present tense, then slips back in time,
the viewer already knows the outcome. The audience is waiting to see
the characters work their way out of the current situation; that action is
forestalled with the intrusion of flashbacks. A television script must
gain the viewer's interest quickly, and—unlike a Fellini film—hold audience interest throughout commercial breaks. If you must use flashbacks, do so sparingly. They may lead you to believe the story is pro-
gressing nicely, when in fact it's stopped the plot cold.

9

The Videotape Script Format

The Wide Margin Format

If a program is produced on videotape, or with multiple cameras, a spacious format is used, derived from the early days of live television. The format uses less camera coverage and fewer angles than film scripts. Moreover, everything on the page is double-spaced—stage directions, scene descriptions, and dialogue. The margins are wider, too (15–55 in *Pica* Type; 18–90 in *Elite* Type). That wide-margin and double-space format allows the director, actor, and technical crew, plenty of room to note specific actions, reactions, and technical requirements from stage blocking to detailed camera coverage.

Since the script is so spacious, the page count is much longer than film—by *half*. A one-hour script in film runs 60 pages; in videotape it might run 90 pages. Here is a rough page count table for videotape script:

Length of Show	Approximate Pages
30 minutes	45 pp. and up
60 minutes	90 pp. and up
90 minutes	135 pp. and up
120 minutes	180 pp. and up

A 30-minute comedy is built around two acts and a short tease (opening) or tag (closing). Each act is about 25–30 pages long.

149

The following script model provides a look at the structure of this format, which is appropriate for any multiple camera comedy, drama, or live action program.

SAMPLE <u>VIDEOTAPE</u> SCRIPT FORMAT ←(*Title*)

by

A Writer for TV ←(*Writer's name*)

(*You can indicate first or final draft*)

FIRST DRAFT ←

                                                    Contact Address

WGAW Reg.

←(*This indicates the project is registered with Writers Guild of America, West*)

(*Your address, production company, agent, or business manager*)

SAMPLE <u>VIDEOTAPE</u> SCRIPT FORMAT *(The title goes here)*

ACT ONE *(This is how to begin a script)*

FADE IN:

INT. HOTEL ROOM-NIGHT *(This is the "slugline" or description line which identifies each new scene)*

(YOU'LL NOTICE THAT NO VIDEO ACTION CAN OCCUR UNTIL YOU'VE

FADED IN. THEN YOU MUST USE A SLUG-LINE, OR DESCRIPTION

LINE, TO SET THE EXTERIOR OR INTERIOR LOCALE, AND THE TIME OF

DAY. PLEASE NOTE THAT YOU MUST USE EXT. OR INT. YOU

DON'T HAVE TO SPELL THEM OUT.) *(Scene descriptions are double-spaced)*

ANGLE ON THE BED *(Here's how to set up a new camera angle)*

(YOU'LL SEE THAT ALL THE NECESSARY INFORMATION IS IN CAPS,

AND IS DOUBLE-SPACED. YOU MUST DESCRIBE YOUR SHOT, THE

CHARACTERS WE SEE, AND THE STAGE ACTION OCCURRING. ALL OF

THIS IS IN PARENTHESIS). *(Scene descriptions and stage directions may or may not be in parentheses)*

FRED

The character's name is capitalized and centered above dialogue

The dialogue is centered under your

character's name, and is double-spaced. That

gives the director room to work on his

dialogue is double-spaced

shooting script.

LINDA

(SMILING)

Character reactions can be suggested in parentheses or written in the stage directions

It also allows the actor and producer to see

the lines at a glance.

(BE SURE TO INCLUDE ANY REACTIONS YOUR CHARACTERS MAY HAVE
TO THE PREVIOUS LINES OR ON-GOING ACTION.)

CLOSE UP-FRED

Here is how to write "CLOSE-UP". It is also written "CU-FRED."

(THIS IS WHERE YOU DESCRIBE HOW YOUR CHARACTER LOOKS IN A

GIVEN SITUATION. HOW DOES HE FEEL ABOUT THIS MOMENT IN THE

SCENE? IT COULD BE A VERY TELLING REACTION, BUT MUST BE

CONSISTENT WITH THE WAY HE'S ACTED BEFORE.)

Writers often suggest new angles, without "overdirecting"

WIDE SHOT OF THE BED

(TRY NOT TO OVER-DIRECT THE SCENE WITH A LOT OF CAMERA

DIRECTIONS. THIS IS THE RESPONSIBILITY OF THE DIRECTOR, NOT

THE WRITER. THERE IS NO NEED TO SPECIFY MED. SHOT,

(CONTINUED)

CONTINUED:

THREE SHOT, CHEST SHOT OR ANY OTHER DESIGNATIONS

THAT ARE NOT TOTALLY NECESSARY TO THE IMPACT AND IMAGE OF

YOUR SCENE.)

                              FRED

This is the way a director might mark the script to indicate precise camera coverage and upcoming technical cuts. The wide margin format allows room for directorial notations

          In some scripts, the writer breaks out the

          video and audio sections into two

① CU- FRED separate columns. This is not really

(Ready cam②)

(Ready music) necessary in television drama, since you have

1 - slow 2 / 1

R /EFX enough room on either side of the directions

          to coordinate and put in appropriate

② WS BED directorial markings. /

(WHEN YOU END YOUR SCENE, TRY TO GO OUT ON A REACTION OR A KEY

PIECE OF VISUAL INFORMATION, AND THEN YOU CAN...)

Here's how to indicate a switch to a totally different location and scene   CUT TO:

INT. HOTEL LOBBY-DAY ← *here's how to set up the new scene*

(AGAIN, YOU MUST DESCRIBE THE SET, DEFINE THE SHOT VISUALLY

FOR THE READER-PRODUCER-DIRECTOR, AND DESCRIBE THE *The new scene is described here*

                                        (CONTINUED)

CONTINUED:

CHARACTERS. BE SURE TO STATE WHO THEY ARE, WHAT THEY LOOK

LIKE, AND WHAT THEY ARE DOING.)

                        FRED

(LIGHTING HIS CIGARETTE)

A small piece of character "business" or action might go in the stage directions above or here

Dialogue, by the way, should be crisp

and to the point. And don't worry if it

doesn't look gramatically correct. People

just don't talk that way. They speak

colloquially, you know? So make your

characters talk like a real person.

                        LINDA

(TRYING TO HIDE HER JEALOUSY)

Attitudes can be suggested here

And don't forget that characters react to

everything they see and hear. Spoken or not.

This helps build credible motivations and

identifiable behavior patterns.

Music or sound effects are set up in a separate line of stage directions

MUSIC UP: IF YOU HAVE MUSIC OR SOUND EFFECTS, THIS IS HOW TO

WRITE THEM IN.

LINDA (Cont'g)

If a character is continuing dialogue from above, uninterrupted

I'd rather listen to the stereo, wouldn't

you?

(FRED GRINS).

here's how to write a reaction without cutting to a CLOSE-UP.

This is the last direction in any script

FADE OUT.

or

FADE TO BLACK.

Capitalizing and Spacing

As you can see, this script format has several distinct features:

1. Everything is capitalized in the script—except dialogue. Set descriptions, character actions and reactions are capitalized, as is every piece of stage direction. The dialogue alone remains in lower case.

2. Every line is double-spaced. From the opening sequence to the final FADE OUT, the script is double-spaced. That includes all dialogue, stage blocking, special effects, and scene descriptions.

3. New sequences are capitalized and underlined. That includes new ACTS, SCENES, TEASERS, TAGS. Moreover, each new sequence begins a new page. When the first scene is over, the next scene begins on a page labeled SCENE TWO. If the first act is over, the next page begins ACT TWO.

4. All new locations, camera directions and special effects are capitalized and underlined: FADE IN, INT. HOTEL ROOM—NIGHT, MUSIC UP, STOP TAPE, FADE OUT.

Typewriter Settings for a Videotape Script

The script can be centered on the page, or shifted to the right or left to accommodate wider margin needs. This is one acceptable typewriter setting for this format:

	Pica	Elite
Script Margins	15–55	18–90
Dialogue	25–55	31–64
Above Dialogue	40	49

Camera Angles and Scene Descriptions

In this script format, camera angles are kept to a bare minimum, with, at most, a reference to NEW ANGLE or CLOSE UP. The scene sets up the basic information concerning place, characters, and action, and the director takes over from that point.

Stage directions are comparatively brief. Compared to film, there is not much latitude for embellishing mood and atmosphere. This, for example, is the opening scene from a videotape script called "The New Little Rascals," a pilot project for Norman Lear's company. Note that the scene is relatively short, stage directions concise, and the angles virtually ignored.

```
''GLUE'S COMPANY''



                            ACT ONE



   SCENE I



   INT. SCHOOLROOM



   SPANKY SITS AT HIS DESK, GLUING TOGETHER A MODEL OF THE

   WRIGHT BROTHERS' AIRPLANE. HE IS USING A LARGE SQUEEZE

   BOTTLE OF GLUE WITH A DISTINCTIVE LABEL: ''FUN-NEE GLUE.

                                            (CONTINUED)
```

CONTINUED:

FAST, FAST, FAST!'' HE IS NOT BEING TOO CAREFUL; AS HE

APPLIES GLUE TO THE PLANE, WE SEE A LARGE DRIP RUN DOWN HIS

SHIRT FRONT. AT A NEARBY DESK, ALFALFA IS METICULOUSLY

LINING UP SEVERAL ROWS OF PLASTIC INDIANS AND OLD-WEST

CAVALRY.

                    SPANKY

    Jeez, this glue is fast! Look at this!

ALFALFA LOOKS. SPANKY TOUCHES A PIECE INTO PLACE ON THE

PLANE IT STICKS IMMEDIATELY, SOUNDLY.

                    ALFALFA

    Wow! Can I borrow that stuff?

                    SPANKY

    Sure, when I'm done. What're you working on?

                    ALFALFA

(WITH A PROUD GESTURE TOWARD THE SOLDIERS AND INDIANS)

    It's Custer's Last Stand!

HIS HAND BRUSHES AGAINST A SOLDIER, WHICH FALLS AGAINST THE

                                        (CONTINUED)

CONTINUED:

NEXT, WHICH FALLS AGAINST THE NEXT...UNTIL WHOLE

ARRANGEMENT HAS FALLEN OVER LIKE SO MANY DOMINOES.

                         SPANKY

          Not any more, it isn't.

WITH A SHRUG, ALFALFA RISES, MOVES TOWARD THE DOOR.

                         ALFALFA

          Oh, well. No point setting 'em up until Jinx

          gets here with the diorama. See you.

                         SPANKY

          See you.

ALFALFA EXITS.

SPANKY APPLIES GLUE TO PLANE, GETTING SOME ON HIS HAND. HE

REACHES OVER WITH GLUEY HAND, PICKS UP PLANE WING. DECIDES

IT ISN'T READY YET, MOVES TO SET WING DOWN: IT WON'T GO. HE

TRIES AGAIN: WING IS STUCK TO HIS HAND.

                         SPANKY (cont'd)

          ...huh?

                                        (CONTINUED)

CONTINUED:

HE SHAKES HAND VIOLENTLY; WING DOESN'T COME OFF. STARING

INTENTLY AT WING, HE PUTS ELBOWS ON DESK, IDLY LAYING FREE

HAND ATOP FUSELAGE. HE THINKS A MOMENT, THEN SITS BACK WITH

RESOLVE.

                    SPANKY (cont'd)

        This glue can't be all that--

HE GESTURES WITH WHAT WAS HIS FREE HAND; THE FUSELAGE STICKS

TO IT. HE DOES TAKE.

                    SPANKY (cont'd)

        Oh no!

HE SHAKES BOTH HANDS VIOLENTLY; NOTHING COMES LOOSE. HE

PULLS AT WING, THEN AT FUSELAGE; NOTHING. HIS EYE FALLS ON

THE GLUE BOTTLE

                    SPANKY (Cont'd)

        The bottle! The bottle'll say what to do!

USING WING AND FUSELAGE AS IF THEY WERE HANDS, HE MANEUVERS

BOTTLE SO HE CAN READ THE LABEL. HE READS AVIDLY...AND HIS

FACE FALLS.

                                        (CONTINUED)

CONTINUED:

               SPANKY (cont'd)

...the bottle says zero!

HE RISES, DETERMINED.

               SPANKY (Cont'd)

O-kay. I'm not gonna panic. I'm not gonna run

around screaming for help.

LOOKING INTENTLY AT HIS HANDS, HE BEGINS TO PACE. HE BUMPS

INTO ALFALFA'S DESK, FALLS SPREADEAGLE, FACE DOWN ATOP THE

PLASTIC FIGURES.

STOP TAPE.

RESUME ON:

ANOTHER ANGLE:

SPANKY RISES FROM ALFALFA'S DESK: ALL BUT ONE OF THE

SOLDIERS AND INDIANS ARE NOW STUCK TO HIS SHIRT FRONT. HE

TUGS HELPLESSLY AT ONE OR TWO OF THEM, THEN LOOKS UP, EYES

WIDE WITH ALARM.

                  SPANKY

Help! Help!

                •   •   •

The whole scene takes place in one set—A SCHOOLROOM—which makes it easier to shoot, and inexpensive to produce. The writer suggests visual blocking and action, but doesn't overdirect with specific angles.

One device the writer employs is the STOP TAPE direction at the closing of the scene. He then resumes the action on ANOTHER ANGLE with SPANKY fully covered by plastic figures. When the sequence is edited together, it will look like SPANKY falls on the plastic figures, then gets right up from the desk with all the figures stuck to his shirt. The STOP TAPE direction allows time for such technical changes required on the set.

Cast and Set Lists

After the script is written, each scene should be reviewed to identify casting and location needs. That information is summarized in a Cast and Set sheet that is placed in the front of the script. This is the Cast and Set list from "The New Little Rascals" script:

''GLUE'S COMPANY''

<u>CAST</u>

ALFALFA

SPANKY

JINX

JO JO

FELIX

TURK

ISH

BELLADONNA

MR. SOPWORTH

POLICEMAN (OFFICER WITOWSKI)

<u>SETS</u>

INT. SCHOOLROOM

EXT. SCHOOL HOUSE (SIDE)

EXT. SCHOOL YARD

EXT. BUSINESS STREET

EXT. VACANT LOT

EXT. RESIDENTIAL STREET   1

EXT. RESIDENTIAL STREET   2

INT. BAG IT 'N BEAT IT

EXT. SPANKY'S HOUSE

The Cast and Set list is only worked up for shows that will be produced on tape or shot with multi-camera set-ups. For the sake of production budgets, it's a good idea to limit the number of sets required and the number of characters needed for casting.

The Variety Show Format

Another multiple-camera program using this format is the variety show. Most variety shows are shot before a live audience with a full complement of cameras. The script conveys the set needs, talent requirements, stage blocking, and basic action for sketches and songs.

In the variety show genre, scenes are referred to as "Segments." Since the segment is shot in relative continuity, each is written as a separate unit: SEGMENT ONE appears at the top left hand corner of the page; the following segment appears on a new page when the previous one is over.

Here's what a sample song segment looks like:

SEGMENT TWO: What's the Sense

(MERV HANDS JODY THE MICROPHONE AS THE LIGHTS BEGIN TO DIM)

(JODY GETS UP, TAKES THE MICROPHONE, AND DOES ''WHAT'S THE

SENSE''* SEGMENT)

                          JODY

                        (SINGING)

What's the sense of talking

If your talking ain't real talking

And if you don't mean anything you're sayin'?

What's the sense of meaning

I´ your meaning is deceiving

And your actions don't believe in what you're

sayin'...

                     JODY (Cont'd)
                       (CHORUS)

Pack your bags, leave me alone, just go away

Your talk is golden but your feet are made of

clay...

                                        (CONTINUED)

_____

CONTINUED:

I'm stronger now than I was stronger

yesterday.

(MERV WALKS OVER TO JODY, SINGS WITH HER)

JODY & MERV

(SINGING)

Mmm Mmm Mmm...

What's the sense of holdin',

If the love I hold is foldin'

And the spark that's left is blowin' in the

wind?

What's the sense of pleading

If I'm pleading for self-pity and

If plastic smiles are painted on my friends?

Pack your bags, leave me alone, just go away

Your talk is golden but your feet are made of

clay...

I'm stronger now than I was stronger

yesterday.

(APPLAUSE)

(CONTINUED)

CONTINUED:

(JODY BOWS, GIVES THE MICROPHONE TO THE HOST, AND MAKES HER

WAY OVER TO THE PLATFORM SET.)

(MERV NODS HIS THANKS TO AUDIENCE AND ORCHESTRA, JOINS JODY

AT THE PLATFORM SET)

• • •

The Double-Column Format

A double-column format is sometimes used for documentary scripts, educational programs, commercials, and other projects requiring a running narrative. This form breaks the script into two columns—the left is for *video* or *picture;* the right is for audio or *sound.* Generally, every camera direction, scene description, and stage direction is capitalized. Only the dialogue remains in lower case letters.

The double-column format is supposed to provide a simultaneous sense of picture and sound. As an example, here is the opening sequence from a non-commercial television project called "The Magic Hearing Box." The script deals with the ramifications of hearing loss in children, and how they learn to cope.

Video	Audio
FADE IN:	SNEAK IN MUSIC:
WE SEE AN ALBUM PHOTO OF A SMILING BABY.	UNDER MUSIC, WE HEAR THE MUTED SOUNDS OF A BABY CRYING.

(CONTINUED)

CONTINUED:

WE SEE A BABY'S RATTLE POKING OUT OF A CARDBOARD BOX.	THE SOUND OF A RATTLE, AND A BABY COOING.
A SPINNING TOP RESTS QUIETLY ON ITS SIDE.	WE HEAR A BABY BABBLING, CONTINUED FROM ABOVE.
A SCRATCHED PLASTIC FERRIS WHEEL SITS ON TOP OF A DRESSER.	THE SUSPENDED SOUNDS OF A MUSICAL LULLABY FROM SOME FARAWAY MUSIC BOX.
A RAGGEDY ANN DOLL SITS ON THE HEAD OF AN OVER-STUFFED LION.	WE HEAR A CHILD GIGGLE, PLAYING WITH HER TOYS.
A SMALL, SCRATCHED ROCKING HORSE.	THE SEQUENCE OF A ROCKING HORSE, A CHILD RIDING, LAUGHING.
CUT TO CLOSE UP-FRAMED	MOTHER (V.O.)
PHOTO OF MELISSA. TEN YEARS OLD, A WIDE GRIN, A HAPPY	Melissa was about two when we found out she had hearing

                                              (CONTINUED)

CONTINUED:

FACE. SLOW ZOOM-IN TO ECU	problems. It was a hard
MELISSA, UNTIL PICTURE	thing for us to accept at
BECOMES GRAINY.	first.

This format is generally reserved for more narrative or documentary purposes than for comedy, drama, or variety. If you're writing comedy or tape drama, the wide margin format is the most widely accepted, and the most likely to be used. Only if your program is more narrative in structure would the double-column approach be suitable.

Once you've completed the script, whether for film or tape, the process of revising is the next phase. It requires fierce objectivity on your part. You'll be examining the format and style, story content and dramatic effectiveness, production values and characterization. It's all fair game for revision.

10

A Check-List for
Script Revision

Rewriting is a time-consuming process that can help make your script more competitive in the marketplace. With a good degree of objectivity you can approach the story's pacing, the visual imagery, and the credibility of the characters and dialogue. The script can be analyzed for strengths and weaknesses on several important levels. Here is a check-list of some critical areas to question as you analyze the first draft of your work.

1. Is the Script Visual?

A script should make the best use of the television medium. As you read the draft, can you actually visualize the scene unfolding? Descriptions should be clear and cinematically interesting. Camera angles can be suggested, character actions amplified, locations sharply defined. As you spot problems in the draft, note in the margins that it may need more visual development.

2. Is the Script Produceable?

No matter how good the script, it won't be produced if it calls for $35 million worth of sets, period costumes, world-wide locations, hundred of stars, thousands of extras, and impossible camera shots. The

script should be realistically conceived in terms of production requirements, locations, and casting needs.

3. Is the Script Format Professional and the Content Readable?

Even the most powerful script can slip by the wayside if the format
looks amateurish to a reader. If you have questions about script form,
check the sample formats in this book as a guide. In addition, look at the
clarity of writing in the script. Sometimes scene descriptions are too
choppy, cluttered with information, or too repetitious. Smooth out the
writing style for the most effective impact on the reader.

4. Is the Story Focused and Well-Developed?

Here you must examine the structure of the dramatic action points.
Some scene may lag, others may be redundant. As you read the script,
assess the effectiveness of the plot sequences. If the story is unclear or
erratic, it's time to "snip and tape." One sequence might work better
at the beginning or end, which means reorganizing the entire story line,
dropping scenes, adding new ones, polishing others.

5. Is the Dramatic Conflict Strong and the Pacing Effective?

The script should hold and build audience interest throughout each
act. If the conflict is cleverly set up, and the stakes are high (i.e., *sense of
urgency* is great), audience involvement with the characters and conflicts increase. The pacing is most effective when scenes build upon
each other in a careful, logical sequence of dramatic action.

6. Is the Mood Accurately Conveyed?

Each scene should help create the atmosphere of the show. If the
descriptions are not vivid enough, take time to rewrite them. Don't set-
tle for less than the most illustrative images of the place, action and
characters.

7. Are the Characters Likeable, Identifiable, and Consistently Developed?

Be sure the characters are fully and credibly motivated. Are the
interrelationships clearly drawn? If not, see if you can strengthen them

through the *Method*-writer constructs, using super-objectives, through-line-of-action, intentions, motivations, sense of urgency, and moment-to-moment realities.

8. Is the Dialogue Realistic and Sharply Defined?

If the dialogue appears to be awkward in some places, check all the pertinent problems. Characters are unique individuals, and their dialogue should reflect that individuality. If a word is off, write "*b.w.*" (find a "better word") in the margin or write "b.l." (find a "better line") to correct the problem. It may seem like nit-picking, but don't let those little problems slip away. If your show reaches the air, those lines will make you cringe in living color.

Once all the points are addressed, and the major revisions are incorporated into the script, there's one more stop-check point. It's called the *polish*. Once more, go over the script with a fine-tooth comb. Be sure the story is focused, the characters are three-dimensional, dialogue is refined, action is visual, the mood is conveyed, and the pacing is effective. After all, this is the script that may eventually wind up in the archives of the Academy of TV Arts and Sciences—or at least in the hands of a reputable agent.

PART FOUR

MARKETING

11

The Cable and Pay TV Marketplace

Background on Cable and Pay TV

When Comsat launched the first communication satellite, the world of television programming would never be the same. Companies that purchased space on the transponder became instant television networks. They could develop, produce or acquire any programming for their scheduling needs, and could target that programming for any specialized audience.

Cable franchisers were on the receiving end of those transmissions, and found themselves having to program an unwieldy number of channels. One channel might be reserved for local original programming, but it would be impossible to rely on that resource for supplying all new programs to all their subscribers. It would make more sense for them to buy produced programs offered by the satellite services.

The satellite companies offered two types of programming services: *Basic*, which was free to all subscribers, and *pay TV*, which was considered a premium service that required additional monthly fees from cable subscribers. In addition, some efforts were made to offer viewers special-event programming that was on a one-time basis, and appropriately called *Pay Per View* (PPV). That concept ran into some problems since viewers already had a healthy choice of cable and pay TV viewing options.

Basic Cable was supposed to be advertiser-supported, and offered to viewers as part of a basic package (for one monthly service fee, viewers could get several program services). However, advertisers were very scarce. As a result, some of the basic services began charging cable operators a fee, based on the numbers of subscribers involved.

Pay TV proved to be a bonanza for a select few companies, most notably Home Box Office (HBO) and Showtime/The Movie Channel. First-run movies, uncensored films, nightclub acts, and major sporting events became very big business. By 1984, pay TV was a multi-billion-dollar business.

Cable and pay TV seemed to be the land of infinite opportunity for creators. However, instead of concentrating on the quality of programming, franchisers became obsessed at an early stage with winning more geographical franchises. Little attention was given to the kinds of shows that would be made available to subscribers; maximum attention was given to lobbying efforts for more county franchises.

The initial programming rationale for cable was based on the concept of *narrowcasting*, i.e., providing relevant shows to limited target audiences. That philosophy equated cable audience subscribership with special-interest magazine publishing. Readers buy daily newspapers, and still subscribe to *Sports Illustrated*, *Teen Magazine*, *Working Woman*, *Psychology Today*, *Ebony*, *Wall Street Journal*, and *Playboy*. The same should hold true for cable viewers, or so the philosophy maintained.

The onslaught of cable TV program services surged, filling every interest gap imaginable. Each service wanted to corner the marketplace, proclaiming sovereignty in the areas of movies, sports, health, women's issues, minority issues, children's programming, adult programming, cultural programming, rock music programming, concerts, news, weather, finances, religion, games, politics, comedy, and the list grew from day to day. One service after another sprang up with a new modification, intending to corner the marketplace, win coveted narrow audiences, and beat out the fierce competition.

Unfortunately, but predictably, the marketplace simply couldn't handle the overload of competing services and channels. Viewers were confused by the diluted programming marketplace. Probably most significantly, viewers in major cities couldn't even have access to many of those start up services. Cable franchisers were now clamoring for programming to back up their promises, but the cost factor became prohibitive. Viewers expected network-quality shows, but the number of homes actually receiving cable services made that unrealistic. In the jargon of the trade, the market penetration could not justify additional expenditures of any magnitude. Some services relied on low cost acquisitions, re-packaging of old material on the shelf, and finally resorted to running repeats regularly to fill up the schedule (some cable services artfully refer to reruns as "premiere encores"). The boat was clearly sinking for many services.

Some of the early front runners pulled away from the rest, most notably HBO, which dug into the game early, offering strong box office hits. HBO came onto the scene in the mid 1970s, leasing a transponder on the Satcom I satellite, and it achieved instant success. It set the demand in major cities for pay channels that offered uncensored entertainment and features without any advertising. HBO has maintained a powerful position in the pay TV market, programming current theatrical features, big name concerts, and top name events. It was a smash with viewers, who felt they were getting something unique for their money.

Its nearest competitor, Showtime, programmed concerts, family entertainment, and theatrical features. To compete head-on with HBO, Showtime teamed with The Movie Channel and invested millions of dollars in program development, production, and acquisition.

HBO and Showtime/The Movie Channel developed original pay TV series and films, and entered into a multi-million-dollar exclusive development deals with major studios to acquire motion picture rights to projects still in development. HBO lined up with Columbia Pictures (and partnered with Columbia and CBS to create a feature company, TRI-STAR). Showtime/The Movie Channel lined up exclusive feature deals with Paramount Studios.

On a smaller scale, some other success stories emerged. ESPN made an impressive splash with all sports programming. In fact, sports programming became one of the indelible hallmarks of basic cable. The U.S. Football League was partially created because professional football was barred from ESPN. In addition to ESPN, sports programming became a staple for WTBS (Atlanta's Super Station), USA Network, and a host of other cable and pay TV services. Even regional pay TV networks formed, e.g., Group W's The Sports Network, to compete for the voracious sports fans.

MTV has had an enormous impact on the rock video scene. Owned by Warner Amex Satellite Entertainment, the company acquired rock video promos from record companies, and air them 24 hours a day. These highly visual clips have changed the face of music on television. Rock video programming is now an integral part of programming for Showtime/The Movie Channel, USA, BET, and the major networks. MTV not only revamped the way music is presented on television, but it also breathed new life in the record industry.

In other areas of successful programming, Cable News Network (CNN) offered worldwide coverage of events, all day, every day. WTBS, Ted Turner's Super Station, successfully offered its Atlanta-based programming for national audiences. Playboy pulled out the bunny ears and cornered the soft-core marketplace. Nickelodean and Disney were the lone contenders fighting for the children's audience. One cultural service, ARTS, became the token survivor of that unusually volatile marketplace.

The demise of the cultural marketplace provides a fascinating glimpse into the risks of programming for cable. At the beginning, CBS Cable held the greatest promise for development and production of original programs. A corporate subsidiary of CBS, it paid handsomely for writers and producers to create new shows for the cultural network. It budgeted $15 million annually for drama, opera, and ballet. Unfortunately, it ended up losing $30 million in just two years of existence, and closed down in 1982. It could not find advertiser support for its programming. Not more than six months later, its major competitor, The Entertainment Channel, a corporate venture of RCA and Rockefeller Center, announced that it, too, would close down—with a loss of $80 million. It could not find *viewer* support for its programming.

A much smaller service, ARTS, owned by ABC Video Enterprises and Hearst, was programming more modest efforts, mostly acquired from independent producers. As opposed to lavish new productions, Broadway shows, or BBC-produced drama, ARTS programmed small concerts and documentaries about creative artists in different fields. Then, with the demise of the two corporate giants, all of the cultural programming produced for CBS Cable and the Entertainment Channel was suddenly made available at dirt cheap prices. ARTS could literally hand pick from an array of high-quality programming at buy-out prices. In fact, ARTS purchased much of the BBC programming from the Entertainment Channel, and now offers a joint service, ARTS & ENTERTAINMENT. Given the glut on the marketplace of programs already produced, it was highly unlikely that any new program concepts would be developed. It was a buyer's market and no new programming was required.

A capsule history of cultural programming would not be complete without some mention of BRAVO, the first pay TV service dedicated to the performing arts. A joint venture of Cablevision, Cox Broadcasting, and Daniels & Associates. BRAVO was the cultural arm of Rainbow Programming Services. The other programming arms included Escapade/The Playboy Channel (partnered with Playboy Enterprises), and The Sport Channel in New York. BRAVO was initially committed to developing and producing high-quality programming at modest costs, but within a short period of time it became apparent that the Playboy Channel was in much greater demand. The late night adult program service grew by leaps and bounds. In the brief time BRAVO struggled for a reasonable number of subscribers, Playboy boasted over three times as many. As a result, Rainbow cut back entirely on new cultural programming efforts, and simply relied on low-cost acquisitions, films on the shelf, and reruns for BRAVO viewers.

In retrospect, it's not too difficult to see why some large companies failed in their initial cable efforts. For one thing, large sums of money were needed for development, production, and acquisition—but the level of cable penetration couldn't support that effort. In some cases, cable companies were competing for advertisers in the same market, while the top ten markets weren't even wired.

Another reason for the collapse of certain services in the program marketplace is that viewers sought greater levels of entertainment. They wanted something that networks couldn't provide. The winners offered the right mix of theatrical first runs, major sports events, big-name concerts, and uncensored films. The original concept of low-budget narrow-casting simply didn't fit in with the pragmatic wishes of viewers who pay for what they see.

HBO and Showtime/The Movie Channel survived the shake-out with a strong base of original entertainment programming and Hollywood feature tie-ins. Similarly, some of the more narrowly targeted programming services have found relatively safe niches for themselves. But the cable and pay TV ground is still shaky, with mergers just around the corner, new ventures looming, and established companies falling by the wayside. The only way to keep track of them all is with an industry scorecard.

Marketing Your Projects for Cable and Pay TV

If you're going to develop a project for the marketplace, become familiar with the current trends. The only way to stay on top of the mergers, declines, and survivors is to read the papers regularly: *Cable Vision, View, Multi Channel News, Cable Marketing.* The trades are published regularly for program executives and producers in the cable and pay TV field.

It's also important to know who is producing what for cable and pay TV. With a list of producers who have programmed for cable, you can identify those who have successfully developed and sold projects similar to your own. Then you can develop your own marketing strategy, sending your proposal to the most appropriate production companies for consideration. A list of independent producers for cable appears regularly in such resources as *Cable File.*

Aside from independent producers, you can send the project directly to program executives at individual cable companies. To help identify the most appropriate companies, you can cluster the market ac-

cording to programming needs. For example, this is one way to analyze
the current programming marketplace:

Basic Cable and Pay TV Marketplace

Programming	Programming Service
Movies	HBO, SHOWTIME/THE MOVIE CHANNEL, CINEMAX
General Entertainment	HBO, SHOWTIME, USA, WTBS, NASHVILLE
Cultural	ARTS, BRAVO
Women's	LIFETIME, USA
Minority	BET, GALAVISION, RELIGIOUS NETWORKS, SILENT NETWORK
News	CNN, AP NEWS, UPI, FNN, INN, BIZNET
Music	MTV, ARTS, NASHVILLE, USA, WTBS, BET
Children's	NICKELODEAN, DISNEY, USA
Sports	ESPN, SHOWTIME, USA, WTBS, WGN, WOR, RSVP
Adult Entertainment	PLAYBOY, ON-TV
Adult Education	ACSN, SPN
Politics	C-SPAN

The chart is not meant to be complete, but you can use it as a model
to build, change, and update information you receive from the trade
publications. Modifying the chart can help you tailor specific projects
to the needs of specific companies in the cable and pay TV area. A
directory of Cable and pay TV companies, and a breakdown of their
program content, is provided in *Appendix B*.

What You Can Expect in Negotiations

HBO and Showtime/The Movie Channel deal regularly with Hollywood writers and producers, and pay the same fees that are expected in
network prime-time situations. The larger companies have reached an
agreement with the Writers Guild, and minimums have been estab-

lished. The smaller companies can hardly afford to compete with that production arrangement, and are more likely to structure a co-venture arrangement, offering a small licensing agreement for exclusive rights to the show. For example, they may offer $10,000 for a one hour special, which *includes* their share of production costs. Most likely you, or a producer working with you, will have to find additional sources of financing for production. A licensing agreement means that the company has an exclusive "window" on your project, and no other cable or pay TV service can show it within a given period of time stipulated in the agreement.

Other Avenues for Marketing:
MSOs, DBS, STV, Home Video, Access, LPTV

Multiple System Operators (MSOs)

MSOs are cable companies that own several systems. Some of them boast millions of subscribers. Among the largest companies are American Television and Communication (ATC), Tele-Communications, Inc. (TCI), Group W Cable, Cox Cable, Storer Cable, Warner Amex Cable, Times Mirror, Newhouse Broadcasting, Rogers U-A Columbia Cable, and Viacom Cablevision.

MSOs need programs to supplement basic and pay services for their respective systems. Although they primarily purchase shows already produced, they may be interested in developing or financing projects that would have strong subscriber appeal. These projects are called "stand-alone programming," since they augment existing programming in the cable systems.

The vice-president of programming or the vice-president of marketing is the likely contact for stand-alone programming. A directory of MSO program buyers is published in *The Cable TV Program Data Book* and in *Cable File* (for these and other "Marketing Resources," see pp. 274–275 in the *Annotated Bibliography*).

Direct Broadcast Satellite (DBS)

Even as cable and pay TV battle between themselves to lure viewers from the networks, new competitors loom hot and heavy. DBS is one of the most intriguing. It offers subscribers an opportunity to select their own program without the franchise operator, and with their own satellite dish on the roof.

One of the giants in the field is Satellite TV Corporation (STC), a subsidiary of Comsat, and a partner with CBS, Inc. During the early start-up phases, United Satellite Communications (USCI) edged the programming marketplace that much closer to reality with plans to provide DBS service before the others. No sooner did they announce, then STC joined CBS; yet another venture, *Skyband* (Rupert Murdoch's entry), sprang up, waiting in the wings with the other licensed DBS companies (RCA, Hubbard, Western Union).

The programming strategy for the DBS companies sound like a rubber-stamp version of the pay TV formula: five channels, with a mix of motion pictures, news, sports, and general entertainment programming. Like all new ventures, they are going to need a great deal of programming to satisfy the appetites of potential viewers. The question is what proportion will be originally produced and how much will be acquired programming from various sources.

Plans are big for DBS and the contenders have anted up millions of dollars to get on the drawing boards. Technology is in place, the next step is programming the big bird in the sky.

Subscription TV Companies (STVs)

Subscription TV is an over-the-air service that broadcasts its programming on a UHF frequency. Subscribers receive a decoding box, which allows them to see adult movies, sports events, concerts, and other programming fare. STV companies are in constant need of strong programming to bolster the schedule and keep subscribers content.

STV is having a rough time finding sufficient programming to schedule regularly, and competing with cable. Subscribers seem to sign up when cable is not available, and abandon STV when cable and pay systems are intact.

There are a great number of STV stations around the country, and it is possible to interest the director of programming in your ideas. However, a commitment from one STV service is not likely to pay the bills; they pay a small percentage based on the numbers of subscribers to their service. You can try to market your ideas to a large number of STVs simultaneously, and that can be more profitable. Unlike cable systems, they don't require a two year "window" (exclusivity) on your project. Instead, they expect exclusivity for their immediate geographical area (which is likely to be small) for a reasonable period of time.

A directory of STV stations is published in cable TV resources, e.g., *Cable File.* You'll find contact names and addresses, current programming and subscriber base information for each STV operation.

Home Video

This is an area that is expanding enormously, but not with new programming. Corporate hopefuls like CBS Fox Video anticipate a wide market for rentals and sales of video entertainment programs and how-to programs. However, the marketplace at this point remains the domain of theatrical features, rock video concerts, and various film classics. Occasionally, an independent program breaks through, e.g., "Jane Fonda's Workout," but original programming is still the stepchild of major theatrical motion pictures and rock concert events.

Public Access

This is a smaller marketplace that might be of interest to some local writers. When cable franchisers were awarded to cable operators, one of the provisions was for public-access programming channels. It's a logical avenue for new writers with an interest in local programming. In most situations, the local cable operator will provide access to facilities and even help train you in production requirements. Any idea is fair game, from local talk shows to variety shows, concert programs to political meetings. For more information, you can contact your local cable access channel, or the National Federation of Local Cable Programmers (NFLCP) in Washington, D.C.

Low Power TV (LPTV)

At the other extreme of technological advancement in the marketplace is Low Power TV (LPTV), which is considered a grass roots approach to television. It's designed around the interests of small communities and minority concerns. With only a 10 to 15-mile radius for broadcasting, however, the costs for developing, producing, or acquiring programs is likely to be a challenging effort.

12

The Network and Studio Marketplace

What You Should Know before Marketing

Marketing a script requires strategy, determination, and a realistic understanding of the industry. The marketplace is extremely competitive, and even the best projects written by established professionals might end up on the shelf. Still, an *excellent* original script—submitted to the right person at the right time—might suddenly break through all barriers. The key word in *excellent*. It makes no sense to submit a script unless you feel that it is in the most polished form (even then it will be subject to rewrites), and that it represents the highest calibre of your creative potential. One might think producers are inclined to see the masterpiece lurking behind a rough draft script. More likely, they'll focus on the weaknesses, compare it to top submissions, and generalize about the writer's talents. So, if you feel uncertain about the professional quality of work, hold off submitting it. Your next work might show you off to better advantage.

How Many Copies of the Project Are Needed

Since unsolicited scripts tend to be lost or "misplaced" by production companies, it's a good idea to have a sufficient number of copies. The *minimum* number you will need is three—one for your files, one for submission, and one for inevitable rewrites. More realistically, you'll probably want additional copies for two or three producers, an agent or two, and your own reserve file for unanticipated submissions. Incidentally, fancy covers and title designs are totally unnecessary. Three inexpensive paper brads can be punched through the left hand margins of the manuscript. Scripts are usually photocopied to avoid the smudged look of carbons.

Script Registration

Any writer can register a story, treatment, series format, or script with the Writers Guild of America. The service was set up to help writers establish the completion dates of their work. It doesn't confer statutory rights, but it does supply evidence of authorship which is effective for ten years (and is renewable after that). If you want to register a project, send one copy along with the appropriate fee ($15 nonmembers; $5 members) to: Writers Guild of America Registration Service, 8955 Beverly Blvd., Los Angeles, California 90048, or WGA East, 555 W. 57th St., New York, New York 10019.

You can also register dramatic or literary material with the U.S. Copyright Office—but most television writers rely on the Writers Guild. The Copyright Office is mainly used for book manuscripts, plays, music or lyrics, which the Writers Guild will not register. For appropriate copyright forms (covering dramatic compositions), write to: Register of Copyrights, Library of Congress, Washington, D.C. 20540.

The Release Form or Waiver

If you have an agent, there is no need to bother with release forms. But if you're going to submit a project without an agent, you'll have to send for a release form—a waiver—in advance. Most production companies will return your manuscript without it. The waiver states that you won't sue the production company and that the company has no obligations to you. That may seem unduly harsh, but consider the fact that millions of dollars are spent on fighting plagiarism suits, and that hundreds of ideas are being developed simultaneously and coincidentally by writers, studios, and networks.

The waiver is a form of self-protection for the producer who wants to avoid unwarranted legal action. But it also establishes a clear line of communication between the writer and producer. So rest assured, if legal action is warranted, it can be taken.

Writing a Cover Letter

When you prepare to send out your project, draft a cover letter that is addressed to a *person* at the studio, network, or production company. If you don't know who is in charge of program development, look it up in the trade papers, or call the studio receptionist. If she says, "Mr. So-and-So handles new projects," ask her to *spell* "Mr. So-and-So." That courtesy minimizes the chance of embarrassment, and maximizes the chance that the project will wind up at the right office.

The letter you write should sound professional. There's no need to offer apologies for being an unsold writer, or to suggest that the next draft will be ten times better than this one. If a cover letter starts off with apologies, what incentive is there to read the project?

Here's the tone a cover letter might have:

Dear _____

I've just completed a mini-series called FORTUNES, based on the book by Marian Sherry. I've negotiated all TV and film rights to the property, which is a dramatic adventure series about a family caught in the California Gold Rush. I think you'll find the project suitable for the mini-series genre. It's highly visual in production values and offers unusual opportunities for casting.

I look forward to your reactions. Thank you for your cooperation.

Sincerely,

The letter doesn't say I'm an unsold writer in the midwest or that Marian Sherry is my sister-in-law who let me have the rights for a handshake. Nor does it take the opposite route, aggressively asserting that it is the best project the studio will ever read. There's no need for such pretentions. The cover letter sets the stage in a simple and dignified manner. The project will have to speak for itself.

Where to Submit Your Project

Independent producers represent the widest span of marketing potential for the freelance writer. If one producer turns down an idea, there are many others who might still find it fresh and interesting. However, the smaller independent producer is not likely to have the financial resources to compete with the development monies available at the network or studio.

Production companies do have that bargaining power. The distinction between smaller independents and larger production companies is their relative financial stability and current competitive strength on the airwaves. Production companies form and dissolve according to the seasonal marketing trends and network purchases. The more successful production companies have become mini-studios in their own right, with a great number of programs on the air and in development. Some of the more recognizable entities are M.T.M. Enterprises (Mary Tyler Moore), Embassy Communications (Norman Lear), and Lorimar Productions (Lee Rich). For a listing of networks, studios, and independent production companies, see *Appendix A*.

The major motion picture studios are in keen competition with production companies. Only seven major studios have aggressive and viable television divisions: Columbia; Disney; Paramount; M.G.M.; 20th Century-Fox; Universal; and Warner Brothers. They represent highly fertile ground for program development. Strong deals can be negotiated for the right project.

At the top of the submission ladder is the network oligarchy: ABC, CBS, NBC. Once a project is submitted at this level, there's no turning back. If a project is "passed" (i.e., turned down), it's too late to straddle down the ladder to independent producers. *Their* goal is to bring it back up to the networks (who in turn must sell to the sponsors).

A visual model of the writer's marketplace in network television is shown on the next page.

As the model shows, the closer the project comes to the network, the more limited the number of buyers. As the submission moves up the ladder, it faces stiffer competition and fewer alternatives. So you see that the marketplace is highly competitive, although not totally impenetrable. Your submission strategy will depend on knowing the marketplace trends and organizing a campaign to reach the most appropriate people and places.

Other Commercial Markets:

A different avenue for exploration is the advertising agency. Many of the larger agencies are heavily involved in program development activities for their clients. It is not unusual for major clients to commit to a number of television films, comedy shows, or variety specials—with the provision that the advertising agency find the product. Many of the agencies buy into projects at an early stage and these shows are almost guaranteed placement at the networks, in syndication, and in cable TV. Among the largest and most active agencies to investigate: Benton & Bowles, BBD&O, Ted Bates, Doyle Dane Bernbach, Foote Cone & Belding, Grey Advertising, Needham Harper Steers, Ogilvy & Mather, J. Walter Thompson, Young & Rubicam. Some of these com-

Where to Submit Your Property

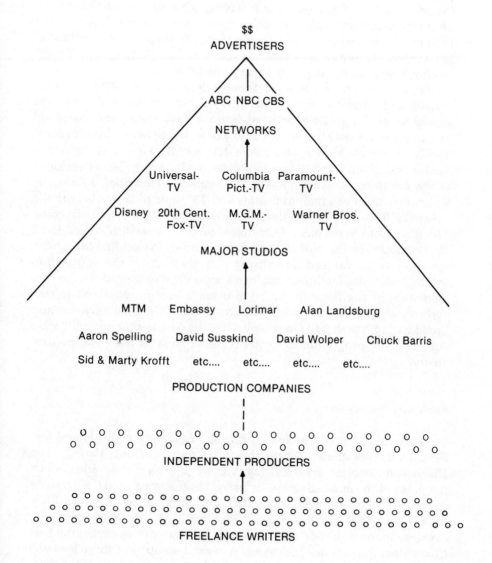

$$
ADVERTISERS

ABC NBC CBS

NETWORKS

Universal-TV   Columbia Pict.-TV   Paramount-TV

Disney   20th Cent. Fox-TV   M.G.M.-TV   Warner Bros. TV

MAJOR STUDIOS

MTM   Embassy   Lorimar   Alan Landsburg

Aaron Spelling   David Susskind   David Wolper   Chuck Barris

Sid & Marty Krofft   etc....   etc....   etc....   etc....

PRODUCTION COMPANIES

INDEPENDENT PRODUCERS

FREELANCE WRITERS

panies have their own production subsidiaries, but are still open to new programming concepts. The person to contact is the vice-president of broadcast programming (or some recognizable variant of that title)—*after* you have thoroughly investigated their clients' needs. You can find out more about the latest advertising trends through regular perusal of the trades, including *Advertising Age, Television/Radio Age, Broadcasting, Cable Marketing,* and *Multi Channel News.*

On a more pragmatic level, independent stations, O&Os (stations owned and operated by the networks), and Group-owned stations should be explored. Group-owned stations have been particularly active in program development. These are stations owned by broadcast entities such as Metromedia, Post Newsweek, Group W (Westinghouse), Storer, and Taft. Some important projects have been developed at the group level, most notably Metromedia's *Operation Primetime,* which produced original miniseries and TV films to compete with the networks. These shows involved top writers, producers, and directors. The financial clout comes from the stations' ownership status. Each station shares in the cost of production, and in the profits. Moreover, the show is guaranteed advertising and distribution through station owned broadcast facilities. You can contact the vice-president of programming of any flagship station to discuss your proposal. Addresses and contacts are in marketing resources, e.g., *Television Factbook* and *Broadcasting Yearbook.* Once again, the trade papers can familiarize you with the programming patterns and trends in the broadcast industry.

Analyzing the Market

There's no better way to stay on top of marketing trends and personnel changes than reading the trade papers—*Daily Variety, The Hollywood Reporter, Broadcasting, Variety* (weekly). The trades reflect the pulse of the entertainment industry. On the West Coast, each trade paper publishes a weekly compilation of production activities ("TV Production Chart," "Films in Production,") listing companies, addresses, phone numbers, and producers for shows in work. On the East Coast, *Ross Reports* does the same. A careful scrutiny of those lists will provide helpful clues to the interests and current activities of independent producers, production companies, and studios.

Another comprehensive marketing source is *The Pacific Coast Studio Directory,* which identifies key contacts at major studios and production companies. A similar resource is the "Television Market List" published regularly in the *Writers' Guild of America Newsletter.* It lists all current shows in production or pre-production, and identifies the story consultant or submission contact for each show. It also states whether or not a show is "open" for submissions, and who to contact for assignments. A careful reading of these and other publications can help bring you closer to making knowledgeable and practical decisions about marketing your own projects. For a list of Trade Publications, see *Appendix G*. A separate listing of Marketing Resources appears in the *Annotated Bibliography*.

How to Submit Your Project

Submission Status Reports

In the network marketplace, you have a choice of *flooding the market* with a project (i.e., submitting it to a great number of sources at the same time) or *shopping it selectively* to a few individuals. The specific strategy depends on the needs of the marketplace at the time, and the strength of your particular project. You should determine which producers and production companies are particularly interested in the type of project you've developed.

Marketing a television property requires time and patience. Each project needs an individual marketing strategy with independent files and records. It's helpful to keep a "Project Status Report," summarizing pertinent information about marketing contacts, dates, reactions, and follow-ups to each project. That information can be kept on 5 × 7 cards or on regular typing paper. This is one way it might be set up:

```
PROJECT STATUS REPORT
PROJECT TITLE:
DATE COMPLETED/REGISTERED:
SEND TO:        DATE MAILED:    RESPONSE:    FOLLOW-UP:
1.
2.
3.
4.
5.
```

Under the first column (*SEND TO*) you can pre-select names and addresses of producers, program development executives, agents who might be interested in your project. If the first person turns down the project, or doesn't respond in a reasonable period of time (4–6 weeks) send it to the next person on the list. This pre-selected listing provides you with a planned strategy for an erratic marketplace.

The second column (*DATE MAILED*) indicates when you for-warded—or *plan* to forward—the project to each person on the list.

In the next column (*RESPONSE*) you can summarize reactions received, e.g., "received letter from studio. They're not interested in this genre, but like my writing style. Asked to see more material."

The final column (*FOLLOW-UP*) leaves room for your initiatives, e.g., "if no word from studio, phone them"; "sent copy of another screenplay, per their request."

Project status reports can help keep track of submission strategies, problems, and solutions on a day-to-day basis.

How to Get an Agent

A good agent is one with a respectable track record, a prestigious list of clients, and a reputation for fairness in the industry. There is no magical list of good agents, although the Writers Guild does publish a list of agents who are franchised by the Guild. (See *Appendix F.*) If you have no agent representing you, it's difficult to get projects considered by major producers.

One of the best ways to make headway is to submit your work to an agent who already represents a friend, a professor, a long-lost uncle in the industry. If you are recommended by someone known to the agency, it makes you less of an unknown commodity. If you have no contact, the quest for representation can still be handled effectively through the concept of marketing strategy. Work up a list of possible agents for your project, and prioritize them in your submission status file. You might send the project to one top agency for consideration, or to a select number of agencies at the same time. There is nothing wrong with a limited organized campaign which seeks representation for your project.

A brief cover letter might introduce you as a freelancer looking for representation on a specific project. If you don't get a response within six to eight weeks, you can follow up with a phone call or letter, and submit the project to the next agent on your list. Don't be discouraged if you get no response at first; just keep the project active in the field. If the script or presentation is good enough, you might eventually wind up with some positive and encouraging feedback from the agency.

If an agent is interested in your work, he or she will ask to represent it in the marketplace. If the work sells, the agent is entitled to 10% com-mission for closing the deal. If the work elicits interest but no sale, you have at least widened your contacts considerably for the next project.

Large and Small Agencies

The larger agencies—William Morris Agency, Inc., and International Creative Management (I.C.M.)—are virtually impenetrable to new writers. These agencies have a long list of clients in every field from variety and concerts to film, television, and the legitimate stage. They handle writers, producers, directors, actors, and even production companies. For that reason, a major agency can *package* top clients into a new project with a massive price tag attached. If the package is attractive enough, the script may sell at a very lucrative price for the writer.

The *package* is a strong way to present a new series presentation or script, but it is not without its drawbacks. The process may take as long as three or four months to set up, and may stretch out some additional months before getting a reading from the network. The most erratic aspect of packaging is the marketplace response. An entire deal can be blown if a key executive dislikes *any* of the elements attached. If one actor is preferred to another, or if the director is disliked by the executive's wife, months of waiting can explode into fragments of frustration. The project may never get off the ground.

The larger agencies offer an umbrella of power and prestige, but that elusive status is seriously undermined by the sheer size of the agency itself. Many clients inevitably feel lost in an over-crowded stable, and newcomers can hardly break into that race. In contrast, a smaller literary agency might provide more personalized service, and might be more open to the work of new talent. If you're going to seek representation, the smaller agency is the likely place to go. But don't be fooled by the label "small." Many of these agencies are exceptionally strong and have deliberately limited their client roster to the cream of the crop. In fact, many smaller agents have defected from executive positions at the major agencies. So you'll have to convince them you're the greatest writer since Shakespeare came on the scene—and that your works are even more saleable.

How do you prove that you have the talent to be a star talent? It's all in the writing. If your projects look professional, creative, and stylistically effective, you're on the right track. Indeed, you can call yourself a writer. If the artistic content is also marketable and you back it up with determination and know-how, you might just become a *selling* writer.

And that is the "bottom line" for success in the television industry.

13

Writers' Fees and Contracts

How Do You Join the Writers Guild?

The Writers Guild of America protects writers' rights, and establishes minimum acceptable arrangements for fees, royalties, credits, and so on. You are eligible to join the Guild as soon as you sell your first project to a signatory company (one who has signed an agreement with the Guild). A copy of your contract is automatically filed and you will then be invited to join the membership. Before you sell the next project, you *have* to be a member of the Guild; otherwise, no signatory company can hire you.

For the Writers Guild of America, West (Los Angeles), the one-time membership fee is $1,500. In addition, dues are assessed quarterly at $25, plus 1 percent of yearly earnings as a writer. For the Writers Guild of America, East (New York), the membership fee is $750. Dues are $50 per years plus 1–½ percent of annual earnings as a writer. (Addresses of WGAW and WGAE are in *Appendix E*.)

Options, Contracts, and Pay Scales: What Happens if a Producer Is Interested

If a producer is interested in a project he or she will propose a *deal*, i.e., the basic terms for a contract. If you have no agent, now is the time to get one. *Any* agent will gladly close the deal for the standard 10%

commission. An attorney would be equally effective. The need for counsel depends on the complexity of the proposed deal, and the counter-proposals you wish to present.

On the basis of your discussions, a *Deal Memo* is drawn up which outlines the basic points of agreement—who owns what, for how long, for how much, with what credits, royalties, rights, and so on. The deal memo is binding, although certain points may be modified if both parties agree. The *Contract* is based on the terms of the deal memo and is the formal legal document. If you're dealing with a producer who is a signatory to the Writers Guild (most established producers are), the contract will adhere to the terms of the Minimum Basic Agreement (M.B.A.) negotiated by the Writers Guild of America.

Options and Step Deals

A producer can either option your work, purchase it outright, or assign you to write new material. If the property is *optioned,* the producer pays for the right to shop it around (which means the project can be submitted by the producer to a third party, e.g., the network). During the option period, you can't submit the project to any one else. Typically, option money is relatively small; perhaps $1,500 or $2,500 for a six-month period. But the writer will be paid an additional sum of money if the producer elicits interest and moves the project forward. If the producer fails to exercise the option (i.e., if the option expires), the rights revert back to the writer.

A *Step Deal* is the most common form of agreement between producers and freelance writers. It sets forth fees and commitments for story and teleplay in several phases. The first step is at the *story* stage. When the writer turns in a treatment, the producer pays for it—at least 30% of the total agreed upon compensation—but the producer does not have to assign that writer to do the script. If the writer *is* retained, the producer exercises the *first draft* option. When that draft of the script is turned in, the writer receives a minimum of 40% of the total agreed upon compensation. Now the producer has the final option—putting the writer to work on the *final draft.* Once that script is received, the writer is entitled to the balance of payment. The *Step Deal* is a form of protection for the producer who can respond to the quality of content, the inviolability of delivery dates, and the acceptability of the project to the networks. It also guarantees the writer that his or her work will be paid for, whether there is a cut-off or a go-ahead on the project.

Here is a copy of the standard contract form for freelance film television writers:

STANDARD FORM FREELANCE FILM TELEVISION
WRITER'S EMPLOYMENT CONTRACT.

Agreement entered into at _____, this _____ day of _____,

19_____ between _____, hereinafter called "Company"
and _____, hereinafter called "Writer",

WITNESSETH:

1. Company hereby employs the Writer to render services in the writing, composition, preparation and revision of the literary material described in subsection 2. hereof, hereinafter for convenience referred to as the "work". The Writer accepts such employment and agrees to render his services hereunder and devote his best talents, efforts and abilities in accordance with the instructions, control and directions of the Company.

2. **FORM OF WORK:**
(   ) Plot outline (based on _____   ).
(   ) Story (based on _____   ).
(   ) Story and teleplay (based on _____   ).
(   ) Teleplay (based on _____   ).
(   ) Rewrite (of _____   ).
(   ) Polish (of _____   ).
(   ) Other material (described as _____   ).

3. **DELIVERY:**
If the Writer has agreed to complete and deliver the work, and/or any changes and revisions, within a certain period or periods of time, then such agreement will be expressed in this paragraph as follows:

4. **RIGHT TO OFFSET:**
With respect to Writer's warranties and indemnification agreement, the Company and the Writer agree that upon the presentation of any claim or the institution of any action involving a breach of warranty, the party receiving notice thereof will promptly notify the other party in regard thereto. Company agrees that the pendency of any such claim or action shall not relieve the Company of its obligation to pay the Writer any monies due hereunder, and the Company will not have the right to withhold such monies until it has sustained a loss or suffered an adverse judgment of decree by reason of such claim or action.

5. **COMPENSATION:**
As full compensation for all services to be rendered hereunder, the rights granted to the company with respect to the work, and the undertakings and agreements assumed by the Writers, and upon condition that the Writer shall fully perform such undertakings and agreements, Company will pay the Writer the following amounts:

    a. Compensation for services $_____
    b. Advance for television re-runs $_____
    c. Advance for theatrical use $_____

No amounts may be inserted in b. or c. above unless the amount set forth in a. above is at least twice the applicable minimum compensation set forth in the Writers Guild of America Theatrical and Television Basic Agreement (herein "Basic Agreement") for the type of services to rendered hereunder.

If the assignment is for story and teleplay or teleplay the following amounts of the compensation set forth in a. above will be paid in accordance with the provisions of Article 13B of said Basic Agreement.

    (1) $_____ following delivery of story.
    (2) $_____ following delivery of first draft teleplay.
    (3) $_____ following delivery of final draft teleplay.

In the event Writer receives screen credit as provided in Article 15B 13. of the Basic Agreement on the television film based on the above work and said film is exhibited theatrically. Company shall pay to the Writer the additional sum of $_____.

6. MINIMUM BASIC AGREEMENT:

The parties acknowledge that this contract is subject to all of the terms and provisions of the Basic Agreement and to the extent that the terms and provisions of said Basic Agreement are more advantageous to Writer than the terms hereof, the terms of said Basic Agreement shall supersede and replace the less advantageous terms of this agreement. Writer is an employee as defined by said Basic Agreement and Company has the right to control and direct the services to be performed.

7. GUILD MEMBERSHIP:

To the extent that it may be lawful for the Company to require the Writer to do so. Writer agrees to become and/or remain a member of Writers Guild of America in good standing as required by the provisions of said Basic Agreement. If Writer fails or refuses to become or remain a member of said Guild in good standing, as required in the preceding sentence, the Company shall have the right at any time thereafter to terminate this agreement with the Writer.

IN WITNESS WHEREOF, the parties hereto have duly executed this agreement on the day and year first above written.

                                           _____
                              By_____
                                          Company

                                           _____
                                         Writer

(The foregoing Freelance Film Television Writer's Contract may contain any other provisions acceptable to both Writer and company and not less favorable to, inconsistent with or violate of any of the terms or provisions of the Basic Agreement above mentioned.)

A Word About Credits and Arbitration

Screen credits literally equate to money in the bank. If a writer receives sole credit—WRITTEN BY—he or she is entitled to full residual payment as well as payment for story and teleplay. An additional CREATED BY credit entitles the writer to 100% of royalties every time the show airs (that can translate to thousand of dollars each week for a new series).

If a producer employs another writer to revise a project—which happens frequently—the credit problem is automatically referred to the Writers Guild for arbitration. All written materials are reviewed by Guild members who agree to review projects anonymously. It's their job to decide who is entitled to what credit. If the final credit is sole story or teleplay (STORY BY or TELEPLAY BY), the residuals will be based on that contribution alone. If a credit is shared with another writer (STORY BY "A" AND "B"), so are the residual checks that come in the mail.

The issue of television credits is to important and complex that many pages of legal definitions and regulations are included in the Writers Guild *M.B.A.* In an effort to stay on top of credit problems, the Guild requires the production company to send a *Notice of Tentative Writing Credits* to Writers Guild headquarters, and to all participating writers on a show. If a writer protests the credits for any reason, the project automatically goes into the arbitration process. A sample *Notice of Tentative Writing Credits* follows.

NOTICE OF TENTATIVE WRITING CREDITS

TO: Writers Guild of America, West, Inc. 8955 Beverly Boulevard, Los Angeles, California 90048 and Participating Writers

NAMES OF PARTICIPATING WRITERS   ADDRESS

_____

_____

_____

Title of Episode _____ Production # _____
(indicate if pilot)

Series Title: _____

Producing Company: _____

Executive Producer: _____

Producer: _____ Assoc. Producer: _____

Director: _____ Story Editor (or Consultant): _____

Other Production Executives, if Participating Writers _____

TENTATIVE WRITING CREDITS (cont'd)

Writing credits on this episode are tentatively determined as follows:

ON SCREEN:
Source material credit ON THIS EPISODE (On separate card, unless otherwise indicated) if any:

Continuing source material or Created By credit APPEARING ON ALL EPISODES OF SERIES (on separate card, unless otherwise indicated) if any:

The above tentative credits will become final unless a protest or request to read the final script is communicated to the undersigned not later than 6:00 P.M. _____

_____ BY: _____

What Do Writers Get Paid?

Television writers are covered by the Minimum Basic Agreement (*M.B.A.*) of the Writers Guild of America. The going rates for television and film are published in the *Schedule of Minimums: Writers Guild of America Theatrical and Television Basic Agreement* (available from the Writers Guild of America).

The tables on the following pages outline some of the minimums for specific writing services. Be sure to ask for the latest contracts. New writers generally receive minimum while writers with credits might negotiate higher rates.

If a writer has not been previously employed in television, films, or dramatic radio, there is a reduced rate that can be used for "flat deals." That rate can be determined by contacting the Guild. If the script is produced, using the writer's material, the payment will automatically be adjusted upward to the full minimum.

On the following pages you will find various sample minimums for writing network prime time and non-network prime time shows.

Sample W.G.A. Minimums—Drama Programs
(7/18/84–2/28/85)

A. New Series Presentations

Format for New Series	$ 3,817
"Bible" for Multi-Part Series*	
(complete presentation)	19,296
Each story line over 6	1,929

*Discount of 20% if "bible" is intended for non-prime-time or non-network

B. Plot Outlines
(narrative synopsis of story)**

30 min.	$ 918
60 min.	1,742
90 min.	2,576
120 min.	3,395

**Company might ask writer to prepare narrative synopsis of plot to determine suitability for teleplay. Company must acquire outline and employ writer in 14 days, or all rights revert to writer.

C. Stories and Teleplays

(High Budget TV Films)

(Note: Minimums for Pilot Stories and Teleplays are 150% of the applicable rates below.)

	Network Prime time	[Addt'l monies if another writer does script)	Non-network Prime time
Story			
30 min.	$ 2,793	$ 452	$ 2,020
60 min.	4,959	754	3,669
90 min.	6,877	755	5,511
120 min.	9,137	1,057	7,223
Teleplay			
30 min.	6,983		3,278
60 min.	9,420		6,354
90 min.	13,571		9,771
120 min.	17,414		12,960

Story and Teleplay (same writer is assigned to both, i.e., no options involved for teleplay.)

30 min.	9,737	5,045
60 min.	14,318	9,171
90 min.	20,145	13,781
120 min.	26,506	18,060

Back-up Scripts—115% of minimums for story and/or teleplay above.

D.   Sequel Payments, Character Spinoffs, Recurring Characters
(Writer of a new series is entitled to sequel payments if company exploits the series and separation of rights applies; character spinoffs payment for introducing new characters; recurring character payments for each new character appearing in an episodic series.)

	Sequel Payments; Character Spinoffs	Recurring Character
30 min.	$ 716	203 per character
60 min.	1,360	
90 min.	1,792	

E. Rewrites and Polishes

	Network (high budget)
Rewrites	
30 min.	$ 1,989
60 min.	3,758
90 min.	5,534
120 min.	7,310
Polishes	
30 min.	991
60 min.	1,879
90 min.	2,767
120 min.	3,654

Note: High Budget TV Films are considered those in which negative costs are equal or greater than these amounts:

	Network Prime time	Non-network Prime time
30 min.	$175,000	$ 82,500
60 min.	250,000	156,750
90 min.	400,000	276,000
120 min.	750,000	375,000

Low Budget TV Films are considered those in which negative costs are less than the amounts above.

Comedy-Variety

Variety programs have a different fee structure based on the length of the show, the numbers of writers on staff, the number of shows per week, the sketches written, and so on. These are sample Writers Guild minimums for programs in the variety genre:

Sample W.G.A. Minimums—Comedy-Variety Programs
(7/1/84–2/28/85)

Program Minimums:

15 min.	$ 1,835
30 min.	3,988
60 min.	5,486
90 min.	7,478

One Program A Week (Minimum Variety Show Commitment):

If all writers are employed under a contract for guaranteed employment in cycles of 13 or more weeks, the weekly minimum for each writer is $1,448.

The aggregate minimum for each program is based on the number of writers employed, for example:

No. of writers	Program Minimums
1	100%
2	150%
3	175%
4	200%

Five Programs A Week (Minimum Variety Show Commitment):

If all writers are employed under a contract for guaranteed employment in cycles of 13 or more weeks, the weekly minimum for each writer is $1,448.

The aggregate minimum for each weekly unit of programs is as follows:

Time Bracket	2 writers	3 writers	4 writers
15 min. Prime Time	7,061	7,979	8,897
(Non-prime)	5,649	6,383	7,118
30 min. Prime Time		11,925	13,069
(Non-prime)		9,540	10,457
60 min. Prime Time			22,470
(Non-prime)			17,975

Sketch Minimums

Prime time	1,351
Non-prime	1,079

Lyrics

(Unaccompanied by music)	1,064

Quiz and Audience Participation

Quiz programs also have minimums based on the number of weeks committed and units of programs involved. WGA provides applicable minimums for staff writers as well as writers of questions and answers for quiz show material. These are sample minimums:

Sample W.G.A. Minimums—Quiz and Audience Participation
(7/1/84–2/28/85)

Applicable minimum per weekly units of not more than five programs:

Weekly Units	Minimums
13 units	$1,087
14–19 units	1,009
20 or more units	927

Writers of questions, answers, and/or ideas for stunts, where writer supplies no other material:

Weekly Units	Minimums
13 units	$ 577
14–19 units	534
20 or more units	493

For Syndication, the applicable minimum is two-thirds of the compensation applicable to network programs.

Serials

Writers for television serials are covered by Guild minimums, with fees worked out for weekly units of programs, scriptwriting services, and long-term story projections. Here is a sample of minimums for writers of serials (other than prime time).

Sample W.G.A. Minimums-Serials
(7/1/84–2/28/85)

Aggregate minimum for each weekly unit of five programs:

30 min.	$ 7,498
60 min.	13,870
90 min.	20,804

Script Fee

For each script on which a writer performs writing services:

30 min.	743
60 min.	1,374
90 min.	2,064

Long-term Story Projections

Minimum for long-term story projections *not* written by a head writer:

Months Projections	Minimum
3 months or less	$ 6,432
6 or less	9,648
12 or less	12,864

Minimums for PBS Programs

W.G.A. has signed an agreement with several PBS stations and PBS producers. That agreement is part of "Schedule A" which is available from the Writers Guild along with the minimum basic agreement.

Sample Minimums for PBS
(7/2/84–7/1/85)

A. New Series Presentations

Format for New Series	$ 3,745
Bible for Multipart Series	14,983
Each storyline over 6	1,498

Back-up Scripts—115% of compensation for applicable story & teleplay below.

Plot Outlines
(narrative synopsis of story)

30 min.	$ 901
60 min.	1,710
90 min.	2,520
120 min.	3,331

B. National Dramatic Programs

(Note: *High Budget* refers to programs that equal or exceed the following negative costs: 30 min. = $82,500; 60 min. = $156,750; 90 min. = $276,000; 120 min. = $375,000.)

	High Budget	Low Budget
30 min		
Story	$ 1,981	$ 1,532
Teleplay	4,641	3,481
*Additional Compensation	2,207	1,658
TOTAL	$ 8,829	$ 6,671
60 min.		
Story	$ 3,599	$ 2,897
Teleplay	7,992	5,994
*Additional Compensation	3,863	2,898
TOTAL	$15,454	$11,789
90 min.		
Story	$ 5,217	$ 4,261
Teleplay	10,587	7,993
*Additional Compensation	5,268	3,950
TOTAL	$21,072	$16,204
120 min.		
Story	$ 6,837	$ 5,628
Teleplay	11,486	8,614
*Additional Compensation	6,110	4,582
TOTAL	$24,432	$18,824

*This additional compensation is payable only if the teleplay is produced.

C. Documentary & Public Affairs Programs

	High Budget	Low Budget
Story & Telescript		
30 min.	$ 4,452	$ 3,442
60 min.	8,099	6,530
90 min.	11,740	9,588
120 min.	15,383	12,660
Story Only		
30 min.	1,205	1,002
60 min.	2,274	1,896
90 min.	3,332	2,797
120 min.	4,391	3,693
Telescript Only		
30 min.	3,470	2,609
60 min.	6,586	4,974
90 min.	8,558	7,349
120 min.	12,803	9,723

(Note: High budget refers to programs that equal or exceed the following negative costs: 30 min. = $100,000; 60 min. = $200,000; 90 min. = $300,000; 120 min. = $400,000.)

Plot Outline: A company may request a writer to prepare a narrative synopsis of the plot outline of a story owned by the writer to determine if it is suitable for telescript purposes. The company has 14 days to elect to acquire the outline and employ the writer. If the company does not proceed, all rights to the outline revert to the writer.

30 min.	$ 823
60 min.	1,559
90 min.	2,292

D. Children's, Special Interest, & Regional Programs

Children's programs, Special Interest Programs, and Regional Programs are 75% of minimums applicable for national programming.

The Guild M.B.A. (minimum basic agreement) covers every conceivable writing service, from staff writing to freelance writing on network and non-network shows. If you have any questions about the applicable rates for any writing service, contact the Writers Guild for a copy of the latest M.B.A.

Royalties and Residuals

The Guild has also negotiated a strong royalty and residual rate. A writer is guaranteed 100% of the applicable minimum for all reruns in network primetime. However, that minimum is based on non-network prime time rates.

If a show is rerun in non-network prime time, 40% of the applicable minimum applies for the second run, 30% for the next run, and 25% for each of the next three. There is a built-in sliding scale for network and non-network reruns, continuing throughout the entire run of the program, into perpetuity.

APPENDIXES:
WHERE TO GO NEXT

Appendix A
Networks, Studios, and
Production Companies

(*Note:* New submissions should be addressed to the Head of Program Development, and should be submitted through an agent, if possible.)

ABC-TV
2040 Ave. of the Stars
Century City, CA 90067
(213) 557-7777

ABC-TV
1330 Ave. of the Americas
New York, NY 10019
(212) 887-7777

CBS-TV
7800 Beverly Blvd.
Los Angeles, CA 90036
(213) 852-2345

CBS-TV
51 W. 52nd St.
New York, NY 10019
(212) 975-4321

NBC-TV
3000 W. Alameda
Burbank, CA 91523
(818) 840-4444

NBC-TV
30 Rockefeller Plaza
New York, NY 10020
(212) 664-4444

Major Studios

Columbia Pictures-TV
3000 Colgems Square
Burbank, CA 91505
(818) 954-6000

Walt Disney Productions
500 S. Buena Vista
Burbank, CA 91521
(818) 840-1000

M.G.M.-TV
10202 W. Washington Blvd.
Culver City, CA 90230
(213) 836-3000

Paramount Pictures-TV
5555 Melrose Ave.

Los Angeles, CA 90038
(213) 468-5000

20th Century Fox-TV
10201 W. Pico Blvd.
Los Angeles, CA 90064
(213) 277-2211

Universal Studios-TV
100 Universal City Plaza
Universal City, CA 91608
(818) 985-4321

Warner Bros. TV
4000 Warner Blvd.
Burbank, CA 91522
(818) 954-6000

Selected Independent Production Companies

ABC Pictures, Inc.
2040 Avenue of the Stars
Los Angeles, CA 90067
(213) 557-7777

The Aldrich Company
606 N. Larchmont
Los Angeles, CA 90004
(213) 462-6511

Irwin Allen Productions
Columbia Plaza
Burbank, CA 91505
(818) 954-3601

Lucille Ball Productions
10201 W. Pico Blvd.
Los Angeles, CA 90035
(213) 203-3650

Bob Barker Prods./Prappas Co.
9201 Wilshire Blvd., Suite 210
Beverly Hills, CA 90210
(213) 278-1160

Barris Industries
9100 Wilshire Blvd., Suite 411E
Beverly Hills, CA 90210
(213) 278-1160

Barry & Enright Productions
1888 Century Park East
Los Angeles, CA 90067
(213) 277-3414

Batjac Productions
9570 Wilshire Blvd.
Beverly Hills, CA 90212
(213) 278-9870

Chris Bearde Productions
225 Santa Monica Blvd.
Santa Monica, CA 90401
(213) 394-9606

Warren Beatty
5555 Melrose Ave.
Los Angeles, CA 90038
(213) 468-5000

Tony Bill
73 Market St.
Venice, CA 90291
(213) 396-5937

Steve Binder Productions
666 N. Robertson Blvd.
Los Angeles, CA 90069
(213) 652-4422

The Burbank Studios
4000 Warner Blvd.
Burbank, CA 91522
(818) 954-6000

Bill Burrud Productions
1100 S. LaBrea Ave.
Los Angeles, CA 90019
(213) 937-0300

Steven J. Cannell Prods.
7083 Hollywood Blvd.
Los Angeles, CA 90028
(213) 465-5800

William Carruther Company
200 N. Larchmont
Los Angeles, CA 90004
(213) 465-0669

Carson Productions
4123 Radford Ave.
Studio City, CA 91604
(818) 506-5333

CBS/Fox
4024 Radford Ave.
Studio City, CA 91604
(818) 760-5000

Ernest Chambers Productions
1438 N. Gower St.
Los Angeles, CA 90028
(213) 464-6158

Chartoff-Winkler Productions
10125 W. Washington Blvd.
Los Angeles, CA 90230
(213) 204-0474

Dick Clark Productions
3003 W. Olive Ave.
Burbank, CA 91505
(818) 841-3003

Francis Coppola
1040 N. Las Palmas Ave.
Los Angeles, CA 90038
(213) 463-7191

Corday Productions
300 Colgems Plaza
Burbank, CA 91522
(818) 954-2637

Pierre Cossette Productions
8899 Beverly Blvd.
Los Angeles, CA 90048
(213) 278-3366

The Cousteau Society
8430 Santa Monica Blvd.
Los Angeles, CA 90048
(213) 656-4422

Douglas S. Cramer Company
1041 N. Formosa
Los Angeles, CA 90046
(213) 850-2500

Disney Productions
500 S. Buena Vista St.
Burbank, CA 91521
(818) 840–1000

Blake Edwards Entertainment
1888 Century Park East, Suite 1616
Los Angeles, CA 90067
(213) 553-6741

Embassy Television Corporation
100 Universal City Plaza
Universal City, CA 91608
(213) 985-4321

EMI Films
9489 Dayton Way
Beverly Hills, CA 90210
(213) 278-4770

Robert Evans
5555 Melrose Ave.
Los Angeles, CA 90038
(213) 468-5000

Don Fedderson Productions
12735 Ventura Blvd. Suite 12
Studio City, CA 91604
(818) 985-4736

Freddie Fields
10202 W. Washington Blvd.
Culver City, CA 90004
(213) 558-5000

Carl Foreman
Universal Studio Bldg. 448
Universal City, CA 91608
(818) 508-3117

Four D Productions
9200 Sunset Blvd., Suite 920
Los Angeles, CA 90069
(213) 466-8231

Frankovich Productions
9220 Sunset Blvd., Suite 230
Los Angeles, CA 90069
(213) 278-0920

Charles Fries Productions
9200 Sunset Blvd. Suite 700
Los Angeles, CA 90069
(213) 859-9957

Greg Garrison Productions
3400 W. Alameda
Burbank, CA 91505
(818) 849-2471

David Gerber Company
9336 W. Washington Blvd.
Culver City, CA 90230
(213) 836-5537

Golden West TV
5800 Sunset Blvd.
Los Angeles, CA 90078
(213) 460-5500

Samuel Goldwyn Company
10203 Santa Monica Blvd.
Los Angeles, CA 90046
(213) 552-2255

Goodson-Todman Productions
6430 Sunset Blvd., Suite 1400
Hollywood, CA 90028
(213) 464-4300

Lawrence Gordon
Universal Studio Bldg. 112
Universal City, CA 91608
(818) 508-2373

Merv Griffin Productions
1541 N. Vine St.
Los Angeles, 90028
(213) 461-4701

Group W
5800 Sunset Blvd.
Los Angeles, CA 90078
(213) 460-5207

Robert Guenette Productions
8489 W. Third St.
Los Angeles, CA 90048
(213) 658-8450

Hanna-Barbera Productions
3400 Cahuenga Blvd. West
Los Angeles, CA 90068
(213) 851-5000

Hill-Mandelker
10201 W. Pico Blvd.
Los Angeles, CA 90035
(213) 203-1584

Hope Enterprises, Inc.
3808 Riverside Dr., Suite 100
Burbank, CA 91505
(818) 841-2080

Ron Howard/Major H Prods./
   New World
1888 Century Park East, 5th fl.
Los Angeles, CA 90067
(213) 551-1444

Henry Jaffe Enterprises
1420 N. Beachwood Dr. Bldg. 50
Los Angeles, CA 90028
(213) 466-3543

Richard Linke Associates
4055 Kraft Ave.
Studio City, CA 91604
(818) 760-2500

Stacey Keach Productions
5216 Laurel Canyon
North Hollywood, CA 91607
(818) 762-0966

Lorimar Productions
3970 Overland Ave.
Culver City, CA 90230
(213) 202-2000

Harlan Kleiman Company
1533 N. Fairfax Ave.
Los Angeles, CA 90046
(213) 874-0187

Major League Productions
4605 Lankershim Blvd., Suite 220
North Hollywood, CA 91602
(818) 508-7712

Howard Koch Productions
5555 Melrose Ave.
Los Angeles, CA 90038
(213) 468-5000

The Malposa Company
4000 Warner Blvd.
Burbank, CA 91522
(818) 954-6000

Kragen & Company
1112 N. Sherbourne Dr.
Los Angeles, CA 90069
(213) 854-4400

Garry Marshall Productions
5555 Melrose Ave.
Los Angeles, CA 90038
(213) 468-5000

Kristofferson Productions
1800 N. Vine, Suite 202
Hollywood, CA 90028
(213) 467–5217

Quinn Martin
1041 N. Formosa Ave.
Los Angeles, CA 90046
(213) 850-2653

Krofft Entertainment
7200 Vineland Ave.
Sun Valley, CA 91352
(213) 875-0324

Paul Mazursky
4000 Warner Blvd.
Burbank, CA 91522
(818) 954-3481

The Ladd Company
4000 Warner Blvd.
Burbank, CA 91522
(818) 954-4400

McCann-Erickson Productions
6420 Wilshire Blvd.
Los Angeles, CA 90048
(213) 655-9420

Alan Landsburg Productions
11811 W. Olympic Blvd.
Los Angeles, CA 90064
(213) 208-2111

Metromedia Producers Corporation
5746 Sunset Blvd.
Los Angeles, CA 90028
(213) 462-7111

Glen A. Larson Productions
10201 W. Pico Blvd.
Los Angeles, CA 90035
(213) 203-1076

MTM Enterprises
4024 Radford Ave.
Studio City, CA 91604
(818) 760-5000

New World Pictures
1888 Century Park East
Los Angeles, CA 90067
(213) 551-1444

Nicholson Films, Inc.
4372 Tujunga Ave.
Studio City, CA 91604
(818) 769-5089

NRW Company
5746 Sunset Blvd.
Hollywood, CA 90028
(213) 856-1746

Orion Pictures Corporation
1875 Century Park East
Los Angeles, CA 90067
(213) 557-8700

Pasetta Productions
8322 Beverly Blvd., Suite 205
Los Angeles, CA 90048
(213) 655-8500

Playboy Productions
8560 Sunset Blvd.
Los Angeles, CA 90069
(213) 659-4080

Sydney Pollack Productions
4000 Warner Blvd.
Burbank, CA 91522
(818) 954-1711

PolyGram Television
3940 Overland Ave.
Culver City, CA 90230
(213) 202-4400

Post-Newsweek Productions
4676 Admiralty Way, Suite 520
Marina Del Rey, CA 90291
(213) 823-5218

Q-M Productions
10960 Wilshire Blvd.
Los Angeles, CA 90024
(213) 208-2000

Rastar Films, Inc.
300 Golgems Sq.
Burbank, CA 91505
(818) 954-6000

River City Productions
1015 Galey Ave., Suite 214
Los Angeles, CA 90024
(213) 208-8711

Al Ruddy Productions
10201 W. Pico Blvd.
Los Angeles, CA 90035
(213) 203-3053

Edgar J. Scherick Associates
5746 Sunset Blvd.
Hollywood, CA 90028
(213) 462-7111

Schlatter Productions
8321 Beverly Blvd.
Los Angeles, CA 90048
(213) 655-1400

Showtime Entertainment
10900 Wilshire Blvd., 4th fl.
Los Angeles, CA 90024
(213) 208-2340

The Sidaris Company
1891 Carla Ridge
Beverly Hills, CA 90210
(213) 275-2682

Melvin Simon Productions
260 S. Beverly Drive
Beverly Hills, CA 90212
(213) 273-5450

Smith and Hemion Productions
1438 N. Gower, Box 15
Hollywood, CA 90028
(213) 871-1200

Smothers, Inc.
8489 W. 3rd St., Suite 38
Hollywood, CA 90028
(213) 651-0200

Aaron Spelling Productions
1041 N. Formosa
Los Angeles, CA 90046
(213) 850-2413

Steven Spielberg
4000 Warner Blvd.
Burbank, CA 91522
(213) 954-3961

Lyn Stalmaster/Howard & Assoc.
9911 W. Pico Blvd., Suite 1580
Los Angeles, CA 90035
(213) 552-0983

Marty Starger Productions
Universal Studio Bldg. 69
Universal City, CA 91608
(818) 508-2095

Robert Stigwood Productions
5555 Melrose Ave.
Los Angeles, CA 90038
(213) 468-5000

Burt Sugarman Inc.
Beverly Wilshire Hotel
Beverly Hills, CA 90212
(213) 273-0900

David Susskind
10202 W. Washington Blvd.
Culver City, CA 90230
(213) 558-5000

D. L. Taffner, Ltd.
5455 Wilshire Blvd., Suite 1908
Los Angeles, CA 90036
(213) 973-1144

Tomorrow Entertainment
4421 Riverside Dr., Suite 100
Burbank, CA 91505
(818) 849-3116

UA Productions
10202 W. Washington Blvd.
Culver City, CA 90230
(213) 202-0202

Renee Valente
10201 W. Pico Blvd.
Los Angeles, CA 90035
(213) 203-2012

Viacom Enterprises
10900 Wilshire Blvd.
Los Angeles, CA 90024
(213) 208-2700

Jerry Weintraub
9744 Wilshire Blvd.
Beverly Hills, CA 90212
(213) 550-7100

Fred Weintraub Productions
9884 Santa Monica Blvd.
Beverly Hills, CA 90212
(213) 203-0722

Jay Weston Productions
1041 N. Formosa Ave.
Hollywood, CA 90047
(213) 850-2461

Daniel Wilcox
4024 Radford Ave.
Studio City, CA 91604
(818) 760-6148

Wildwood Enterprises
4000 Warner Blvd.
Burbank, CA 91522
(818) 954-6000

Henry Winkler Productions
Universal Studio Bldg. 507/2E
Universal Studios, CA 91608
(818) 508-3277

Robert Wise Productions
1438 N. Gower
Los Angeles, CA 90028
(213) 461-3864

Witt-Thomas-Harris Productions
1438 N. Gower
Los Angeles, CA 90028
(213) 464-1333

Robert Wold Company
10880 Wilshire Blvd.
Los Angeles, CA 90024
(213) 474-3500

Wolper Organization
4000 Warner Blvd.
Burbank, CA 91522
(818) 954-1707

Wrather Corporation
270 N. Canon Dr.
Beverly Hills, CA 90210
(213) 278-8521

Zanuck/Brown Company
P.O. Box 900
Beverly Hills, CA 90213
(213) 203-3215

Zoetrope Studios
1040 N. Las Palmas
Los Angeles, CA 90038
(213) 463-7191

Appendix B
Cable and Satellite TV Companies

National Associations

Cable Communications Resource
  Center
2000 K St., N.W.
Washington, DC 20006
(202) 857-4800

Cable TV Information Center
1800 N. Kent St., Suite 1007
Arlington, VA 22209
(703) 528-6846

National Cable TV Association
1724 Massachusetts Ave., N.W.
Washington, DC 20036
(202) 775-3550

National Federation of Community
  Broadcasters
1314 14th St., N.W.

Washington, DC 20005
(202) 797-8911

National Federation of Local Cable
  Programmers
906 Pennsylvania Ave., S.E.
Washington, DC
(202) 544-7272

Public Service Satellite Consortium
1660 L St., N.W.
Washington, DC 20006
(202) 331-1154

Women in Cable
2033 M St., N.W.
Washington, DC 20006
(202) 296-7245

Basic Cable Program Services

These are some of the basic cable programming services that produce or acquire new shows. To discuss original programming concepts, contact the director of programming for the company.

Program Service	*Type of Programming*
ACSN-The Learning Channel 1200 New Hampshire Ave., N.W. Washington, DC 20036 (202) 331-8100	Adult personal enrichment, telecourses, how-to's
AP Newscable 50 Rockefeller Pl. New York, NY 10020 (212) 621-1500	Text news service
ARTS & ENTERTAINMENT (Hearst/ABC Video/RCTV) 555 Fifth Ave. New York, NY 10017 (212) 661-4500	Adult cultural programming on performing arts, drama, entertainment, documentaries
BET-Black Entertainment Television (TCI/Taft Broadcasting) 1050 31st St., N.W. Washington, DC 20007 (202) 337-5260	Music, public affairs, talk shows, movies geared toward Black audiences
CNN-Cable News Network (Turner Broadcasting Systems) 1050 Techwood Dr., N.W. Atlanta, GA 30318 (404) 892-1717	Hard news with live coverage of breaking events, features subjects in many areas
C-SPAN (Cable Satellite Public Affairs Network) 444 N. Capitol St., N.W. Washington, DC 20001 (202) 737-3220	House of Representative debates, congressional hearings, government events, public affairs

ESPN-Entertainment &
  Sports Programming Network
  (Getty Oil)
ESPN Plaza
Bristol, CT 06010
(203) 584-8477
	Major sports events, U.S. Football
	League games, sports coverage 24
	hours per day

Program Service	*Type of Programming*
Financial News Network (Merrill Lynch/Biotech) 2525 Ocean Park Blvd. Santa Monica, CA 90405 (213) 450-2412	Live reports on financial news, stocks, commodities, interviews
Independent Network News (WPIX) 220 E. 42nd St. New York, NY 10017 (212) 210-2411	News, *Wall Street Journal Report*, magazine series, panel/discussion
Lifetime (Viacom, Hearst/ABC) 1211 Ave. of Americas New York, NY 10036 (212) 719–7230	Merger of Cable Health Network and daytime programming for women; self-improvement, magazine series, health and enrichment for women
MSN-The Information Channel (Modern Satellite Network) 45 Rockefeller Center New York, NY 10011 (212) 765-3100	Consumer information and business news; producers pay for time
MTV (Warner Amex Satellite Entertainment Co.) 1211 Ave. of the Americas New York, NY 10036 (212) 944-5380	Rock video record promos, top name acts, interviews, latest releases, 24 hours per day
The Nashville Network (WMS/Group W) 2806 Opryland Dr. Nashville, TN 37214 (615) 889-6840	Country & western music and entertainment, variety, dance, comedy, sports, movies
Nickelodean (Warner Amex) 1211 Ave. of the Americas New York, NY 10036 (212) 944-4250	Children's programming, originally produced and acquired, comedy, concerts, films, teen talk show, new series
Satellite Program Network (Satellite Syndicated Systems) 8252 South Harvard Tulsa, OK 74136 (918) 481–0881	Classic feature films, series on hobbies, how to's, music video, health, entertainment, international programming, 24 hours per day

Program Service	*Type of Programming*
The Silent Network P.O. Box 1902 Beverly Hills, CA 90213 (213) 654-6972	Original captioned programming for deaf audiences, news, magazine shows, teen, children's, aerobics, drama
United Press International 220 E. 42nd St. New York, NY 10017 (212) 850-8600	Text news service
USA Cable Network (Time/MCA/Paramount) 208 Harristown Rd. Glen Rock, NJ 07452 (201) 445-8550	Professional and college sports, women's programming for enrichment, Night Flight (video rock), movies, specials, series

Super Stations

WTBS-TV (Turner Broadcasting) 1050 Techwood Dr., N.W. Atlanta, GA 30318 (404) 892-1717	Feature films, sports, original programming, soaps, rock video, news, documentaries, network reruns
WGN-TV (Tribune) 2501 West Bradley Pl. Chicago, IL 66618 (312) 528-2311	Feature films, sports, syndicated and public affairs, network reruns
WOR-TV (RKO/Eastern Microwave/ Newhouse) 3 Northern Concourse Box 4827 Syracuse, NY 13221 (315) 455-5955	Feature films, sports, news, public affairs

Pay TV Program Services

These are some of the pay TV services that produce or acquire programming for cable, subscription TV (STV), multipoint distribution systems (MDS), and direct broadcast satellite (DBS). To discuss original programming concepts, contact the director of programming for the company.

Program Service	*Type of Programming*
Biznet (U.S. Chamber of Commerce) 1615 H St., N.W. Washington, D.C. 20062 (202) 463-5808	Business news and information
BRAVO (Rainbow Programming) 100 Crossways Park West Woodbury, NY 11797 (516) 364-2222	Art films (American and foreign), small number of specials on performing arts (dance, music, opera)
Cinemax (Time, Inc.) 1271 Ave. of the Americas New York, NY 10020 (212) 484-1100	Movies, women's programming, family features, SCTV comedy network, adult features
The Disney Channel (Walt Disney Productions) 4111 W. Alameda Ave. Burbank, CA 91505 (818) 846–6661	Disney features, new series and specials for children
Galavision (Spanish International Network) 250 Park Ave. New York, NY 10017 (212) 953-7500	Spanish language features, music and variety, drama, sports
HBO (Home Box Office) (Time, Inc.) 1271 Ave. of the Americas New York, NY 10020 (212) 484–1000	Feature films, sports events, specials, new series and films
Home Entertainment Network (United Cable TV) 5179 Fishwick Dr. Cincinnati, OH 45216 (513) 641-4400	Feature films, specials, sports
HTN-Home Theatre Network (Group W) 465 Congress St. Portland, ME 04101 (207) 774-0300	Feature films, concerts, travel

Program Service	*Type of Programming*
ON-TV (Oak Media) 16935 W. Bernardo San Diego, CA 92128 (619) 485-9300	Feature films, adult programming, original and local productions

The Playboy Channel (Rainbow
  Programming Service/Playboy
  Enterprises)
100 Crossways Park West
Woodbury, NY 11797
(516) 364-2222
	Soft-core features, specials, comedy,
	variety, original series

Preview (Time, Inc.) 1271 Ave. of the Americas New York, NY 10020 (212) 484-1000	Features, specials, pay per view (sports, specials), adult late-night programming for STV
Prism 50 Monument Rd. Bala Cynwyd, PA 19004 (215) 668-2210	Feature films, sports, specials
QUBE (Warner Amex) 75 Rockefeller Pl. New York, NY 10019 (212) 750-0929	Programming determined by individual systems, including interactive programming
RSVP Sports (ABC Video/ESPN) ABC Video Enterprises 1330 Ave. of Americas New York, NY 10019 (212) 887-7297	Live sports events on pay per view basis
Satellite TV Corporation (STC) (Comsat) 1301 Pennsylvania Ave., N.W. Washington, DC 20004 (202) 626-3600	DBS programming plans call for movies, children's and family, news, sports
Showtime/The Movie Channel (Viacom/Warners/MCA/Paramount) Paramount Plaza Building 1633 Broadway New York, NY 10019 (212) 708-1600	Feature films, specials, concerts, new series and films

Program Service	Type of Programming
United Satellite Communications (USCI) 919 Third Ave., 27th fl. New York, NY 10022 (212) 750-8666	DBS programming includes first run features, news, sports, variety

Appendix C
National Funding Sources:
Agencies, Resource Groups,
Foundations

Funding Agencies and Resource Groups

American Council for the Arts
570 7th Ave.
New York, NY 10018
(212) 354-6655

American Film Institute (AFI)
2021 N. Western Ave.
Los Angeles, CA 90028
(213) 856-7600

American *Playhouse* (Drama)
365 W. 58th St.,
New York, NY 10019
(212) 664–7272

Center for Arts Information
80 Centre St.
New York, NY 10013
(212) 587-4967

Children's & Family Programming
  Consortia
WQED-TV

4802 Fifth Ave.
Pittsburgh, PA 15213
(412) 622-1300

Corporation for Public
  Broadcasting (CPB)
1111 16th St., N.W.
Washington, DC 20036
(202) 293-6160

The Film Fund
80 E. 11 St.,
New York, NY 10003
(212) 475-3720

The Foundation Center
808 7th Ave.
New York, NY 10019
(212) 489-8610

The Foundation Center
1001 Connecticut Ave., N.W.
Washington, DC 20036
(202) 331-1400

Foundation for Independent Video &
  Film
625 Broadway
New York, NY 10012
(212) 473-3400

Frontline (Documentaries)
WGBH-TV
125 Western Ave.
Boston, MA 02134
(617) 492–2777

Global Village
454 Broome St.
New York, NY
(212) 966-7526

Grantsmanship Center
1031 S. Grand
Los Angeles, CA
(213) 749-4721

Independent Documentary Fund
WNET Television Lab
356 W. 58th St.
New York, NY 10019
(212) 560-3910

National Endowment for the Arts
1100 Pennsylvania Ave., N.W.
Washington, D.C. 20506
(202) 682-5452

National Endowment for the
  Humanities
1100 Pennsylvania Ave., N.W.
Washington, DC 20506
(202) 786-0278

National Public Radio
2025 M St. NW
Washington, DC 20036
(202) 822-2000

Public Broadcasting System (PBS)
475 L'enfant Plaza, S.W.
Washington, DC 20024
(202) 488-5000

Sundance Institute for Film &
  Television
19 Exchange Place
Salt Lake City, UT 84111
(801) 521-9330

Private Foundations

Annenberg/CPB Project
1111 16th St., N.W.
Washington, DC 20036
(202) 955-5245

Carnegie Foundation
437 Madison Ave.
New York, NY
(212) 371-3200

Ford Foundation
320 E. 43rd St.
New York, NY
(212) 573-5000

John Simon Guggenheim Memorial
  Foundation
90 Park Ave.
New York, NY 10016
(212) 687-4470

Jerome Foundation
West 1052 First National Bank Bldg.
St. Paul, MN 55501
(612) 224-9431

Lilly Endowment
2801 N. Meridian St.
Indianapolis, IN 46208
(317) 924-5471

John & Mary Markle Foundation
50 Rockefeller Plaza
New York, NY 10036
(212) 489-6655

Andrew W. Mellon Foundation
140 E. 62nd St.
New York, NY 10021
(212) 838-8400

Rockefeller Foundation
1133 Ave. of Americas
New York, NY 10036
(212) 869-8509

Sears Roebuck Foundation
Dept. 703, Sears Tower
Chicago, IL 60684
(312) 875-2500

Alfred P. Sloan Foundation
630 Fifth Ave.
New York, NY 10020
(212) 582-0450

Tinker Foundation
645 Madison Ave.
New York, NY 10022
(212) 421-6858

Writers Guild of America
  Foundation
555 W. 57th St.
New York, NY 10019
(212) 245-6180

Appendix D
Regional and State
Funding Contacts

Regional Public Broadcasting Networks

Central Educational Network (CEN)
4300 W. Peterson Ave.
Chicago, IL 60625
(312) 545-7500

Eastern Educational Network (EEN)
120 Boylston St.
Boston, MA 02116
(617) 338-4455

Pacific Mountain Network (PMN)
2480 W. 26th Ave.
Denver, CO 80211
(303) 455-7161

Southern Educational
Communications Association
(SECA)
Woodrow St., P.O. Box 5966
Columbia, SC 29250
(803) 799–5517

Regional Media Arts Centers

The following regional media arts centers offer fellowships for independent film and TV creators. They are supported by NEA, AFI, state arts agencies, private foundations and corporations. For information and application forms, contact the center nearest you.

Central Mid-West
Illinois, Indiana, Kansas, Michigan, Missouri, Nebraska

Center for New Television
11 East Hubbard St.
Chicago, IL 60611
(312) 565-1787

Mid-Atlantic
Delaware, District of Columbia, Maryland, New Jersey, New York, Ohio,
Pennsylvania, West Virginia

Pittsburgh Filmmakers, Inc.
P.O. Box 7467
Pittsburgh, PA 15213
(412) 681-5449

New England
Connecticut, Maine, Massachusetts, New Hampshire, Rhode Island, Vermont

The Boston Film/Video
   Foundation, Inc.
1126 Boylston St.
Boston, MA 02215
(617) 536-1540

Southeast
Alabama, Florida, Georgia, Kentucky, Mississippi, North Carolina, South
Carolina, Tennessee, Virginia

Appalshop Inc.
Box 743
Whitesburg, KY 41858
(606) 633-0108

Southwest
Arkansas, Arizona, Louisiana, New Mexico, Oklahoma, Texas, Puerto Rico,
Caribbean

Southwest Alternate Media
   Project, Inc.
1519 West Main
Houston, TX 77006
(713) 522-8592

Upper Mid-West
Iowa, Minnesota, North Dakota, South Dakota, Wisconsin

Film in the Cities
2388 University Ave.
St. Paul, MN 55114
(612) 646-6104

West
Alaska, California, Colorado, Hawaii, Idaho, Montana, Nevada, Oregon, Utah,
Washington, Wyoming, and Pacific Territories

Rocky Mountain Film Center
University of Colorado—Box 316
Boulder, CO 80309
(303) 492-7903

State Arts Agencies

Alabama State Council on the
Arts and Humanities
Gallagher House
114 North Hull St.
Montgomery, AL 36130
(205) 832-6758

Alaska State Council on the Arts
619 Warehouse Ave.
Suite 220
Anchorage, AK 99501
(907) 279-1558

American Samoa Council on
Culture, Arts, and Humanities
P.O. Box 1540
Office of the Governor
Pago Pago, American Samoa 96799
9-011-684-633-4347

Arizona Commission on the
Arts and Humanities
2024 North Seventh St.
Suite 201
Phoenix, AZ 85006
(602) 255-5884

Arkansas Arts Council
Continental Building, Suite 500
Main and Markham Streets
Little Rock, AR 72201
(501) 371-2539

California Arts Council
1901 Broadway, Suite A
Sacramento, CA 95818
(916) 445-1530

Colorado Council on the
Arts and Humanities
Grant-Humphreys Mansion
770 Pennsylvania St.
Denver, CO 80203
(303) 866-2617

Connecticut Commission on
the Arts
340 Capitol Ave.
Hartford, CT 06106
(203) 566-4770

Delaware State Arts Council
State Office Building
820 N French St.
Wilmington, DE 19801
(302) 571-3540

District of Columbia Commission
on the Arts and Humanities
420 Seventh St., N.W., 2nd Floor
Washington, D.C. 20004
(202) 724-5613 or 727-9332

Florida, Arts Council of
Division of Cultural Affairs
Department of State
The Capitol
Tallahassee, FL 32301
(904) 487-2980

Georgia Council for the
Arts and Humanities
2082 East Exchange Place
Suite 100
Tucker, GA 30084
(404) 656-3967

Guam, Insular Arts Council of
Office of the Governor
P.O. Box 2950
Agana, Guam 96910
477-9845 (must go through overseas
   operator)

Hawaii State Foundation on
   Culture and the Arts
335 Merchant St.
Room 202
Honolulu, HI 96813
(808) 548-4145

Idaho Commission on the Arts
304 West State St.
c/o Statehouse Mail
Boise, ID 83720
(208) 334-2119

Illinois Arts Council
111 North Wabash Ave.
Room 720
Chicago, IL 60602
(312) 793-6750

Indiana Arts Commission
Union Title Building
155 East Market St.
Suite 614
Indianapolis, IN 46204
(317) 232-1268

Iowa State Arts Council
State Capitol Building
Des Moines, IA 50319
(515) 281-4451

Kansas Arts Commission
112 West 6th St.
Topeka, KS 66603
(913) 296-3335

Kentucky Arts Council
Berry Hill
Louisville Rd.
Frankfort, KY 40601
(502) 564-3757

Louisiana Department of Culture,
   Recreation, and Tourism
Division of the Arts
P.O. Box 44247
Baton Rouge, LA 70804
(504) 925-3930

Maine State Commission on the
   Arts and the Humanities
55 Capitol St.
State House Station 25
Augusta, ME 04333
(207) 289-2724

Maryland State Arts Council
15 West Mulberry St.
Baltimore, MD 21201
(301) 685-6740

Massachusetts Council on the
   Arts and Humanities
1 Ashburton Place
Room 2101
Boston, MA 02108
(617) 727-3668

Michigan Council for the Arts
1200 Sixth Ave.
Executive Plaza
Detroit, MI 48226
(313) 256-3735

Minnesota State Arts Board
432 Summit Ave.
St. Paul, MN 55102
(612) 297-2603
(800) 652-9747—toll free within
   Minnesota

Mississippi Arts Commission
P.O. Box 1341
Jackson, MS 39205
(601) 354-7336

Missouri State Council on the Arts
Wainwright Office Complex
111 N. Seventh St.
Suite 105

St. Louis, MO 63101
(314) 444-6845

Montana Arts Council
1280 South Third St. West
Missoula, MT 59801
(406) 543-8286

Nebraska Arts Council
1313 Farnam-on-the-Mall
Omaha, NE 68102-1873
(402) 554-2122

Nevada State Council on the Arts
329 Flint St.
Reno, NV 89501
(702) 784-6231/2 or 6

New Hampshire Commission
  on the Arts
Phenix Hall
40 North Main St.
Concord, NY 03301
(603) 271-2789

New Jersey State Council
  on the Arts
109 West State St.
Trenton, NJ 08608
(609) 292-6130

New Mexico Arts Division
113 Lincoln Ave.
Santa Fe, NM 87501
(505) 827-6490

New York State Council on the Arts
80 Centre St.
New York, NY 10013
(212) 587-4555

North Carolina Arts Council
N.C. Department of
  Cultural Resources
Raleigh, NC 27611
(919) 733-2821

North Dakota Council on the Arts
Black Building
Suite 811
Fargo, ND 58102
(701) 237-8962

Northern Mariana Islands
  Commonwealth Council for
  Arts and Culture
Ferreira Building, Beach Road
Garapan, Saipan
Commonwealth of the Northern
  Mariana Islands 96950
District office:
2121 R St., N.W.
Washington, DC 20008
(202) 328-3847

Ohio Arts Council
727 E. Main St.
Columbus, OH 43205
(614) 466-2613

Oklahoma, State Arts Council of
Jim Thorpe Building
Room 640
2101 North Lincoln Blvd.
Oklahoma City, OK 73105
(405) 521-2931

Oregon Arts Commission
835 Summer St., N.E.
Salem, OR 97301
(503) 378-3625

Pennsylvania Council on the Arts
Room 216
Finance Building
Harrisburg, PA 17120
(717) 787-6883

Puerto Rican Culture, Institute of
Apartado Postal 4184
San Juan, PR 00905
(809) 723-2115

Rhode Island State Council
  on the Arts

312 Wickenden St.
Providence, RI 02903-4494
(401) 277-3880

South Carolina Arts Commission
1800 Gervais St.
Columbia, SC 29201
(802) 758-3442

South Dakota Arts Council
108 West 11th St.
Sioux Falls, SD 57102
(605) 339-6646

Tennessee Arts Commission
505 Deaderick St.
Suite 1700
Nashville, TN 37219
(615) 741-1701

Texas Commission on the Arts
P.O. Box 13406
Capitol Station
Austin, TX 78711
(512) 475-6593

Utah Arts Council
617 East South Temple St.
Salt Lake City, UT 84102
(801) 533-5895

Vermont Council on the Arts, Inc.
136 State St.
Montpelier, VT 05602
(802) 828-3291

Virginia Commission for the Arts
400 East Grace St.
First Floor
Richmond, VA 23219
(804) 786-4492

Virgin Islands Council on the Arts
Caravelle Arcade
Christiansted, St. Croix
U.S. Virgin Islands 00820
(809) 773-3075 ext. 3

Washington State Arts Commission
9th and Columbia Building
Mail Stop GH-11
Olympia, WA 98504
(206) 753-3860

West Virginia Department of
    Culture and History
Arts and Humanities Division
Science and Culture Center
Capitol Complex
Charleston, WV 25305
(304) 348-0240

Wisconsin Arts Board
123 West Washington Ave.
Madison, WI 53702
(608) 266-0190

Wyoming Council on the Arts
2nd Floor
Equality State Bank Building
Cheyenne, WY 82002
(307) 777-7742

State Humanities Agencies

The Committee for the Humanities
    in Alabama
Box A-40
Birmingham-Southern College
Birmingham, AL 35254
(205) 324-1314

Alaska Humanities Forum
429 D. St., Rm. 312
Loussac Sogn Building
Anchorage, AK 99501
(907) 272-5341

Arizona Humanities Council
First Interstate Bank Plaza
100 W. Washington, Suite 1290
Phoenix, AZ 85003
(602) 257-0335

Arkansas Endowment for the
  Humanities
The Remmel Building, Suite 102
1010 West 3rd St.
Little Rock, AR 72201
(501) 372-2672

California Council for the
  Humanities
312 Sutter St., Suite 601
San Francisco, CA 94108
(415) 391-1474

Colorado Humanities Program
601 Broadway, Suite 307
Denver, CO 80203
(303) 595-0881

Connecticut Humanities Council
195 Church St.
Wesleyan Station
Middletown, CT 06457
(203) 347-6888

Delaware Humanities Forum
2600 Pennsylvania Ave.
Wilmington, DE 19806
(302) 738-8491

D. C. Community Humanities
  Council
1341 G St., N.W., Suite 620
Washington, DC 20005
(202) 347-1732

Florida Endowment for the
  Humanities
LET 468
University of South Florida
Tampa, FL 33620
(813) 974-4094

Georgia Endowment for the
  Humanities
1589 Clifton Rd., NE
Emory University
Atlanta, GA 30322
(404) 329-7500

Hawaii Committee for the
  Humanities
2615 South King St., Suite 211
Honolulu, HI 96826
(808) 947-5891

The Association for the Humanities
  in Idaho
1409 West Washington St.
Boise, ID 83702
(208) 345-5346

Illinois Humanities Council
618 South Michigan Ave.
Chicago, IL 60605
(312) 939-5212

Indiana Committee for the
  Humanities
3135 North Meridian St.
Indianapolis, IN 46208
(317) 925-5316

Iowa Humanities Board
Oakdale Campus
University of Iowa
Iowa City, IA 52242
(319) 353-6754

Kansas Committee for the
  Humanities
112 West Sixth St., Suite 509
Topeka, KS 66603
(913) 357-0359

Kentucky Humanities Council, Inc.
Ligon House
University of Kentucky
Lexington, KY 40508
(606) 257-5932

Louisiana Committee for the
   Humanities
The Ten-O-One Building
1001 Howard Ave., Suite 4407
New Orleans, LA 70113
(504) 523-4352

Maine Humanities Council
P.O. Box 7202
Portland, ME 04112
(207) 773-5051

The Maryland Committee for the
   Humanities
516 N. Charles St., #304-305
Baltimore, MD 21201
(301) 837-1938

Massachusetts Foundation for the
   Humanities and Public Policy
237 E Whitmore Admin. Bldg.
University of Massachusetts
Amherst, MA 01003
(413) 545-1936

Michigan Council for the
   Humanities
Nisbet Building, Suite 30
1407 S. Harrison Rd.
East Lansing, MI 48824
(517) 355-0160

Minnesota Humanities Commission
LL 85 Metro Square
St. Paul, MN 55101
(612) 224-5739

Mississippi Committee for
   Humanities, Inc.
3825 Ridgewood Rd., Rm. 111
Jackson, MS 39211
(601) 982-6752

Missouri State Committee for the
   Humanities
Loberg Building, Suite 204
11425 Dorsett Rd.
Maryland Heights, MO 63043
(314) 738-7368

Montana Committee for the
   Humanities
P.O. Box 8036
Hellgate Station
Missoula, MT 59807
(405) 243-6022

Nebraska Committee for the
   Humanities
Cooper Plaza, Suite 405
211 N. 12th St.
Lincoln, NE 68508
(402) 474-2131

Nevada Humanities Committee
P.O. Box 8065
Reno, NV 89507
(702) 784-6587

New Hampshire Council for the
   Humanities
112 South State St.
Concord, NH 03301
(603) 224-4071

New Jersey Committee for the
   Humanities
73 Easton Ave.
New Brunswick, NJ 08903
(201) 932-7726

New Mexico Humanities Council
1712 Las Lomas NE
University of New Mexico
Albuquerque, NM 87131
(505) 277-3705

New York Council for the
   Humanities
33 West 42nd St.
New York, NY 10036
(212) 354-3040

North Carolina Humanities
   Committee
112 Foust Building,
   UNC-Greensboro
Greensboro, NC 27412
(919) 379-5325

North Dakota Humanities Council
Box 2191
Bismarck, ND 58502
(701) 663-1948

The Ohio Humanities Council
760 Pleasant Ridge Ave.
Columbus, OH 43209
(614) 231-6879

Oklahoma Foundation for the
   Humanities
Executive Terrace Building
2809 Northwest Expressway
Suite 500
Oklahoma City, OK 73112
(405) 840-1721

Oregon Committee for the
   Humanities
418 S.W. Washington, Rm. 410
Portland, OR 97204
(503) 241-0543

Pennsylvania Humanities Council
401 N. Broad St.
Philadelphia, PA 19108
(215) 925-1005

Fundacion Puertorriquena de las
   Humanidades
Box S-4307
Old San Juan, PR 00904
(809) 721-2087

Rhode Island Committee for the
   Humanities
463 Broadway
Providence, RI 02909
(401) 273-2250

South Carolina Committee for the
   Humanities
17 Calendar Court
Suite #6
Columbia, SC 29206
(803) 738-1850

South Dakota Committee on the
   Humanities
University Station, Box 35
Brookings, SD 57007
(605) 688-6113

Tennessee Committee for the
   Humanities
1001 18th Ave. South
Nashville, TN 37212
(615) 320-7001

Texas Committee for the
   Humanities
1604 Nueces
Austin, TX 78701
(512) 473-8585

Utah Endowment for the
   Humanities
10 West Broadway
Broadway Building, Suite 900
Salt Lake City, UT 84101
(801) 531-7868

Vermont Council on the
   Humanities and Public Issues
Grant House, P.O. Box 58
Hyde Park, VT 05655
(802) 888-3183

Virginia Foundation for the
   Humanities and Public Policy
One-B West Range
University of Virginia
Charlottesville, VA 22903
(804) 924-3296

Washington Commission for the
   Humanities
Olympia, WA 98505
(206) 866-6510

The Humanities Foundation of
   West Virginia
Box 204
Institute, WV 25112
(304) 768-8869

Wisconsin Humanities Committee
716 Langdon St.
Madison, WI 53706
(608) 262-0706

Wyoming Council for the
Humanities
Box 3274—University Station
Laramie, WY 82701
(307) 766-6496

State Education Agencies

State education agencies received funds from the Department of Education to support relevant projects that advance educational goals, including the use of television. Contact the "Chapter 2" coordinator of your state agency to discuss project possibilities.

Alabama State Department of
Education
State Office Building-Room 406
Montgomery, AL 36130
(205) 832-3290

Commissioner of Education
Alaska Department of Education
Pouch F, State Office Building
Juneau, AK 99811
(907) 465-2800

Associate Superintendent
Arizona Department of Education
1535 West Jefferson
Phoenix, AR 85007
(602) 255-5754

Assoc. Dir. for Federal Pgms.
Arkansas Dept. of Education
State Education Building
Capitol Mall
Little Rock, AR 72201
(501) 371-1287

Associate Superintendent
Department of Education
State Education Building
721 Capitol Mall
Sacramento, CA 95814
(916) 322-2363

Executive Assistant
Federal Relations
State Office Buiding
201 E. Colfax
Denver, CO 80203
(303) 866-5344

Assistant to the Commissioner for
Federal/State Relations
Room 308, State Office Building
165 Capitol Avenue
Hartford, CT 06106
(203) 566-2137 or 566-3585

Assistant State Superintendent
Administrative Services Branch
Department of Public Instruction
The Townsend Building
P.O. Box 1402
Dover, DE 19901
(302) 736-4661

Director
State-Federal Relations
Florida Department of Education
Tallahassee, FL 32301
(904) 487-2910

Administrator
Textbooks and ECIA, Chapter 2
Georgia Department of Education

1652 Twin Towers East
Atlanta, GA 30334
(404) 656-2404

Director, Planning and
  Evaluation Branch
Hawaii Department of Education
P.O. Box 2360
Honolulu, HI 96804
(808) 548-6485

Chief
Bureau of Special Services
Idaho Department of Education
L. B. Jordan State Office Building
Boise, IO 83720
(208) 334-2186

Manager, Educ. Innovation & Spt.
Illinois State Board of Education
100 North First Street
Springfield, IL 62777
(217) 782-3810

Director, Division of Federal
  Resources and School
  Improvement
Department of Public Instruction
Room 229, State House
Indianapolis, IN 46204
(317) 927-0296

Deputy State Superintendent
Iowa Department of Public
  Instruction
Grimes State Office Building
Des Moines, IA 50319
(515) 281-3436

Director
State and Federal Programs
Kansas Department of Education
120 East Tenth Street
Topeka, KS 66612
(913) 296-2306

Supervisor
Office of Federal Programs

Kentucky Department of Education
930 Capital Plaza Tower
Frankfort, KY 40601
(502) 564-3256

Assist. Superintendent
Office of Elementary Support
Louisiana Department of Education
P.O. Box 44064
Baton Rouge, LA 70804
(504) 342-3589

Assistant to the Commissioner
Maine Department of Educational
  and Cultural Services
State House Station #23
Augusta, ME 04333
(207) 289-2321

Assistant Deputy State
  Superintendent
Maryland Department of Education
200 W. Baltimore Street
Baltimore, MD 21201
(301) 659-2385

Acting Associate Commissioner
Division of Curriculum and
  Instruction
The Commonwealth of
  Massachusetts Department of
  Education
1385 Hancock Street
Quincy, MA 02169
(617) 770-7540

Office of the Superintendent
Michigan Department of Education
P.O. Box 30008
Lansing, MI 48909
(517) 373-8298

Asst. Comm. for Special Svs.
Minn. State Dept. of Educ.
726 Capitol Square Building
550 Cedar Street
St. Paul, MN 55101
(612) 296-5061

Coordinator, Chapter 2
Mississippi Dept. of Education
P.O. Box 771
Jackson, MS 39205
(601) 354-6958

Coordinator of Elem. & Sec.
    Education Act
Dept. of Elem. & Sec. Ed.
P.O. Box 480
Jefferson City, MO 65102
(314) 751-3520

Assistant Superintendent
Special Services
Mont. Office of Public Instr.
State Capitol
Helena, MT 59620
(406) 449-3693

Director, Federal Programs
Nebraska Dept. of Education
P.O. Box 94987
301 Centennial Mall South
Lincoln, NE 68509
(402) 471-2481

Associate Superintendent
Federal Pgms. & Special Svs.
Nevada Dept. of Education
400 W. King Str.-Capitol Complex
Carson City, NV 89710
(702) 885-3106

Director
Accountability Unit
N.H. Department of Education
410 State House Annex
Concord, NH 03301
(603) 271-2657

Director
Federal/State Relations
N.J. Dept. of Education
225 West State Street
Trenton, NJ 08625
(609) 292-5790

State Dept. of Education
300 Don Gaspar
Santa Fe, NM 87501
(505) 827-5441

Exec. Deputy Comm.
N.Y. Dept. of Educ.
Room 125
Albany, NY 12234
(518) 474-5836

Program Coordinator
Office of Federal Relations
N.C. Dept. of Education
Education Building
Raleigh, NC 27611
(919) 733-3614

Coordinator for ECIA, Chapter 2
North Dakota Department of
    Public Instruction
State Capitol
Bismarck, ND 58505
(701) 224-2276

Director
Division of Federal Assistance
933 High Street
Worthington, OH 43085
(614) 466-4161

Dir., Federal Financial Assistance
    Programs
State Dept. of Education
2500 North Lincoln Blvd.
Oklahoma City, OK 73105
(405) 521-2808

Director, Office of Policy and
    Program Development
Oregon Dept. of Education
700 Pringle Parkway, S.E.
Salem, OR 97310
(503) 378-8378

Bureau of Planning, Research,
    Evaluation and Dissemination
Pennsylvania Department of
    Education

12th Floor
333 Market Street
Harrisburg, PA 17108
(717) 787-4097

Coordinator, Chapter 2
Rhode Island Department of
    Elementary & Secondary Ed.
22 Hayes Street
Providence, RI 02908
(401) 277-2617

Director
Federal Programs
S.C. Dept. of Education
Room 211
Columbia, SC 29201
(803) 758-7782

Coord. for ECIA, Chapter 2
S.D. Dept. of Education
Richard F. Kneip Building
Pierre, SD 57501
(605) 773-3327

Deputy Commissioner
Tenn. Dept. of Education
Cordell Hull Building, Rm. 100
Nashville, TN 37219
(615) 741-3647

Deputy Commissioner
Finance and Program Admin.
Texas Education Agency
201 East Eleventh Street
Austin, TX 78701
(512) 475-3723

Administrator
Federal Programs
Utah Office of Education
250 East 500 South Street
Salt Lake City, UT 84111
(801) 533-5434

Vermont St. Dept. of Ed.
120 State Street

Montpelier, VT 05602
(802) 828-3124

Deputy Superintendent
Va. Dept. of Education
Post Office Box 6-Q
Richmond, VA 23216
(804) 225-2024

Chapter 2 Program Supervisor
Office of the Superintendent of
    Public Instruction
Old Capitol Building
7th and Washington
Olympia, WA 98504
(206) 753-1031

Director, ECIA Chapter 2
W.V. Dept. of Education
1900 Washington Street East
Building 6, Room B-346
Charleston, WV 25305
(304) 348-3925

Asst. Spt., Div. for Mgmt.
Planning and Federal Services
Wis. Dept. of Public Instr.
125 South Webster Street
Box 7841
Madison, WI 53707
(608) 266-3903

Department of Education
Hathaway Building
Cheyenne, WY 82002
(307) 777-6207

Director, Division for
    Grants Administration
Room 1004
415-12th Street, N.W.
Washington, DC 20004
(202) 724-4230 or 724-4235

Under Secretary, Puerto Rico
    Department of Education
Apartado 759
Hato Rey, 00919
(809) 753-8109

State Film and TV Commissions

Although film commissions are not in a position to fund scripts or productions, they are excellent resources for learning more about current and future television and film activities in your state.

Alabama Film Commission
340 N. Hull St.
Montgomery, AL 36130
(800) 633-5898

Alaska Film Commission
Division of Tourism
Pouch E, Juneau, AK 99811
(907) 465-2013

Arizona Motion Picture
  Development Office
1700 W. Washington
Phoenix, AZ 85007
(602) 255-5011

Arkansas Office of Motion Picture
  Development
One State Capitol Mall
Little Rock, AR 72201
(501) 371-7676

California Motion Picture Council
6725 Sunset Blvd.
Hollywood, CA 90028
(213) 736-2465

Canadian Film Center
c/o 144 S. Beverly Dr.
Beverly Hills, CA 90212
(213) 859-0268

Colorado Motion Picture & TV
Advisory Commission
1313 Sherman St.
Denver, CO 80203
(303) 866-2778

Connecticut Dept. of
  Economic Development
210 Washington St.

Hartford, CT 06106
(203) 566-3385

Delaware State Travel Service
630 State College Rd.
Dover, DE 19901
(800) 441-8846

D.C. Office of Business & Economic
  Development
1350 Pennsylvania Ave., N.W.
Washington, DC 20004
(202) 727-6600

Florida Division of
  Economic Development
107 West Gaines St.
Tallahassee, FL 23011
(904) 487-1100

Georgia Dept. of Industry & Trade
P.O. Box 1776
Atlanta, GA 30301
(404) 656-3591

Hawaii Film Office
Dept. of Planning &
  Economic Development
P.O. Box 2359
Honolulu, HI 96804
(808) 548-4535

Idaho Film Bureau
Capitol Building
Boise, ID 83720
(208) 334-4357

Illinois Film Office
310 S. Michigan Ave.
Chicago, IL 60604
(312) 793-3600

Indiana Dept. of Commerce
440 N. Merdian St.
Indianapolis, IN 46204
(317) 232-8860

Iowa Development Commission
250 Jewett Building
Des Moines, IA 50309
(515) 281-3185

Kansas Dept. of
  Economic Development
503 Kansas Ave.
Topeka, KS 66603
(913) 296-3481

Kentucky Film Commission
Barry Hill Mansion
Frankfort, KY 40601
(502) 564-2240

Louisiana Film Commission
Box 44185
Baton Rouge, LA 70804
(504) 342-5403

Maine Film Commission
P.O. Box 8424
Portland, ME 04104
(207) 772-8529

Maryland Motion Picture &
  TV Development
2525 Riva Rd.
Annapolis, MD 21401
(301) 269-3500

Massachusetts Film Bureau
100 Cambridge St.
Boston, MA 02202
(617) 727-3330

Michigan Dept. of Commerce
Office of Film & TV Services
1200 Sixth St.
Detroit, MI 48226
(313) 256-9098

Minnesota Film Board
230 Nicollet Mall
Minneapolis, MN 55401
(601) 354-6710

Mississippi Film Commission
P.O. Box 849
Jackson, MS 39205
(601) 354-6710

Missouri Division of Tourism
P.O. Box 1055
Jefferson City, MO 65101
(314) 751-3246

Montana Dept. of Commerce
1424 9th Ave.
Helena, MT 59620
(406) 449-2654

Nebraska State Film Office
Box 94666
Lincoln, NE 68509
(402) 471-3791

Nevada Dept. of
  Economic Development
2501 E. Sahara
Las Vegas, NV 89104
(702) 386-5287

New Hampshire Film & TV Bureau
P.O. Box 856
Concord, NH 03301
(603) 271-2598

New Jersey Motion Picture &
  TV Commission
Gateway 1
Newark, NJ 07102
(201) 648-6279

New Mexico Motion Picture Bureau
1050 Old Pecos Trail
Santa Fe, NM 87503
(505) 827-2880

New York State Office for Motion
Picture & TV Development
230 Park Ave.
New York, NY 10169
(212) 949-8514

North Carolina Office of
Motion Picture Development
430 N. Salisbury St.
Raleigh, NC 27611
(919) 733-7651

North Dakota Dept. of Bus. &
Ind. Development
1050 E. Interstate Ave.
Bismarck, ND 58505
(701) 224-2810

Ohio Film Bureau
P.O. Box 1001
Columbus, OH 43216
(800) 848-1300

Oklahoma Film Industry Task Force
500 Will Rogers Blvd.
Oklahoma City, OK 73105
(405) 521-3525

Oregon Economic
Development Dept.
155 Cottage St. N.E.
Salem, OR 97310
(503) 378-4735

Pennsylvania Dept. of Commerce
461 Forum Bldg.
Harrisburg, PA 17120
(717) 787-5333

Puerto Rico Institute for Film & TV
P.O. Box 4682 Minillas Station
Santcurce, PR 00936
(809) 754-8580

Rhode Island Dept. of
Economic Development
7 Jackson Walkway
Province, RI 02903
(401) 277-2601

South Carolina Educational
TV Network
2712 Millwood Ave.
Columbia, SC 29250
(803) 758-3091

South Dakota Dept. of Economic
&Tourism Development
221 South Central
Pierre, SD 57501
(605) 773-3301

Tennessee Film Commission
James K. Polk Bldg.
Nashville, TN 37219
(800) 251-8594

Texas Film Commission
P.O. Box 12428
Austin, TX 78711
(512) 475-3785

Utah Film Development
200 S. Main
Salt Lake City, UT 84101
(800) 453-8824

Vermont Agency of Development
& Community Affairs
61 Elm St.
Montpelier, VT 05602
(802) 828-3236

Virgin Islands Film Promotion Office
P.O. Box 6400
St. Thomas, VI 00801
(809) 774-8784

Virginia Film Office
282 N. 9th St.
Richmond, VA 23219
(804) 786-4346

Washington Dept. of Commerce
& Economic Development
312 First Ave. North
Seattle, WA 98109
(206) 464-7143

West Virginia Economic &
   Commerce Development Office
Rotunda 150
Charleston, WV 23505
(304) 348-0400

Wisconsin Film &
   TV Administration
123 West Washington St.
Madison, WI 53702
(608) 266-7018

Wyoming Travel Commission
Interstate 25 at Etchepare Circle
Cheyenne, WY 82002
(307) 777-7777

Appendix E
Professional Guilds, Unions, and Associations

Academy of Motion Picture Arts and
  Sciences
8949 Wilshire Blvd.
Beverly Hills, CA 90211
(213) 278-8900

Academy of TV Arts and Sciences
  (Hollywood)
5605 Lankershim Blvd.
N. Hollywood, CA 91609
(818) 506-7880

Actors' Equity Association
1560 Broadway
New York, NY 10036
(818) 869-8530

Alliance of Motion Picture &
  TV Producers
14144 Ventura Blvd.
Sherman Oaks, CA 91423
(818) 995-3600

American Federation of Television
  and Radio Artists (AFTRA)
1717 N. Highland
Hollywood, CA 90028
(213) 461-8111

American Film Institute (AFI)
2021 N. Western Ave.
Los Angeles, CA 90027
(213) 856-7600

American Federation of Television
  and Radio Artists (AFTRA)
1717 N. Highland
Hollywood, CA 90028
(213) 461-8111

American Film Institute (AFI)
2021 N. Western Ave.
Los Angeles, CA 90027
(213) 856-7600

Association of Motion Picture and
  TV Producers, Inc. (AMPTP)
8480 Beverly Blvd.
Los Angeles, CA 90048
(213) 653-2200

Broadcast Education Association
1771 N St., N.W.
Washington, D.C. 20036
(202) 293-3518

Directors Guild of America, Inc.
7950 Sunset Blvd.
Hollywood, CA 90046
(213) 656-1220

Independent Producers Association
10501 Wilshire Blvd.
Los Angeles, CA 90024
(213) 279-2187

Information Film Producers of
  America
750 E. Colorado Blvd.
Pasadena, CA 91101
(213) 795-7866

International Radio and TV Society
420 Lexington Ave.
New York, NY 10017
(212) 532-4546

Motion Picture Association of
  America (MPAA)
14144 Ventura Blvd.
Sherman Oaks, CA 91423
(213) 995-3600

National Academy of TV Arts and
  Sciences
110 W. 57th St.
New York, NY 10019
(212) 586-8424

National Association of Broadcasters
  (NAB)
1771 N Street, N.W.
Washington, DC 20036
(202) 293-3500

PEN (Poets, Playwrights, Essayists,
  Editors, and Novelists)
American Center
47 Fifth Ave.
New York, NY 10010
(212) 255-1977

Producers Guild of America
292 S. La Cienega Blvd.
Beverly Hills, CA 90211
(213) 659-3053

Screen Actors Guild (SAG)
7750 Sunset Blvd.
Hollywood, CA 90046
(213) 876-3030

Story Analysts, Local 854, IATSE
7715 Sunset Blvd.
Los Angeles, CA 90046
(213) 876-4433

Women in Film
8489 W. Third St., Suite 25
Los Angeles, CA 90048
(213) 651-3680

Writers Guild of America, East, Inc.
555 W. 57th St.
New York, NY 10019
(212) 245-6180

Writers Guild of America, West, Inc.
8955 Beverly Blvd.
Los Angeles, CA 90048
(213) 550-1000

Appendix F
Agents for Television and Film Writers

The following is a list of agents who have subscribed to the W.G.A.-Artists' Manager Basic Agreement. It is reprinted with the permission of the Writers Guild of America, West. The Guild does not endorse any of these agencies, nor will it assist writers in finding, selecting, or recommending specific agents.

The Guild suggests that you contact the agency by letter or phone, detailing professional and/or academic credentials, and describing the nature of the project. If the agency expresses interest in seeing the manuscript, a stamped self-addressed envelope should be enclosed. Even so, be advised that the material might not be returned.

Agencies with a single asterisk (*) indicate they will consider unsolicited material from writers. A double asterisk (**) indicates they will consider unsolicited material from writers only as a result of references from people known to the agency. However, the Guild has received a number of complaints from new writers seeking representation. Even though the intent has been expressed, many agents are not able to afford the time or commitment to read unsolicited material.

For an updated listing of agencies signed to the Artists' Manager Basic Agreement, contact the Writers Guild of America, West (8955 Beverly Blvd., Los Angeles, CA 90048). For a list of agents signed through the Society of Authors Representatives, contact the Writers Guild of America, East (555 W. 57th St., New York, NY 10019).

*Act 48 Mgmt., 1501 Broadway #1713, NY (10036), 212/354-4250

Adams Limited, Bret, 448 W. 44th St., NY (10036), 212/765-5630

**Adams, Ray & Rosenberg, (P) 9200 Sunset Blvd. PH 25, LA (90069), 278-3000

**Agency For The Performing Arts, (P), 9000 Sunset Bl., #1200, LA (90069), 273-0744

Agency For The Performing Arts (P), 888 7th Ave., NY (10016), 212/582-1500

*All Talent Agency, 2437 E. Washington Bl., Pasadena (91104), 797-2422

*Allan Agency, Lee, 4571 N. 68th St., Milwaukee, WI (53218), 414/463-7441

**Altoni, Buddy, PO Box 1022, Newport Beach, CA (92663), 714/851-1711

Amsel & Assoc., Fred, 291 S. La Cienega Blvd., #307, BH (90211), 855-1200

Artists Agency, The (P), 10000 Santa Monica Bl., #305, LA (90067), 277-7779

**Artists Career Mgmt., 9157 Sunset Bl., LA (90069), 278-9157

Artists' Entertainment Agency (P), 10100 Santa Monica Blvd., #348, LA (90067), 557-2507

*Artists Group, The, 10100 Santa Monica Bl., #310, LA (90067), 552-1100

Associated Artists Mgmt., 1501 Broadway, #1808A NY (10036), 212/398-0460

**Associated Talent Agency, 8816 Burton Way, BH (90211), 271-4662

Barskin Agency, The, 11240 Magnolia Bl. #201, NY (91601), 985-2992

*Barnett Agency, Gary Jay, Box 333 Bay Station, Brooklyn, NY (11235), 212/332-2894

Beakel & Jennings Agency, 427 N. Canon Dr. #205, BH (90210), 274-5418

Berger Associates, Bill (S), 444 E. 58th St., NY (10022), 212/486-9588

**Berkeley Square Literary Agency, P.O. Box 25324, LA (90025), 478-5745

Berman, Lois, 240 W. 44th St., NY (10036), 212/575-5114

**Berkus-Cosay-Stein (P), 1900 Ave. of the Stars, #1530, LA (90067), 277-9090

**Bernacchi & Assoc., Shauna, 1100 Glendon Ave., LA (90024), 824-0542

Bernstein, Ron, 119 W. 57th St., NY (10019), 212/265-0750

*Big Red Talent Ent., 8330 Third St., LA (90048), 463-4982

**Bloom, Levy, Shorr & Assoc., 800 S. Robertson Blvd., LA (90035), 659-6160

Bloom, Harry, 8833 Sunset Blvd. #202, LA (90069), 659-5985

Bloom, J. Michael, 400 Madison Ave. 20th Fl., NY (10017), 212/832-6900

Bloom, J. Michael, 9200 Sunset Bl., #1210, LA (90069), 275-6800

Boyd Talent Agency, The, 3575 Cahuenga Blvd. West, #240, Hwd. (90068), 876-3102

Brandon & Assoc., Paul. 9046 Sunset Bl., LA (90069), 273-6173

Brandt & Brandt (S), 1501 Broadway, NY (10036), 212/840-5760

Breitner Literary Assoc., Susan, 1650 Broadway #501, NY (10019), 212/246-0546

Brebner Agencies, 185 Berry St., Bldg. 2, #144, SF (94017), 415/495-6700

Brewis Agency, Alex, 8721 Sunset Bl., LA (90069), 274-9874

**Broder/Kurland Agency, The (P), 9046 Sunset Bl. #202, LA (90069), 274-8921

*Brody, Howard T., 11741 NW 33 St., Sunrise, FL (33323) 305/741-1685

Brooke-Dunn-Oliver, 9165 Sunset Blvd., #202, LA (90069), 859-1405

Brown Agency, J., 8733 Sunset Blvd. #102, LA (90069), 550-0296

Brown, Ltd., Curtis (S), 575 Madison Ave., NY (10022), 212/755-4200

Brown, Ned, 407 N. Maple Dr., BH (90210), 276-1131

Buchwald & Assoc., Don, 10 E. 44th St., NY (10017), 212/867-1070

*Butler, Ruth, 8622 Reseda Bl., #211, Northridge (91324), 886-8440

*Calder Agency, 4150 Riverside Dr., Burbank, (91505), 845-7434

Career Mgmt., 435 S. La Cienega Blvd., #108, LA (90048), 657-1020

*Carpenter Co., 1434-6th Ave., San Diego (92101), 619/235-8482

Carroll Agency, William, 448 N. Golden Mall, Burbank (91502), 848-9948

Carvanis Agency, Maria, 235 West End Ave., NY (10023), 212/580-1559

**Case, Bertha, 345 W. 58th St., NY (10019), 212/541-9451

Catalytic Agent, The, 685 West End Ave., NY (10025), 212/666-3991

**Cavaleri & Associates, 6605 Hollywood Blvd. #220, Hwd. (90028), 461-2940

Charter Mgmt., 9000 Sunset Blvd. #1112, LA (90069), 278-1690

Chasin-Park-Citron Agency, 9255 Sunset Bl., LA (90069), 273-7190

Chasman & Strick, Assoc., 6725 Sunset Bl. #506, Hwd. (90028), 463-1115

**Clients' Agency, The, 2029 Century Park East, #1330, LA (90067), 277-8492

*CNA & Associates, 8721 Sunset Blvd., #102, LA (90069), 657-2063

Colton, Kingsley & Assoc., 321 S. Beverly Dr., BH (90212), 277-5491

Conejo Agency, 247 Green Heath, Pl., Thousand Oaks (91361), 805/497-2214

Connell & Assoc., Polly, 4605 Lankershim Bl., NH (91602), 985-6266

Contemporary-Korman Artists, 132 Lasky Dr., BH (90212), 278-8250

**Conway & Assoc., Ben, 999 N. Doheny Dr., LA (90069), 271-8133

*Cooper Agency, The (P), 1900 Ave. of the Stars, #2535, LA (90067), 277-8422

Creative Artists Agency (P), 1888 Century Pk. E., LA (90067), 277-4545

*Cumber Attractions, Lil, 6515 Sunset Bl., Hwd. (90028), 469-1919

*C.W.A. Chateau of Talent, 1633 Vista Del Mar, Hwd. (90028), 461-2727

**D, H, K, P, R, 7319 Beverly Bl., LA (90036), 857-1234

*D.J. Enterprises, 339 S. Franklin St., Allentown, PA (18102), 215/437-0723

DMI Talent Agency, 250 W. 57th St., #713, NY (10107), 212/246-4650

Dade/Rosen Assoc., 9172 Sunset Bl. #2, LA (90069), 278-7077

*Daimler Artists Agency, 2007 Wilshire Blvd., #808, LA (90058), 483-9783

**Davis Agency, Dona Lee, 3518 W. Cahuenga Blvd., Hwd. (90068), 850-1205

*Dellwood Enterprises, 409 N. Camden Dr., #206, BH (90210), 271-7847

DeMille Talent Agency, Diana, 12457 Ventura Blvd., #104, SC (91604), 761-7171

Dennis, Karg, Dennis and Co., 470 S. San Vicente Blvd., LA (90048), 651-1700

Diamant, Anita (S), 51 E. 42nd St., NY (10017), 212/687-1122

**Diamond Artists, 9200 Sunset Bl. #909, LA (90069), 278-8146

Donadio & Associates, Candida (S), 111 W. 57th St., NY (10019), 212/757-7076

**Dorese Agency, Alyss Barlow, 41 W. 82nd St., NY (10024), 212/580-2855

**Dubose Associates, Albert, One Sherman Square, NY (10023), 212/580-9790

Eisenbach-Greene (P), 760 N. La Cienega Bl., LA (90069), 659-3420

Elmo Agency, Ann (S), 60 E. 42nd St., NY (10165), 212/661-2880

Exclusive Artists Agency, 4040 Vineland Blvd., #225, SC (91604) 761-1154

*Ferguson & Berry Talent Agency, 1090 S. La Brea Ave., #201, LA (90019), 857-0519

Film Artists Associates, Inc., 9200 Sunset Bl. #431, LA (90069), 275-6193

Film Artists Mgmt. Enterprises, 8278 Sunset Bl., LA (90046), 556-8071

Fischer Co., Sy, (P), 1 E. 57th St., NY (10022), 212/486-0426

Fischer Co., Sy (P), 10960 Wilshire Blvd. #922, LA (90024), 557-0388

Fox Chase Agency (S), 419 E. 57th St., NY (10022), 212/752-8211

Freeman-Wyckoff & Assoc., 6331 Hollywood Bl. #1122, LA (90028), 464-4866

Frings Agency, Kurt, 415 S. Crescent Dr., #320, BH (90210), 274-8881

*Garrick Int'l Agency, Dale, 8831 Sunset Blvd., LA (90069), 657-2661

**Gerard, Paul, 2918 Alta Vista, Newport Bch, CA (92660), 714/644-7950

**Gerritsen International, 8721 Sunset Blvd., #203, LA (90069), 659-8414

Gersh Agency Inc., The, 222 N. Canon Dr., BH (90210), 274-6611

Gibson Agency, J. Carter, 9000 Sunset Blvd., #811, LA (90069), 274-8813

**GMA, 1741 N. Ivar St., #221, Hwd. (90028), 466-7161

*Gold Talent Agency, Harry, 8295 Sunset Blvd., #202, LA (90064), 654-5550

Goldman & Novell Agency, The, 6383 Wilshire Blvd., #115, LA (90048), 651-4578

Goldstein & Assoc., Allen, 9000 Sunset Bl., #1105, LA (90069), 278-5005

Grashin Agency, Mauri, 8170 Beverly Bl. #109, LA (90048), 651-1828

Green Agency, Ivan, The, 1888 Century Pk. E. #908, LA (90067), 277-1541

Groffsky Literary Agency, Maxine, 2 Fifth Ave., NY (10011), 212/677-2720

Grossman & Assoc., Larry, 211 S. Beverly Dr. #206, BH (90212), 550-8127

Grossman-Stalmaster Agency, 10100 Santa Monica Blvd., #310, LA (90067), 552-0905

**Halsey Agency, Reece, 8733 Sunset Bl., LA (90069), 652-2409

Hamilburg Agency, Mitchell, 292 S. La Cienega. Bl., BH (90211), 657-1501

**Hannaway-We-Go, 1741 N. Ivar St., #102, Hwd (90028), 854-3999

**Harris Mgmt., Mark, 10100 Santa Monica Blvd. #310, LA (90067), 552-1100

Harvey, Helen (S), 410 W. 24th St., NY (10011), 212/675-7445

**Heacock Literary Agency, Inc., 1523 6th St., SM (90401), 393-6227

**Henderson/Hogan Agency, 247 S. Beverly Dr., BH (90212), 274-7815

Henderson/Hogan Agency, 200 W. 57th St., NY (10019), 212/765-5190

**Henry, Kevin Jon, 2301 Westwood Blvd., LA (90064), 475-9737

**Hesseltine/Baker Associates, 165 W. 46th St., #409, NY (10036), 212/921-4460 Letters only

Holland Agency, Calvin Bruce, 1836 E. 18th St., Brooklyn, NY (11229), 212/375-4863

*Hollywood Talent Agency, 213 Brock Ave., Toronto, Ont., Canada M6K 2L8 414/531-3180

**Hunt Mgmt., Diana, 44 W. 44th St., #1414, NY (10036), 212/391-4971

**Hunt & Associates, George, 8350 Santa Monica Bl., LA (90069), 654-6600

*Hyman, Ansley Q., 3123 Cahuenga Bl. W., LA (90068), 851-9198

International Creative Mgmt. (P), 8899 Beverly Bl., LA (90048), 550-4000

International Creative Mgmt. (P), 40 W. 57th St., NY (10019), 212/556-5600

International Literary Agents, 9601 Wilshire Bl. #300, BH (90210), 278-4141

*Jaffe Representatives, 140 7th Ave. #2L, NY (10011), 212/741-1359

*Joseph/Knight Agency, 6331 Hollywood Blvd., #924, Hwd (90028), 465-5474

*Kalmus, Michael L., 90 Gold St., NY (10038), 212/732-0127

Kane Agency, Merrily, 9171 Wilshire Bl. #310, BH (90210), 550-8874

**Kaplan-Stahler Agency, 119 N. San Vicente Blvd., BH (90211), 653-4483

Karlan Agency, Patricia, 3815 W. Olive Ave. #202, Burbank (91505), 954-8848

**Karlin Agency, Larry, 10850 Wilshire Bl. #600, LA (90024), 475-4828

*Kerwin Agency, Wm., 1605 N. Cahuenga Bl. #202, Hwd. (90028), 469-5155

**Keynan-Goff Assoc., 2049 Century Park East, #4370, LA (90067), 556-0339

*Kimberly Agency, 3950 W. 6th St. #203, LA (90020), 738-6087

*King, Ltd., Archer, 1440 Broadway #2100, NY (10018), 212/764-3505

*King Agency, Howard, 9060 Santa Monica Blvd. #104, LA (90069), 858-8048

*Kingsley Corp., 112 Barnsbee Ln., Coventry, CT (06238), 203/742-9575

**Kohner Agency, Paul, (P), 9169 Sunset Bl., LA (90069), 550-1060

**Kopaloff Company, The, 9046 Sunset Blvd. #201, LA (90069), 273-6173

*Kratz & Co., 210 5th Ave., NY (10010), 212/683-9222

Kroll Agency, Lucy (S), 390 West End Ave., NY (10024), 212/877-0627

**Lake Office, Candace, 1103 Glendon Ave., LA (90024), 824-9706

Lantz Office, The, 888 Seventh Ave., NY (10106), 212/586-0200

Lantz Office, The, 9255 Sunset Bl. #505, LA (90069), 858-1144

Lazar, Irving Paul, 211 S. Beverly Dr., BH (90212), 275-6153

*Lee Literary Agency, L. Harry, Box 203, Rocky Point, NY (11778), Letters Only 516/744-1188

Lenny Assoc., Jack, 9701 Wilshire Bl., BH (90212), 271-2174

Lenny Assoc., Jack, 140 W. 58th St., NY (10019), 212/582-0272

Light Co., The, 113 N. Robertson Bl., LA (90048), 273-9602

Light Co., The, 1443 Wazee St., 3rd Fl., Denver, CO (80202), 303/572-8363

**Literary Artists Mgmt., P.O. Box 1604, Monterey, CA (93940), 408/899-7145

*Literary Associates, 9701 Wilshire Blvd. #850, BH (90212), 550-0077

Littman Co., Robert, 409 N. Camden Dr., #105, BH (90210), 278-1572

*London Star Promotions, 7131 Owensmouth Ave., #C116, Canoga Park (91303), 709-0447

Loo, Bessie, 8235 Santa Monica Bl., LA (90046), 650-1300

Lund Agency, The, 6515 Sunset Blvd., #304, Hwd (90028), 466-8280

Lynne & Reilly Agency, 6290 Sunset Bl. #1002, Hwd. (90028), 461-2828

Lyons Agency, Grace, 203 S. Beverly Dr., #102, BH (90212), 652-5290

Major Talent Agency (P), 11812 San Vicente Bl., #510, LA (90049), 820-5841

**Mann Agency, Sheri, 1623 Vista Del Mar Ave., LA (90048), 462-4008

*Maris Agency, 17620 Sherman Way, #8 Van Nuys, CA (91406), 708-2493

Markson Lit. Agency, Elaine, 44 Greenwich Ave., NY (10011), 212/243-8480

**Markson Literary Agency, Raya, 6015 Santa Monica Blvd., Hwd (90038), 552-2083

**Matson Co., Harold, 276 5th Ave., NY (10001), 212/679-4490

McCartt, Oreck, Barrett, 9200 Sunset Bl. #531, Hwd. (90069), 278-6243

McIntosh & Otis (S), 475 5th Ave., NY (10017), 212/689-1050

Medford Agency, Ben, 139 S. Beverly Dr. #329, BH (90212), 278-0017

Merit Agency, The, 12926 Riverside Dr. #C, SO (91423), 986-3017

Merrill, Helen (S), 337 W. 22nd St., NY (10011), 212/924-6314

Messenger Agency, Fred, 8235 Santa Monica Bl., LA (90046), 654-3800

**Miller Agency, Peter, The, P.O. Box 764, Midtown Station, NY (10018), 212/221-8329

**Mills, Ltd., Robert P., 333 5th Ave., NY (10016), 212/685-6575

Morris Agency, William (P), 151 El Camino Dr., BH (90212), 274-7451

Morris Agency, William (P), 1350 Ave/Americas, NY (10019), 212/586-5100

Morton Agency, 1105 Glendon Ave., LA (90024), 824-4089

**Moss, Marvin, (P), 9200 Sunset Bl., LA (90069), 274-8483

Murphy Agency, Mary, 10701 Riverside Dr., NH (91602), 985-4241

**Nachtigall Agency, The, 1885 Lombard St., SF (94123), 415/346-1115

Neighbors, Charles, 240 Waverly Pl., NY (10014), 212/924-8296

*Northern California Casting, 595 Mission St., #404, SF (94105), 415/495-5945

Ober & Associates, Harold (S), 40 E. 49th St., NY (10017), 212/759-8600

Oscard Assoc., Fifi, 19 W. 44th St., NY (10022), 212/764-1100

*Panda Agency, 3721 Hoen Ave., Santa Rosa, CA (95405), 707/544-3671

Paramuse Artists Associates, 1414 Avenue of the Americas, NY (10019), 212/758-5055

Phoenix Literary Agency, 150 E. 74th St., NY (10021), 212/838-4060

Pickman Co., The, 9025 Wilshire Bl. #303, BH (90211), 273-8273

**Pleshette Agency, Lynn, 2700 N. Beachwood Dr., Hwd. (90028), 465-0428

**Preminger Agency, Jim (P), 1650 Westwood Bl. #201, LA (90024), 475-9491

Prescott Agency, Guy, The, 8920 Wonderland Ave., LA (90046), 656-1963

*Professional Authors Literary Services, 4237-2 Keanu St., Honolulu, HI (96816), 808/734-5469

Progressive Artists Agency, 400 S. Beverly Dr., BH (90212), 553-8561

*Protter, Susan Ann, 110 W. 40th St., #1408, NY (10018), 212/840-0480

Raines & Raines (S), 475 5th Ave., NY (10017), 212/684-5160

Raper Enterprises Agency, 9441 Wilshire Bl. #620D, BH (90210), 273-7704

Rappa Agency, Ray, 7471 Melrose Ave., #11, LA (90046), 650-1190

**Regency Artists Ltd., 9200 Sunset Blvd., #823, LA (90069), 273-7103

*Rhodes Literary Agency, 140 West End Ave., NY (10023), 212/580-1300 Letters Only

**Richland Agency, The, 1888 Century Park East, #1107, LA (90067), 553-1257

Roberts Co., The, 427 N. Canon Dr., BH (90210), 275-9384

*Roberts, Flora, 157 W. 57th St., NY (10019), 212/355-4165

Robinson-Luttrell & Assoc., 141 El Camino Dr. #110, BH (90212), 275-6114

**Rogers & Assoc., Stephanie, 9100 Sunset Bl., #340, LA (90069), 278-2015

Rose Agency, Jack, 6430 Sunset Blvd., #1203, Hwd (90028), 463-7300

**Rosenstone/Wender 3 E. 48th St., NY (10017), 212/832-8330

**Ross Assoc., Eric, 60 E. 42nd St. #426, NY (10017), 212/687-9797

Sackheim Agency, The, 9301 Wilshire Bl., BH (90210), 858-0606

Safier, Gloria (S), 667 Madison Ave., NY (10021), 212/838-4868

**Sanders' Agency, Honey, 229 W. 42nd St. #404, NY (10036), 212/947-5555

**Sanders Agency, Norah, 1100 Glendon Ave., PH, LA (90024), 824-2264

**San Fran. Agency, 899 E. Francisco Bl.-E, San Rafael (94901), 415/456-7140

**Sanford-Beckett Agency, 1015 Gayley Ave., LA (90024), 208-2100

*SBK Assoc., 11 Chamberlain, Waltham, MA (02154), 617/894-4037

**Schechter, Irv (P), 9300 Wilshire Blvd., #410, BH (90212), 278-8070

*Schuster-Dowdell Org., The, PO Box 2, Valhalla, NY (10595), 914/761-3106

Seiden & Assoc., 13735 Victory Bl., Van Nuys (91401), 780-2288

*Selected Artists Agency, 12711 Ventura Bl. #460, SC (91604), 763-9731 Calls Only

Shapira & Assoc., David, 15301 Ventura Blvd. #345, SO (91403), 906-0322

*Shapiro-Lichtman, Inc. (P), 2049 Century Pk. E. #1320, LA (90067), 557-2244

**Shaw Agency, Glenn, 3330 Barham Bl., Hwd. (90068), 851-6262

Shedd Agency, Jacqueline, 9701 Wilshire Blvd., BH (90212), 274-0978

Sherrell Agency, Lew, 7060 Hollywood Bl., Hwd. (90028), 461-9955

Shiffrin-Barr Artists, 7466 Beverly Bl., #205, (90036), 937-3937

**Shumaker Talent Agency, The, 10850 Riverside Dr., #410, NY (91609), 877-3370

Siegel Assoc., Jerome, 8733 Sunset Bl., LA (90069), 652-6033

Smith, Gerald K., PO Box 7430, Burbank, CA (91510), 849-5388

**Smith-Freedman & Assoc., 9869 Santa Monica Bl., BH (90212), 277-8464

*Socio-Economic Research Inst. of America, Lamoree Rd., Rhinebeck, NY (12572), 914/876-3036

**Starbrite, 409 Alberto Way #C, Los Gatos, CA (95030), 408/253-1991

Starkman Agency, The, 1501 Broadway, #301 A, NY (10036), 212/921-9191

*Starr Agency, The, Box 546, Jacksonville, FL (32201), 904/743-5807

**Steele & Assoc., Ellen Lively, P.O. Box 188, Organ, (NM) (88052), 505/382-5863

Stone-Masser Agency, 1052 Carol Dr., LA (90069), 275-9599

*Sugho Agency, Larry, 1017 N. La Cienega Bl., #305, LA (90069), 628-6857

**Swanson, H. N., 8523 Sunset Bl., LA (90069), 652-5385

Talent Ent. Agency, 1607 N. El Centro Ave., #2, Hwd. (90028), 462-0913

Talent Mgmt. International, 6380 Wilshire Bl., #910, LA (90048), 273-4000

Targ Literary Agency, Roslyn (S), 250 W. 57th St., NY (10107), 212/582-4210

*Tel-Screen Artists Int'l., 7965 SW 146 St., Miami, FL (33158), 305/235-2722

**Thompson, Willie, 3902 6th St., #213, LA (90020), 380-0676

Tobias & Assoc., Herb, 1901 Ave. of the Stars #840, LA (90067), 277-6211

Twentieth Century Artists, 13273 Ventura Bl., Studio City (91604), 990-8580

**Universal Artists Agency, 9465 Wilshire Blvd., #616, BH (90212), 278-2425

*Vamp Talent Agency, 713 E. La Loma Ave. #1, Somis, CA (93066), 805/485-2001

*Wain Agency, Erika, 1418 N. Highland Ave. #102, Hwd. (90028), 460-4224

Wallace & Sheil Agency (S), 177 E. 70th St., NY (10021), 212/570-9090

Wasserman Co., Hillel Avery, 704 N. Gardner Ave. #3, LA (90046), 653-3616

*Waugh Agency, Ann, 4731 Laurel Cyn. Blvd., #5, NH (91607), 980-0141

Wax & Associates, Elliott (P), 273-8217

Webb, Ruth, 7500 Devista Dr., LA (90046), 874-1700

Weitzman & Assoc., Lew, (P), 14144 Ventura Blvd., #200, SO (91423), 995-4400

**William Jeffreys Agency, 8455 Beverly Blvd., #408, LA (90048), 651-3193

**Witzer Agency, Ted, 1900 Ave. of the Stars #2850, LA (90067), 552-9521

World Class Talent Agency, 8530 Wilshire Bl. #203-A, BH (90211), 655-9326

Wormser, Heldfond & Joseph, 1717 N. Highland Ave., Hwd. (90028), 466-9111

Wosk Agency, Sylvia, 439 S. La Cienega Bl., LA (90048), 274-8063

*Wright Assoc., Ann, 8422 Melrose Pl., LA (90069), 655-5040 Letters Only

Wright Rep., Ann, 136 E. 57th St., NY (10022), 212/832-0110

Writers & Artists Agency (P), 11726 San Vicente Blvd., #300, LA (90049), 820-2240

Writers & Artists Agency (P), 162 W. 56th St., NY (10019), 212/246-9029

**Wunsch Agency, The, 9200 Sunset Blvd., #808, LA (90069), 278-1955

Ziegler Associates, Inc. (P), 9255 Sunset Bl., LA (90069), 278-0070

LA—	Los Angeles	NH—	North Hollywood
BH—	Beverly Hills	NY—	New York, New York
Hwd—	Hollywood	SM—	Santa Monica
SC—	Studio City	SF—	San Francisco
SO—	Sherman Oaks	(P)	Indicates packaging agency.
		(S)	Society of Authors Representatives—signed through WGAE only.

All telephone numbers are Area Code 213 or 818
unless otherwise noted.

Appendix G
Trade Publications and Periodicals

(Note: For a listing of industry directories and other marketing resources, see the *Annotated Bibliography*, pp. 274–275.)

Advertising Age (biweekly)
220 E. 42 St.
New York, NY
(212) 210-0100

American Film (monthly)
American Film Institute
JFK Center for Performing Arts
Washington, D.C. 20566
(202) 828-4000

Backstage (weekly)
1411 Broadway
New York, NY 10036
(212) 391-1030

Broadcasting (weekly)
1735 DeSales St., N.W.
Washington, D.C. 20036
(202) 638-1022

CableVision (weekly)
2500 Curtis St.
Denver, CO 80205
(303) 573-1433

Channels (bimonthly)
Box 2001
Mahopac, NY 10541
(914) 628-1154

Current (public broadcasting)
Box 53358
Washington, D.C. 20009
(202) 332-8580

Daily Variety (daily)
1400 N. Cahuenga Blvd.
Hollywood, CA 90028
(213) 469-1141

Editor and Publisher (weekly)
850 Third Ave.
New York, NY 10022
(212) 752-7050

Emmy (quarterly)
Academy of TV Arts and Sciences
4605 Lankershim Blvd.
N. Hollywood, CA 91602
(213) 506-7885

**Grants and Awards Available to
   American Writers** (annual)
P.E.N.
American Center
47 Fifth Ave.
New York, NY 10010
(212) 255-1977

The Hollywood Reporter (daily)
6715 Sunset Blvd.
Hollywood, CA 90028
(213) 464-7411

Media Report to Women (monthly)
3306 Ross Place, N.W.
Washington, D.C. 20008
(202) 363-0812

MultiChannel News
633 Third Ave.
New York, NY
(212) 741-6208

Ross Reports (monthly)
Television Index, Inc.
150 Fifth Ave.
New York, NY 10011
(212) 924-0320

Show Business News (weekly)
1301 Broadway
New York, NY 10036
(212)354-7600

Television Quarterly (quarterly)
National Academy of TV Arts and
Sciences

110 W. 57th St.
New York, NY 10019
(212) 586-8424

Television/Radio Age
1270 Ave. of Americas
New York, NY 10010
(212) 757-8400

Variety (weekly)
154 West 46th St.
New York, NY 10036
(212) 582-2700

View (weekly)
150 E. 58 St.
New York, NY 10155
(212) 486-7111

WGAW Newsletter (monthly)
Writers Guild of America West
8955 Beverly Blvd.
Los Angeles, CA 90048
(213) 550-1000

The Writer (monthly)
8 Arlington St.
Boston, MA 02116
(617) 536-7420

Writer's Digest (monthly)
9933 Alliance Rd.
Cincinnati, OH 45242
(513) 984-0717

Writers Market (annual)
9933 Alliance Rd.
Cincinnati, OH 45242
(513) 984-0717

The Writer's Yearbook (annual)
9933 Alliance Rd.
Cincinnati, OH 45242
(513) 984-0717

Annotated Bibliography
for the TV Writer

Program Development and the Networks

Bedell, Sally. *Up The Tube: Prime Time TV and the Silverman Years.* New York: Viking Press, 1981. A hard look at the programming activities and competition at the networks during Fred Silverman's reign. A well-documented investigation into network programming practices.

Brown, Les. *Television: The Business Behind the Box.* New York: Harcourt Brace Jovanich, 1971. A straight-from-the-hip account of programming practices and conflicts at the networks.

Froug, William, ed. *The Screenwriter Looks at the Screenwriter.* New York: Dell Publishing, 1972. An informative compilation of interviews with outspoken screenwriters, who discuss their theories and thoughts on writing as a profession.

Goldman, William. *Adventures in the Screen Trade: A Personal View of Hollywood and Screenwriting.* New York: Warner Books, 1983. An excellent account of the development and production problems faced by Goldman in his Academy award winning films. The book offers practical insights into all areas of screenwriting, including studio anecdotes, script samples, and very useful advice for film and television writers.

Levinson, Richard and William Link. *Stay Tuned: An Inside Look at the Making of Prime Time Television.* New York: St. Martin's Press, 1981. Two of the successful writers/producers in Hollywood offer a splendid look at the development stages and management obstacles encountered during the making of their TV series and television films.

Miller, Merle and Evan Rhodes. *Only You, Dick Daring.* New York: William Sloan and Associates, 1964. This remains a classic demonstration of how a pilot is developed by the writer, aborted by the studio, and mangled by the network.

Mitz, Rick. *The Great American TV Sitcom Book.* New York: Marek, 1980. A compilation of sitcom greats.

Shanks, Bob. *The Cool Fire: How to Make it in Television.* New York: Vintage Books, 1977. This paperback is *essential* reading. Shanks offers unique and personal insights into the television industry from programming to production. He also has a very strong chapter on presentations and scripting.

Skaggs, Calvin. *American Short Story,* Vols I, II. New York: Dell, 1980. A collection of short stories adapted for the PBS series and funded by NEH. Includes stories and scenes from the script.

Whitfield, Steve and Gene Roddenberry. *The Making of Star Trek.* New York: Ballantine Books, 1972. This paperback provides a historical account of how the series was put together, from conception and development to sale and production. The original series presentation is included.

Grants and Non-Commercial Funding

AFI Guide to College Courses in Film & TV, 7th ed. N.J.: Peterson's Guides, 1980. A comprehensive profile of over 1,000 colleges and universities offering film and TV courses, including titles, facilities, faculty, undergraduate and graduate programs, scholarships.

Annual Register of Grant Support. Chicago: Marquis Academic Media. This annual register offers information on writing proposals and provides an index to grant programs catalogued by subject, e.g., media.

Brown, James W., ed. *Educational Media Yearbook.* New York: R. R. Bowker. This annual publication lists federal funding sources for new projects in television and film.

Catalog of Federal Domestic Assistance. Washington, D.C.: U.S. Government Printing Office. This is an annual compilation of all RFPs (requests for proposals); available in libraries with U.S. government publications.

Cultural Directory II: Federal Funds and Services for the Arts & Humanities. Washington, D.C.: Smithsonian Institution Press, 1980. This directory identifies the federal funding programs available for individuals in the arts and humanities, as well as for artistic organizations. Written by Federal Council on the Arts & Humanities (1111 N. Capitol St., Washington, D.C. 20560).

Eles, Richard. *The Corporation and The Arts.* New York: MacMillan, 1967. A resource for understanding corporate support of the arts.

Film, Documentary, Media, and A/Vs. New York: Foundation Center. A concise resource about funding opportunities for TV and film projects.

Foundation Center National Data Book. New York: Foundation Center. Annual information on all non-profit organizations in the U.S.

Foundation Directory. New York: Columbia University Press. Extremely useful cross-indexed resource of over 21,000 foundations and subjects funded. Revised editions written by The Foundation Center, New York.

Foundation Grants to Individuals. New York: Foundation Center, 2nd ed., 1979. Lists almost 1,000 foundations awarding grants to individuals, including sample grants and list of recipients.

Gadney's Guide to 1800 International Contests, Festivals, & Grants in Film & Video. Glendale, Calif. Festival Publications. A cross-indexed reference for worldwide grants and competitive events in film, video, writing, and broadcasting.

Global Village Handbook for Independent Producers and Public TV. New York: Global Village, 1980. An exceptionally useful resource for writers and producers of public TV programs, including substantial information on funding sources.

Grants and Awards Available to American Writers. N.Y. PEN. Annual compilation of grants and awards for writers. Compiled by PEN (poets, playwrights, essayists, editors, novelists), American Center, New York.

Guide to Corporate Giving in the Arts. New York, American Council for the Arts, Susan Wagner, ed. A detailed resource on corporate giving patterns in the arts.

Guidelines and Formats for Submitting Program Production Proposals. Washington, D.C.: Corporation for Public Broadcasting. Guidelines established by CPB for submitting new program proposals.

Handbook for Independent Producers, Filmmakers, and Videomakers. New York: WNET-TV, Department of Program Planning. This brochure outlines the submission process for new projects at WNET-TV.

National Endowment for the Arts (NEA), Washington, D.C., publishes annual guidelines pertaining to their grant programs:

———. *Guide to NEA* provides information about the Endowment's major program areas.

———. *Literature Program* describes the support available for creative writers.

———. *Media Arts: Film/Radio/Television* describes the requirements for production aid and fellowships.

———. *Theatre Program* describes the support available to new playwrights and theatre companies.

National Endowment for the Humanities (NEH), Washington, D.C., publishes annual guidelines pertaining to their grant programs:

———. *Program Announcement* provides information about the Endowment's major program areas.

———. *Humanities Projects in Media* describes the requirements for script development and production support.

Milsaps, Daniel. *Grants and Aid to Individuals in the Arts,* 4th ed. Washington, D.C.: Washington International Arts Letter, 1978. This lists over a thousand foundations and agencies which support the arts (including TV and film programs).

———. *National Directory of Arts Support by Business Corporations.* Washington, D.C.: Washington International Arts Letter. Over 700 corporate contacts for arts projects (a plus), but no subject index (a minus).

Penny, Steve. *How to Get Grants to Make Films: A Guide to Media Grants, Film Grants Research.* Santa Barbara, California (P.O. Box 1138, Santa Barbara, CA 93102). A helpful guide to the funding process for filmmakers.

Proposal Writer's SWIPE File I, II. Washington, D.C.: Taft Corporation. The title tells all. These are professional grant proposals with appropriate styles, formats, and content.

Taft Corporation Foundation Directory, Washington, D.C.: Taft Corporation (1000 Vermont Ave., N.W., Washington, D.C. 20005), 1979. This directory lists corporate foundations and profiles their giving patterns.

What Makes a Good Proposal. New York: Foundation Center. A free, informative pamphlet from the Foundation Center.

What Will a Foundation Look for When You Submit a Grant Proposal. New York: Foundation Center. Another free and useful pamphlet available from the Foundation Center.

Periodicals on Grants

"ACA Reports," American Council for the Arts, 570 7th Ave., New York, NY 10018. Periodic reports on the arts in America, and funding activities.

"Arts Management," Arts Management, 408 W. 57th St., New York

NY 10019. Periodical on arts management, for those who finance, manage, and communicate the arts.

"Arts Reporting Service," 9214 Three Oaks Drive, Silver Spring, MD 20910. Bi-weekly newsletter on arts organizations and funding in the area.

"Communication Notes," Council of Communication Societies, P.O. Box 1074, Silver Spring, MD 20910. Monthly listing of events, awards, scholarships in communication.

"Arts Review," National Endowment for the Arts, Washington, D.C. 20506. Periodic publication that gives up-to-date information about grant activities in the arts. Write for free copy and subscription form.

"Foundation Center Source Book Profiles," Foundation Center, 888 7th Ave, New York, NY 10019. Bi-monthly updates on the largest grantmaking foundations in the U.S.

"Foundation News," Box 783, Old Chelsea Station, New York, NY 10011. Bi-monthly index of grants awarded (in excess of $5,000). Published by Council on Foundations.

"The Grantsmanship Center News," 1031 S. Grand Ave., Los Angeles, CA 90012. Bi-monthly newsletter on relevant issues, grant deadlines, new publications of interest.

"Washington International Arts Letter," P.O. Box 9005, Washington, D.C. 20003. Monthly newsletter which covers the spectrum of politics, legislation, and grant opportunities for artists with emphasis on NEA and NEH activities.

Dramatic Theory and Story Development

Archer, William. *Playmaking.* New York: Dodd, Mead & Co., 1912. Archer had no striking dramatic theory, but he sets out to *disprove* Bruntiere's law. He felt that crisis (rather than conflict of wills) is the chief requirement of drama. He was an early 20th century English critic.

Aristotle. *The Poetics.* (See S. H. Butcher.) Aristotle provided the first codification of dramatic theory in classic Greek times. He thought plot was the most important element in a play, and that it should be unified in time, place and action. He defined drama, partially, as an imitation of an action that is serious, complete, and of a certain magnitude. In his view, the impact of good drama creates an emotional catharsis for the audience.

Baker, George Pierce. *Dramatic Technique.* Boston: Houghton, Mifflin Co., 1919. Baker was the granddaddy of American playwriting teachers. He felt that a writer's major objective is to create an action which is capable of arousing audience emotions. The chief essential of drama is *action.*

Bentley, Eric. *Life of the Drama.* New York: Atheneum, 1964. This is a thought-provoking work by an outstanding contemporary American critic. Bentley parallels Aristotelian theory.

————. *The Playwright as Thinker: A Study of Drama in Modern Times.* New York: Harcourt, Brace, & World, rev. 1967. An excellent work of dramatic criticism, pointing to the problem of commercialism vs. art in theatre, and examining the work of selected playwrights.

Bruntiere, Ferdinand. *The Law of the Drama.* (1914). In Barrett H. Clark, *European Theories of the Drama.* Rev. ed. New York: D. Appleton-Century Co., 1965. Bruntiere was an important late 19th century French critic, extending Aristotle's concept of "conflict" in drama. Bruntiere proposed that drama is based on the conflict of wills among characters.

Butcher, S. H. *Aristotle's Theory of Poetry and Fine Art, With a Critical Text and Translation of the Poetics.* (Prefatory essay by John Gassner). New York: Dover Publications, 1951. This is one of the best translations of Aristotle's *Poetics.*

Clark, Barret H., ed. *European Theories of the Drama.* Rev. ed. New York: Crown Publishers, 1945; 1965. This is a classic resource for European dramatic theory.

Cole, Toby, ed. *Playwrights on Playwriting.* New York: Dramabook, 1961. An excellent compilation of theories, philosophies, and creative techniques expressed by a range of 20th century playwrights.

Dukore, Bernard, ed. *Dramatic Theory & Criticism: Greeks to Grotowski.* New York: Holt, Rinehart, & Winston, 1974. An excellent volume of dramatic criticism, excerpted from major writings of each period (classic times through late 20th century).

Egri, Lajos. *The Art of Dramatic Writing.* New York: Simon and Schuster, 1966. This is one of the most important and useful books for any writer of television, film, or the stage. Egri deals with the theory and technique of character development, premise construction, and building of conflict.

Olson, Elder. *Tragedy and Theory of Drama.* Detroit: Wayne State University Press, 1961. Olson agrees with Aristotle that plot governs character, but feels that any formal ordering of dramatic elements is too restrictive. Dramatic action is primarily interpersonal in Olson's point of view.

"The Method" and Character Development

Blum, Richard A. *American Film Acting: The Stanislavski Heritage.* Ann Arbor: UMI Research Press, 1984. This book traces the history and impact of Stanislavski's system on American film acting. You'll recognize the author of this one.

Easty, Edward. *On Method Acting*. New York: House of Collectibles, Inc., 1966. This is a book that is used by actors trained in the Lee Strasberg Theatre Institute, where "The Method" is still being taught, in New York and Los Angeles.

Hethmon, Robert, ed. *Strasberg at the Actors Studio*. New York: The Viking Press Inc., 1965. This book is transcribed from tape recordings of Lee Strasberg teaching "The Method" at the Actor's Studio.

Lewis, Robert. *Method—or Madness*. New York: Samuel French, Inc., 1958. A down-to-earth discussion of the Stanislavski system which was modified by Lee Strasberg at the Actor's Studio. "The Method" is defined, with strong points and weak points illuminated.

Magarshack, David. *Stanislavski on the Art of the Stage*. New York: Hill and Wang, 1961. Includes a collection of lectures by Stanislavski, "The System and Method of Creative Art." The introduction offers a simple and useful summary of Stanislavski's theory and techniques.

Moore, Sonia. *The Stanislavski System*. New York: The Viking Press, 1974. An easy-to-read handbook of Stanislavski's system of acting and character development.

Stanislavski, Constantin. *An Actor Prepares*. Trans. Elizabeth Reynolds Hapgood. New York: Theatre Arts Books, 1936. This book outlines the basic principles of finding inner truth, objectives, super-objectives, and through-lines of action.

———. *Building a Character*. Trans. Elizabeth Reynolds Hapgood. New York: Theatre Arts Books, 1949. This work concentrates on "outer technique" for the actor. Initially it was not as well known as the other two Stanislavski works.

———. *Creating a Role*. Trans. Elizabeth Reynolds Hapgood. New York: Theatre Arts Books, 1961. This book covers script analysis and character development techniques for the actor.

TV Writing Techniques

Brady, Ben. *The Keys to Writing for Television and Film*, Dubuque, Iowa: Kendall-Hunt, 3rd ed., 1978. Examines the dramatic structure of writing for TV and films, with script samples.

Coopersmith, Jerome. *Professional Writer's Teleplay/Screenplay Format*. New York: Writers Guild of America, East, 1977. A very concise and informative booklet that provides detailed script models and formats. This is a must for the new TV writer.

Cousin, Michelle. *Writing a Television Play*. Boston: Writer, Inc.,

1975. A sensitive guide to visual and dramatic requirements in scripting.

Field, Syd. *Screenplay*. New York: Dell, 1979. A good foundation for screenwriting.

Herman, Lewis. *A Practical Manual of Screen Playwriting*. Cleveland: World Publishing, 1963. Offers solid theory and practice of writing for motion pictures and TV films.

Hilliard, Robert L. *Writing for Television and Radio*. 3rd ed. New York: Hastings House, 1976. Presents concrete approaches to professional writing in all TV program formats and genres. In addition, each chapter is supplemented by practical exercises and suggested reference sources.

Lee, Robert and Robert Misiorowski. *Script Models: A Handbook for the Media Writer*. New York: Hastings House, 1978. Offers specific formats and script samples.

Swain, Dwight V. *Film Scriptwriting: A Practical Manual*. Woburn, MA: Focal Press, 1980. This book deals with the basic techniques and tools of writing fact films (for clients) and feature films, with samples.

Trapnell, Coles. *Teleplay: An Introduction to Television Writing*. New York: Hawthorn Books, 1974. A basic introduction to form and technique.

Vale, Eugene. *Technique of Screenplay Writing*. New York: Grosset and Dunlap, 1972. A practical approach to scriptwriting, with samples.

Willis, Edgar E. and Camille D'Arienzo. *Writing Scripts for Television, Radio and Film*. New York: Holt, Rinehart and Winston. An update of Willis' earlier book, this explores dramatic and nondramatic writing, with script samples.

Marketing Resources

Broadcasting Yearbook, 1735 DeSales St., N.W., Washington, DC 20036, (202) 638-1022. This is an annual compilation of facts and figures about the broadcast industry, including information on all television stations across the country. If you need to find out anything about the television industry, this is one major directory to consult.

Cable File, Titsch Communications, 2500 Curtis St., Denver, CO 80217, (303) 295-0900. An invaluable semi-annual resource, including profiles on all pay and basic programming, program producers, and satellite TV companies. Also includes profiles of top advertising agencies, MSOs, MDS and STV operations. *Cable File/Update* offers periodic revisions throughout the year, updating all information on program services, systems, and industry trends.

Cable TV Program Data Book, Kagan Associates, Inc., 26386 Carmel Rancho Lane, Carmel, CA 93923, (408) 624-1536. Another important semi-annual "who's who" in cable, including national contacts for program production and distribution, advertising agencies developing and producing cable programs, sources for financing, in-depth profiles of basic cable program services and pay TV program services (including STV operations and DBS). Lists program buyers for MSOs, and selected programmers for local cable access.

Pacific Coast Directory, 6331 Hollywood Blvd., Hollywood, CA 90028, (213) 467-2920. A quarterly listing of all production companies in California and in 15 different states. Includes lists of agents, advertising agencies, producers, TV stations, and film commissions. A very useful directory for finding names, addresses, and phone numbers.

Ross Reports, Television Index, Inc., 150 Fifth Ave., New York, NY 10011. A monthly publication on the East Coast that lists all national production activity, including network, syndicated, and cable TV programming. Lists names, addresses, and contacts for all the current shows in work, as well as agents handling new projects.

Television Factbook, 1836 Jefferson Pl., NW, Washington, D.C. 20036, (202) 872-9200. Another major annual directory that encompasses the entire spectrum of the television industry. It includes a list of all independent stations, group-owned stations, network O&O's advertisers, cable TV and satellite companies. There is a wealth of information compiled in its pages, and it is a chief resource for any information you may need.

Writers Guild of America, 8955 Beverly Blvd., Los Angeles, CA 90048. The Writers Guild has copies of the latest "Schedule of Minimums, WGA, Theatrical and Television Basic Agreement," which lists all negotiated writing fees. Also available is the list of "Agents That Have Subscribed to the WGA-Artists Manager Basic Agreement."

Word Processing

Publications and Books

An enormous number of books and publications are available on technical and creative uses of word processing systems. These are some of the more readable and accessible:

Consumer Reports, *Computers at Home*, Mt. Vernon, N.Y.: Consumer
    Union, 1983. A special publication of Consumer Reports offering a
    concise exploration of computers and word processing systems. It
    includes an unbiased evaluation of eleven word processing pro-
    grams.
Elman, Barbara, ed., *Word Processing News*, a bi-monthly newsletter
    for writers, published in Burbank, California (211 E. Olive Ave.,
    Burbank, CA 91502).
Flugelman, A. and Hewes, J. J., *Writing in the Computer Age*, N.Y.:
    Doubleday, 1983. Easy to read, lots of information, and written
    specifically for writers.
McWilliams, Peter, *The Word Processing Book*, Los Angeles, Prelude
    Press, 5th ed., 1983 (Box 69773, Los Angeles, CA 90069). If you are
    not familiar with word processing or not familiar with McWil-
    liams, you *owe* it to yourself to read this book. It's a charming and
    witty book, that is jam-packed with relevant information. McWil-
    liams has written screenplays and poetry, as well as computer
    books. He publishes regular updates to this book and his many
    others.

Software for Script Writers

The software available for word processing is vast, and some of the
resources above will help you wade through the maze of possibilities.
They offer specific comparative information on some of the most
prominent, including *WORDSTAR, EASY WRITER II, PERFECT
WRITER, PEACH TEXT, VOLKSWRITER, SELECT, SPELLBINDER*
and many others. Regular publications such as *Byte* (P.O. Box 590,
Martinsville, NJ 08836), *Personal Computing* (4 Disk Drive, Box 1408,
Riverton, NJ 08077), and *Popular Computing* (P.O. Box 307, Martinsville, N.J. 08836) publish articles in their magazines on computing and
word processing.

In addition to the basic software for text editing, two software programs have been designed exclusively for the television and script
writer. Any of the programs listed above will handle margins and for-
matting creditably, but for reformatting (specifically revisions) you
might want to look into these offerings:
Screenplay (Automated Screenplay Systems, P.O. Box 1823, Beverly
    Hills, CA 90213).
Scriptor (Screenplay Systems, 211 E. Olive #210, Burbank, CA 91502).

Index

ABC Video Enterprises, 178
Academy of Motion Picture Arts and
    Sciences, 63, 249
Academy of TV Arts and Sciences
    Library, 123, 249
Act, structure of, 115–120
Adams Chronicles, 59
Adaptations, 10, 88–96
Advertising Age, 190, 265
Advertising agencies, 188–190
Agents, 186, 192–193, 195, 251–263
American Film Institute, 63, 227, 249
    Center for Advanced Film
        Studies, 123
    Independent Filmmaker Program,
        58
American Playhouse, 55, 58, 64
American Short Story, 59
American Television and
    Communication (ATC), 181
Annenberg/CPB project, 55, 228
Anthology series, 10, 14–15
Aristotle, 77, 81
Art of Dramatic Writing (Egri), 77
ARTS & ENTERTAINMENT, 178,
    220
Audience interest, plotting, 86–88

Background action, 129
Back to shot, 131
Baker, George Pierce, 77
Basic Cable, 175, 221
BBC, 178
BBD&O, 188

"Beats" (dramatic), 25, 97–101,
    128–129
Belushi, John, 44
Bentley, Eric, 81
Benton & Bowles, 188
Best of Families, 59
"Bible" (Series presentation), 10
Black Entertainment Television
    (BET), 177, 220
Blues Survivors, 45
Book adaptations, 10, 69, 88–89
BRAVO, 178–179, 223
Broadcasting, 190
Broadcasting Yearbook, 190
Brown, Clarence ("Gatemouth"),
    42–43
Bruntiere, Ferdinand, 77

Cable File, 179, 181, 182
Cable Marketing, 179, 190
Cable News Network (CNN), 177,
    220
Cable TV, 1, 175–183
    marketing for, 179–183
    national associations, 219–220
    variety specials, 37, 38–48
Cable TV Program Data Book, 181
Cable Vision, 179
Cablevision systems, 178
Camera angles, 117–119, 125
    and film script format, 126, 128,
        129, 130–133
    and videotape format, 152, 154,
        157

Carnegie Commission on the Future
    of Public Broadcasting, 53–54
CBS, 177
CBS Cable, 178, 182
CBS Fox Video, 183
Central Educational Network (CEN),
    56–57, 231
Character development, 2
    and adaptation, 88
    and dialogue, 102–112
    and "method," 91–101
    and plot, 77–78
    and presentation, 16, 19–22, 34
    and revision, 170–171
Charles Ford Band, 43–44
Charles K. Feldman Library, 123
Chenier, Clifton, 42
Children's programs, 55, 62, 178, 180
Close up (CU), 23, 30
    and film script format, 127, 130
    and videotape format, 153
Collins, Albert, 43
Columbia Pictures, 177
Commerce Business Daily, 62
Comsat, 175, 182
Consultants, 71
Contract, 196–199
Coopersmith, Jerome, 116
Copies of script, number of, 185–186
Corporation for Public Broadcasting
    (CPB), 53, 54–55, 69, 71–72, 227
Corporations, 63, 64–65
Cost-sharing, 67–68
Cover letter, 187, 192
Cox Broadcasting, 178, 181
Cray, Robert, 44
Credits, 196, 199
Cultural television, 178–179, 180

Daily Variety, 190, 265
Daniels & Associates, 178
Deal memos, 196
Dialogue, 2
    and character development,
        102–112
    and film script format, 125, 129
    problems and solutions, 102–112
    revision, 171
    and treatment, 24, 25, 29

Direct broadcast satellite (DBS),
    181–182, 222–225
Directing, training program, 63
Disney, 178, 223
Documentaries, 55, 64
Double-column format, 165–167
Doyle Dane Bernbach, 188
Dramatic action points, 81–86, 88,
    170
Dramatic Technique (Baker), 77
Dream sequence, 145–147

Eastern Educational Network (EEN),
    56, 72, 231
Egri, Lajos, 77
Electric Company, 62
Embassy Communications, 188
Entertainment Channel, 178
Episodic series, 10
Escapade/The Playboy Channel, 178
ESPN, 177, 220
Establishing shot, 118
Exxon, 64

Face sheet, 57, 65–68
Fade in, 22, 23, 151
Fade out, 22, 30, 128, 155
Fantasy sequence, 145–147
Federal agencies as market, 2, 61–62,
    72
Federal Domestic Assistance
    Catalogue, 62
Fees
    cable/pay TV, 180–181
    comedy-variety, 202–203
    drama, 201–202
    minimum, 52, 54–55, 71, 196, 198,
        199–209
    public TV, 54–55, 205–207
    quiz shows, 52, 204
    serials, 204–205
Film Fund, 63
Film script
    development, 115–121
    format, 123–148
Flashbacks, 147–148
Foote Cone & Belding, 188
Ford Foundation, 64, 228
Foreground action, 129

Format
  and film script, 123–148
  and presentation, 16–19, 34
  and quiz shows, 49–50
  and series, 9, 16–19
  and videotapes, 149–167
For Us The Living, 59
Foundations, 63, 64–65, 228–229
Foundation Center, 64–65, 227
Foundation Directory, 65
Frontline, 55, 228

Gifts and matching funds, 67
Glenn, Lloyd, 44
Grants, 1, 54–55, 60, 63
Great Performances, 58
Grey Advertising, 188
Group-owned stations, 190
Group Theatre, 98
Group W, 177, 181, 190
Guggenheim foundation, 64, 228
Guide to NEA, 59
Guilds, 249–250

Hammond, John, 43
Hearst, 178
Herman, Lewis, 80
Hollywood Reporter, 190, 266
Home Box Office (HBO), 176, 177,
  179, 180–181, 223
Home video, 183
"Hook," 11, 15–16, 78–79, 115
Hubbard Broadcasting, 182
Humanities Projects in Media, 60
Humanities Projects in Media
  program, 59–60

Independent Documentary Fund, 64
Independent producers, 187, 212–218
Intentions of characters, 99, 104
Intercuts, 142–143
International Creative Management
  (ICM), 193
Interregional Program Service (IPS),
  56

"Jane Fonda's Workout," 183
J. Walter Thompson, 188

Klein, Paul, 9

Law of the Drama (Bruntiere), 77
Lear, Norman, 156, 188
Least objectionable programming
  thoery, 9
Length
  of act, 116
  of pilot story, 32
  of teaser, 116, 149
  of videotape, 149
Life of the Drama (Bentley), 81
Lilly Endowment, 64, 228
Literature program (NEA), 59
Little Charlie & the Nightcaps, 44
Littlejohn, Johnny, 44
"Live from the Met," 58
Local stations
  group O&Os, 190
  public access, 183
  public TV, 55, 56, 72
  variety specials, 37
Locale of action, 117
  and film script format, 125,
    126–127
  and videotape, 157
Lorimar Productions, 188
Low power TV (LPTV), 183

"Magic Hearing Box," 165–167
Margin settings, 129, 149–155
Markle Foundation, 64, 228
Mark Twain Series, 59
Master scene script, 133–142
Masterworks of Civilization, 60
Media Arts program (NEA), 57–58
Mellon Foundation, 64, 228
Method acting and characterization,
  2, 92–101
Metromedia, 190
"Middletown," 59
Minelli, Liza, 46, 47
Mini-series, 10
Minorities, 54, 180
Mobil, 64
Moment-to-moment realities, 100–101
Montage, 144–146
Motion picture studios, 177, 188
Motivation of characters, 97, 104

Movie Channel, 176, 177, 179,
    180–181, 224
M.T.M. Enterprises, 188
MTV, 177, 221
Multi Channel News, 179, 190, 266
Multi-part series. See Mini-series
Multiple System operators, 181
Multipoint distribution systems
    (MDS), 222–225
Murdoch, Rupert, 182
Music, use of, 118–119, 154

Narrowcasting, 176
National Council on Arts, 73
National Council on the Humanities,
    72
National Endowment for the Arts
    (NEA), 57–59, 63, 64, 73, 228
National Endowment for the
    Humanities (NEH), 59–60, 69, 72,
    228
National Federation of Local Cable
    Programmers, 183, 219
National Science Foundation (NSF),
    62
Needham, Harper, Steers, Ogilvy &
    Mather, 188
Networks, 211
    marketing to, 185, 188, 191–193
    program development, 8–9
    and variety specials, 45–48
New angle, 131, 156
Newhouse Broadcasting, 181
"New Little Rascals," 156–160
Nickelodean, 178, 221
Nielsen ratings, 8, 80
Nova, 62

Odyssey, 59
Off screen (O.S.), 23, 126, 127
Olson, Elder, 81
O&O stations, 190
Operation Primetime, 190
Options, 196–199

Pacific Coast Studio Directory, 190
Pacific Mountain Network (PMN),
    57, 231
Packages, 37, 45–48, 193

Paramount, 177
Pay Per View TV (PPV), 175
Pay TV, 175–183, 222–223
Phillips, David Graham, 69
Pilot show, 2, 16, 22–32, 34–35
Plagiarism and unsolicited material,
    8, 186
Playboy, 177–178, 224
Plot, 77–78, 79–80, 86–88
Point of view (P.O.V.), 23, 28, 31, 128
Polish, 171
Polti, Georges, 80
Post Newsweek, 190
Practical Manual of Screenplay
    Writing, (Herman), 80
Presentation
    and characters, 16,19–22, 34
    and format, 16–19, 34
    and future storylines, 32–34
    and pilot, 16, 22–32, 34–35
    for series, 10, 16–35
Production companies, 187–188,
    212–218
Professional Writer's Teleplay/
    Screenplay Format (Coopersmith),
    115–116
Program Fair, 55–56
Program Services Endowment, 53–54
Pronoun confusion, 120–121
Proposals
    for network TV series, 10–16
    for public TV, 54, 57, 60, 62, 65–71
    for quiz show, 48–52
    requests for, 62, 72
    for variety special, 38–48
Public-access programming, 183
Public Broadcasting Service (PBS),
    54, 55–56, 205–207, 228
Public Telecommunications Trust, 53
Public TV, 53–73
    and budgets, 54–55, 69–71
    and evaluation of projects, 71–73
    and proposals, 54, 57, 60, 62, 65–71
    and rights and royalties, 73
Public Television: A Program for
    Action, 53

Que Pasa, USA?, 62
Quiz shows, 2, 48–52

Radio Production programs, 58
Rate sheets, 71
RCA, 178, 182
Reactions, indication of characters,
  125, 151–152, 154–155
Rebop, 62
Reddy, Helen, 45, 46
Redford, Robert, 64
Regional media arts centers, 58, 62,
  231–233
Regional media arts fellowships, 58,
  63
Regional pay TV networks, 177
Regional public TV networks, 56–57,
  72, 231
Registration of scripts, 186
Repetitiousness, 104–105, 121
Requests for proposals (RFPs), 62, 72
Reruns, 176–177, 207
Research, 55, 71
Residuals, 207
Revision of scripts, 169–171
Rich, Lee, 188
Rickles, Don, 46, 47
Rights, 73, 88, 181, 182
Rockefeller Center, 178
Rock video, 177
Rocky Mountain Public Broadcasting
  Network, 57
Rogers U-A Columbia Cable, 180
Rolling Stones, 45–46
Rosie the Riveter, 59
Ross Reports, 190, 266
Royalties, 73, 207
Rundown sheets, 46
Run time, 46

Salgado, Curtis, 44
San Francisco Blues Festival, 38–48
Satcom I satellite, 177
Satellite TV Corporation (STC),
  181–182
Scarlet Letter, 59
Scene, structure of, 116–119
Scene description, 119–121
  and film script format, 129, 133,
    142
  and videotape format, 151, 153,

154–156
Schedule of Minimums, 199, 205–207.
  See also Fees
Seg time, 46
Series, 2, 7–8
  development, 8–9
  fees, 204
  format, 9, 16–19
  presentation, 10, 16–35
  types, 10, 14
Sesame Street, 62
Set-ups, 119
Short films, 58, 64
Showtime, 176, 177, 179, 180–181,
  224
Sinatra, Nancy and Frank, Jr., 45–48
Skyband, 182
Slug lines, 23, 26, 28, 31
  and film script format, 124, 131
  and videotape format, 150–151
Somebody Else's Place, 62
Songs, 119
Sound effects, 129, 154
Southern Educational
  Communications Association
  (SECA), 54, 231
Spaces, 62
Special effects, 31, 130
Sport Channel, 178
Sports, 58, 177, 180
Sports Network, 177
Stage directions, 157–163
"Stand alone programming," 181
Stanislavski, Constantin, 98, 272–273
States
  arts and humanities agencies,
    62–63, 233–240
  education agencies, 240–241
  film and television commissions,
    63, 244–247
Station Independent Program
  Cooperative, 56
Step deal, 196–199
Step outline, 80–86
Storer Cable, 181, 190
Story development, 77–96
Strasberg, Lee, 98
Submissions, 7–8, 185–191
  status reports, 191–192

Subscription TV companies (STVs), 182, 222–225
Sundance Institute for Film and Television, 64
Super-objective, 99
Susan Lennox, 69

Taft Communication, 190
"Tags," 151, 157
Teaser, 115, 116, 149, 156
Teaspoon of Honey, A, 89–96
Ted Bates, 188
Tele-Communications, Inc., 181
Television Factbook, 190
"Television Market List," 190–191
Television/Radio Age, 190, 266
Theatre Program (NEA), 59
Theme, 78
3-2-1 Contact, 62
Through-line-of-action, 99
Times Mirror, 181
To Be Young, Gifted and Black, 59
Trade papers, 179, 190, 265–266
Tragedy and the Theory of Drama (Olson), 81
Training programs, 63
Travel expenses, 55, 71
Treatment, 22–32
    development of, 77–96
    narrative style, 26
    and public TV proposals, 69
TRISTAR, 77
Turner, Ted, 177
"TV Production Chart," 190
Typewriter settings, 130, 149–156

Unions, 249–250
Unit series, 10
United Satellite Communications, 182
U.S. Copyright Office, 186
U.S. Department of Defense, 61
U.S. Department of Education, 62
U.S. Information Agency, 62
Urgency, sense of, 99–100, 170
USA Network, 177

Variety, 190, 266
Variety specials, 2, 37–48, 162–165, 202–203
Vegetable Soup, 62
Viacom Cablevision, 181
Videotape script, 149–167
Vietnam: The Television History, 59
View, 179
Villa Allegre, 62
Voice of America, 62
Voice over (V.O.), 126

Waiver, 186
Warner Amex Satellite Entertainment, 177, 181
"Watchmaker, The," 89–96
Western Educational Network, 57
Western Union, 182
WGBH-TV, 55, 56
"What if—?" technique, 101–102
Wide angle shot, 131–133
William Morris Agency, Inc., 193
"Window" (for exclusivity) 181, 182
Winkler, Henry, 46, 47
WNET-TV, 55, 56, 72
Women, 54, 58, 180
Word processor, 130, 275–276
WQED-TV, 55
Writers Guild
    and agents, 192, 251
    and arbitration of credits, 199
    joining, 195
    Minimum Basic Agreement, 52, 54–55, 71, 196, 198, 199–209
    registration of scripts, 186
    residuals and royalties, 207
Writers Guild of America Foundation, 64
Writers Guild of America Newsletter, 190–191
WTBS, 177, 222

Xerox, 64

Young and Rubicam, 188